Animacies

PERVERSE MODERNITIES

*A series edited by Judith Halberstam
and Lisa Lowe*

Animacies

Biopolitics, Racial Mattering, and Queer Affect

MEL Y. CHEN

Duke University Press

Durham and London

2012

© 2012 Duke University Press
All rights reserved
Printed in the United States of America
on acid-free paper ∞
Designed by C. H. Westmoreland
Typeset in Monotype Bembo
with Gill Sans display
by Tseng Information Systems, Inc.
Library of Congress Cataloging-
in-Publication Data appear on the last
printed page of this book.

Contents

Acknowledgments

I've always struggled to find truly reflective words of thanks, and these acknowledgments are no exception. The ideational and affective matter of a book travels long and far; in my case, all the way back to the toads hopping in my backyard in Illinois at a time when I seemed only a bit bigger than them. So I begin with heartfelt thanks to the toads: literally grubby and ponderous yet lightning fast with food items; squinting as they sloughed off their own molting skin, seemingly neckless but surprisingly flexible; walking, hopping, and swimming; and hunched and still when I came upon them in their cold hibernations. Toads infused my lifelong experience with their peculiar, but resolute, grace, with a style of creatureliness that I could and could not occupy. And though they were only sporadically visible, I could be certain a toad was somewhere near.

Yet toads and frogs may not be long for this world. The latest theory involves a destructive fungus, apparently created within particularly benevolent lab conditions where *Xenopus* frogs were being studied; the fungus was distributed globally by the popular trade in *Xenopus* frogs and spread back into various ecosystems by released *Xenopus* and herpetologists themselves in search of undocumented species. I must admit to the possibility of writing into a world in which toads may no longer be near. The style of their disappearance reminds me of the complexities of identity, environment, and transaction, and even of the retroactive "discovery" between a historical trace of material conveyance and a diagnosis of present-day loss. Toads, too, teach me again that toxicities have retrospective temporalities and affects, as do my acknowledgments.

In perhaps less "earthly" but more "worldly" circumstances, given how such segregations have come to work: enormous thanks are due to the many humans and domesticated animals populating the words in this book affectively, informedly, notionally, diagnostically, insinuatingly. The following categories most certainly bleed into one another; I think of collegiality as always containing the possibility of friendship, and of friendship as always containing the possibility of avocation. All were important to the making of this book, and much, much more.

For my evolution in learning, I begin with thanking the University of California, Berkeley, Linguistics Department for fostering my PhD work, as well as its essential partner, the Designated Emphasis in Women, Gender, and Sexuality. Both were represented in my dissertation committee, mentors all in their own respects: Eve Sweetser, Judith Butler, George Lakoff, and Trinh T. Minh-ha. Eve Sweetser shared her brilliant, always persuasive explorations of grammar, culture, and criticism, while modeling for me a way to rejoice unreservedly in the realm of inquiry. Carolyn Dinshaw offered encouragement in my first course outside of linguistics and handed me my own issue of GLQ 1, no. 1. Trinh T. Minh-ha began with me what is already a years-long trajectory of engagement, for which I am immensely grateful. For life-changing new collectivities and the provision of the best kind of collective support, I thank the President's Postdoctoral Fellowship, including Kimberly Adkinson and Sheila O'Rourke. I also thank my UCLA home for the fellowship, particularly Patricia Greenfield, Marjorie Orellana, and the Center for Culture, Brain, and Development.

My colleagues in the Department of Gender and Women's Studies at Berkeley have been stellar, both formidable intellects and devoted colleagues. I thank Paola Bacchetta, Evelyn Nakano Glenn, Minoo Moallem, Juana María Rodríguez, Charis Thompson, and Barrie Thorne, along with Eileen Andrade, Althea Grannum-Cummings, Linda Baker, and Gillian Edgelow, for providing a stimulating environment that is fiercely supportive to all. At Berkeley, I have been privileged to know so many outstanding students, undergraduate and graduate. My first graduating class (in 2007) of senior honors students, the "F6," went far beyond my call to reflective investment, and mutual dedication: Ian Livengood, Nikiko Masumoto, Liz Padilla, Drea Scally, and Tamar Shirinian. My past and current graduate students are all sources of inspiration, including Laura Horak, Amy Fujiwara Shen, and Katrina Dodson. Anastasia Kayiatos was a research assistant for an early version of this book and the kind of graduate student who exemplifies utterly why I can thrive here. There are many intellectually generative centers at Berkeley with which I've been affiliated. I thank them all for fostering the growth of collegial engagement beyond the departmental level, hence working as a form of inter- and transdisciplinary mattering so essential to this university. They include the Center for Race and Gender; the Science, Technology, and Society Center; and the Institute for Cognitive and Brain Sciences.

For always insightful commentary and probing questions, I thank audiences at Mills College, University of Leeds, University of Maryland, Humboldt University, UC Berkeley, UCLA, UC Irvine, UC Santa Cruz, the Crossroads Conference in Cultural Studies, the Society for Disability Studies, the American Studies Association, and especially the insightful audience at the keynote I delivered at UC Davis's "Queer Privates." I also benefited from UCLA's "First Books, Feminism, and the Future" workshop, with thanks especially to Laura Kang, Rachel Lee, Martin Manalansan, and Lucy Burns, for whom the workshop was convened. I thank colleagues and friends within the Society for Disability Studies for modeling so beautifully how to unthink the habit of bodily optimization. I benefited from several reading and writing groups, including the Queer of Color writing group (Huma Dar, Roshy Kheshti, Fouzieyha Towghi), and Gender Workers (Julian Carter, Rita Alfonso, Don Romesburg, Rebekah Edwards, and Nan Alamilla Boyd), and more recently, the Mediating Natures group, with whom I had a delightful conversation.

My thinking was very much informed by an intense quarter spent as the convener of a University of California Humanities Research Institute Residential Research Group, "Species Spectacles." I owe a debt of intellectual, and gustatory, gratitude to all the participants: Carla Freccero, J. Jack Halberstam, Tamara Ho, Tonglin Lu, and Kyla Schuller; in addition, I am grateful for the acumen and thoughtful support of David Theo Goldberg and the assistance of the UCHRI staff. I completed the revisions of this book as a guest in the carefully cultivated peace of the Clark Art Institute, and for that very productive atmosphere, I thank Michael Ann Holly and Aruna D'Souza, as well as the fellows who provided company and support, not least the irrepressible Griselda Pollock. In addition to resources from the Williams College

Library, special thanks are due to Karen Bucky for ample interlibrary loan help, which I had never used to such a degree. She enabled me to rebuild my book library away from home, which was no small task. Uncategorizable but perhaps all the more valuable for their remarkable incidence in my life are my colleagues within and beyond Berkeley: Dana Luciano, Cori Hayden, Sunaura Taylor, James Kyung-jin Lee, Margaret Price, Eliza Chandler, Sarah Snyder, Lilith Mahmud, Arlene Keizer, Laura Kang, and Teenie Matlock. Alison Kafer simply knew there was a place for me to participate in disability-studies dialogues, and with that brought me the community and scholarship of the Society for Disability Studies, after which I cannot ever go back. Eli Clare has shown me integrity and commitment to social justice at its deepest. Judith Butler and Susan Schweik were supportive in many ways.

For friendship and community over the years, knowing that not all can be listed here, I wish to thank Margo Rivera-Weiss, Hadas Rivera-Weiss, Willy Wilkinson, Georgia Kolias, Jolie Harris, Jian Chen, Kyla Schuller, Huma Dar, Emma Bianchi, Lann Hornscheidt, Roslyn McKendry, Sophia Neely, Amber Straus, Angie Wilson, Quang Dang, Katrin Pahl, Cory Wechsler, Alicia Gilbreath, Amy Huber, Gayle Salomon, Karen Tongson, Karin Martin, Amy Yunis, Susan Chen, Keri, Ella and Omri Kanetsky, Lize van Robbroeck, Madeleine Lim, Kebo Drew, the Queer Women of Color Media Arts Project, Gwen d'Arcangelis, Rob and Julie Edwards, Laurie Olsen, Mike Margulis, Jesse Olsen, Josh Olsen, Carol Tseng, Stan Yogi and David Carroll, Kathryn Socha, Elizabeth Jockusch, Jim Voorheis, Nate Padavick, and Mary Lum. I am fortunate that Rebekah Edwards believed quite fiercely in this book well before its genesis as such; I thank her for many years of creatively inspiring companionship and helping to create an environment where I could focus entirely on healing, for being strong and steadfast for so many. I thank Gil Hochberg for the combination of great spirit, face-breaking laughter, and friendship at many critical times over all these years, and for letting me meet Ella on the very first day of her life. Dev Rana provided years of important friendship; I keep with me our many unforgettable conversations about race, food, toxicity, and illness into the night.

I have indescribable gratitude for the family who raised me: Ruth Hsu and Michael Ming Chen, my brother Derek, and my sister Brigitte. Mom and Dad have always modeled fierce interest in justice, studying through ignorance, and compassion; the ways they continue to change and the celebration with which they apprehend the world astounds me. I grew up into the legacy of Brigitte's love; her early death shaped my senses in ways that I continue to discover. Derek is both my brother and my friend; I feel lucky to continue to know and grow with him. He is a model of deep thoughtfulness and great generosity, and his constant inventiveness is contagious. I have been so nourished by all my extended family, with special thanks to cousins Janet and Andy Tao, David Lee, and Stanley Wang, and Aunty Elizabeth Lee and Wu Jie Jie (Cheryl Wang). Bibim Bap and Mikey, Fabiola and Giovanni, my present and departed cats, taught me how to be present, to witness, to touch, to hold. Finally: Julia Bryan-Wilson, in such a short time you have changed my life, made fulfillment possible in every direction; in part this has come from acknowledging where I am and welcoming it more openly than I've ever experienced. I honor all the hours of work you spent on *Animacies* in its many drafts, but I also want to mark that it's because of you that joy has found its way into this book; in turn, this book breathes with you.

At Duke, I thank two anonymous readers for simultaneously incisive and generous analyses of the book, attentive to detail and to the multidisciplinary implications of my arguments. Courtney Berger is an author's dream editor in every respect; she ushered this manuscript through with integrity, sharp thinking, and personalized consideration. I also wish to thank Ken Wissoker for identifying the value of this project, as well as the editorial associate Christine Choi. I thank J. Jack Halberstam and Lisa Lowe for finding my book worthy of inclusion in Perverse Modernities, a commitment that condemns them to having my book included in their Amazon searches forevermore.

My research was supported by a UC President's Postdoctoral Fellowship, an Abigail Hodgen Publication Fund, a Hellman Faculty Family Fund, a UC Humanities Research Institute Convener's Fellowship, and UC Berkeley's Committee on Research. Portions of chapters 4, 5, and 6 underwent earlier development in three essays: "Racialized Toxins and Sovereign Fantasies," *Discourse: Journal for Theoretical Studies in Media and Culture* 29, no. 2 (2007); "Animals without Genitals," *Women in Performance: A Journal of Feminist Theory* 20, no. 3 (2010); and "Toxic Animacies, Inanimate Affections," *GLQ: A Journal of Lesbian and Gay Studies* 17, no. 2–3 (2011).

Introduction

Animating Animacy

Recently, after reaching a threshold of "recovery" from a chronic ill-ness—an illness that has affected me not only physically, but spatially, familially, economically, and socially, and set me on a long road of thinking about the marriage of bodies and chemicals—I found my-self deeply suspicious of my own reassuring statements to my anxious friends that I was feeling more alive again. Surely I had been no *less* alive when I was *more* sick, except under the accountings of an intu-itive and immediately problematic notion of "liveliness" and other kinds of "freedom" and "agency." I felt unsettled not only for reasons of disability politics—for "lifely wellness" colludes with a logic that troublingly naturalizes illness's morbidity—but also because I realized that in the most containing and altered moments of illness, as often occurs with those who are severely ill, I came to know an incredible wakefulness, one that I was now paradoxically losing and could only try to commit to memory.[1]

In light of this observation, I began to reconsider the precise condi-tions of the application of "life" and "death," the working ontologies and hierarchicalized bodies of interest. If the continued rethinking of life and death's proper boundaries yields surprising redefinitions, then there are consequences for the "stuff," the "matter," of contemporary biopolitics—including important and influential concepts such as Achille Mbembe's necropolitics, the "living dead," and Giorgio Agam-ben's "bare life."[2] This book puts pressure on such biopolitical factors, organized around a multipoint engagement with a concept called *animacy*.

Animacies: Biopolitics, Racial Mattering, and Queer Affect draws upon recent debates about sexuality, race, environment, and affect to consider how matter that is considered insensate, immobile, deathly, or otherwise "wrong" animates cultural life in important ways. *Animacies* interrogates how the fragile division between animate and inanimate—that is, beyond human and animal—is relentlessly produced and policed and maps important political consequences of that distinction. The concept of animacy undergirds much that is pressing and indeed volatile in contemporary culture, from animal rights debates to biosecurity concerns, yet it has gone undertheorized. This book is the first to bring the concept of animacy together with queer of color scholarship, critical animal studies, and disability theory.

It is a generative asset that the word *animacy*, much like other critical terms, bears no single standard definition. Animacy—or we might rather say, the set of notions characterized by family resemblances—has been described variously as a quality of agency, awareness, mobility, and liveness.[3] In the last few decades, *animacy* has become a widely debated term within linguistics, and it is in fact within linguistics that animacy has been most extensively developed and applied. A pathbreaking work written in 1976 by the linguistic anthropologist Michael Silverstein suggested that "animacy hierarchies" were an important area of intersection between meaning and grammar, on the basis of evidence that spanned many languages.[4] Within linguistics today, animacy most generally refers to the grammatical effects of the sentience or liveness of nouns, but this ostensibly simple meaning opens into much wider conversations.

How does animacy work linguistically? To take one popular example involving relative clauses, consider the phrase "the hikers that rocks crush": what does this mean?[5] The difficulty frequently experienced by English speakers in processing this phrase has much to do with the inanimacy of the rock (which plays an agent role in relation to the verb *crush*) as compared to the animacy of the hikers, who in this scenario play an object role. "The hikers that rocks crush" thus violates a cross-linguistic preference among speakers. They tend to prefer animate head nouns to go with subject-extracted relative clauses (the hikers *who ___ crushed the rock*), or inanimate head nouns to go with object-extracted relative clauses (the rock *that the hiker crushed ___*). Add to this that there is a smaller plausibility that rocks will agentively crush hikers than that hikers will agentively crush rocks: a conceptual order of things, an animate hierarchy of possible acts, begins to take shape. Yet more contentious examples belie the apparent obviousness of this hierarchy, and even in this case, it is within a specific cosmology that stones so obviously lack agency or could be the source of causality. What if nonhuman animals, or humans stereotyped as passive, such as people with cognitive or physical disabilities, enter the calculus of animacy: what happens then?

Using animacy as a central construct, rather than, say, "life" or "liveliness"—though these remain a critical part of the conversation in this book—helps us theorize current anxieties around the production of humanness in contemporary times, particularly with regard to humanity's partners in definitional crime: animality (as its analogue or limit), nationality, race, security, environment, and sexuality. Animacy activates new theoretical formations that trouble and undo stubborn binary systems of difference, including dynamism/stasis, life/death, subject/object, speech/nonspeech, human/animal, natural body/cyborg. In its more sensitive figurations, animacy has the capacity to rewrite conditions of intimacy, engendering different communalisms and revising biopolitical spheres, or, at least, how we might theorize them.

Interestingly, in most English language dictionaries, including *Merriam-Webster's* and the *Oxford English Dictionary* (OED), the word *animacy* does not appear, though the related adjective *animate* does. The related senses of *animate* (ppl., adj., n.) found in the OED—of which only the adjective remains contemporary—are denoted as having the following Latin etymology: "ad. L. *animātus* filled with life, *also*, disposed, inclined, f. *animāre* to breathe, to quicken; f. *anima* air, breath, life, soul, mind." As an adjective, *animate* means "endowed with life, living, alive"; "lively, having the full activity of life"; "pertaining to what is endowed with life; connected to animals"; and "denoting living beings." *Animus*, on the other hand, derives from the Latin, meaning "(1) soul, (2) mind, (3) mental impulse, disposition, passion," and is defined as "actuating feeling, disposition in a particular direction, animating spirit or temper, usually of a hostile character; hence, animosity." We might find in this lexical soup some tentative significations pertaining to materialization, negativity, passion, liveness, and a possible trace of quickened breath. Between these two, *ani-*

mate and *animus*, is a richly affective territory of mediation between life and death, positivity and negativity, impulse and substance; it might be where we could imagine the territory of animacy to reside. As I argue, animacy is much more than the state of being animate, and it is precisely the absence of a consensus around its meaning that leaves it open to both inquiry and resignification.

Construals of Life and Death

Concepts related to animacy have long shadowed Western philosophical discussions: Aristotle's *De Anima*, subtly presaging the present-day debates about the precise status of animals and things, proposed that "soul" could be an animating principle for humans, animals, and vegetables, but not "dead" matter such as stones (or hypothetical rocks that crush hikers).[6] There are many implications in this work: not only did Aristotle provocatively include "animal" as a possessor of soul, he proposed the blending of two disciplines of thought, psychology and biology (to the extent they were then segregated). Though it is beyond the intent of this book to wholly revive Aristotle, it is compelling nonetheless to recall the outlines of his image of the "soul" as a suggestive invitation to think contemporarily of "soul" as an "animating principle" rather than the proverbial "spark of life" ignited by a set of strictly biological processes, such as DNA.

It is further compelling to understand that such an animating principle avowedly refused a priori divisions between mind and body, the philosophical legacy of Descartes which today remains cumbrous to scholars of material agency. Michael Frede has explained that "the notion of the soul attacked by Aristotle is the historical ancestor of Descartes's notion of the mind: a Platonist notion of the soul freed of the role to have to animate a body."[7] We might therefore say, if we took Aristotle to one end point, that it is possible to conceive of something like the "affect" of a vegetable, wherein both the vegetable's receptivity to other affects and its ability to affect outside of itself, as well as its own animating principle, its capacity to animate itself, become viable considerations.

I note, too, that Aristotle's exclusion of stones itself rubs up against other long-standing beliefs according to which stones are animate or potentially animate; his ontological dismissal anticipates the affective economies of current Western ontologies that are dominant, in which stones might as well be nothing. Carolyn Dean usefully observes that "Western tradition does not generally recognize a 'continuum of animacy.' . . . Denying the constant (though imperceptible) changeability of rocks, Western thought has most often identified stone as the binary opposite of, rather than a complement to, things recognized as animate."[8] While in my own perusing of linguistic theory and philosophy of language I have certainly seen prolific examples of stones as "bad" verbal subjects, I will insist in this book that stones and other inanimates definitively occupy a *scalar* position (near zero) on the animacy hierarchy and that they are not excluded from it altogether and are not only treated as animacy's binary opposite.

New materialisms are bringing back the inanimate into the fold of Aristotle's animating principle, insisting that things generate multiplicities of meanings while they retain their "gritty materiality," to use Lorraine Daston's phrase.[9] The history of objects is a combination of intuitive phenomenologically acquired abstractions and socially acquired histories of knowledge about what constitutes proper "thingness."[10] Throughout the humanities and social sciences, scholars are working through posthumanist understandings of the significance of stuff, objects, commodities, and things, creating a fertile terrain of thought about object life; this work asserts that "foregrounding material factors and reconfiguring our very understanding of matter are prerequisites for any plausible account of coexistence and its conditions in the twenty-first century."[11] At the forefront of this field, Jane Bennett, in her book *Vibrant Matter*, extends affect to nonhuman bodies, organic or inorganic, averring that affect is part and parcel, not an additive component, of bodies' materiality.[12] This book builds on these insights by digging into animacy as a specific kind of affective and material construct that is not only nonneutral in relation to animals, humans, and living and dead things, but is shaped by race and sexuality, mapping various biopolitical realizations of animacy in the contemporary culture of the United States.

Recent critical theory has considered the believed-to-be-given material world as more than provisionally constituted, illusorily bounded, and falsely segregated to the realm of the subjective. Such work includes, for instance, Donna Haraway's feminist dismantling of the binary of nature and culture in terms of "naturecultures," Bruno Latour's "hybrids," Karen Barad's agential realism, and Deleuze and Guattari's "assemblages" of objects and affects.[13] Thinking twice about such givens means that we might further reconceive how matter might contribute to the ongoing discussions about the conceptual, cultural, and political economies of life and death. That is, what are the creditable bodies of import, those bodies whose lives or deaths are even in the field of discussion? If we should rethink such bodies—and I argue that we should—then how might we think differently if nonhuman animals (whom both Haraway and Latour point out have been ostensibly, but in fact not neatly, bracketed into "nature," despite already being hybrids) and even inanimate objects were to inch into the biopolitical fold? Nicole Shukin's *Animal Capital*, for instance, reads biopolitics as having been theorized only in relation to *human* life, arguing that, in fact, "discourses and technologies of biopower hinge on the species divide."[14]

If contemporary biopolitics is already troubling the living with the dead, this book, in a way, continues to crash the party with protagonists which hail from animal studies (monkeys) and science studies (pollutant molecules), bringing humanism's dirt back into today's already messy biopolitical imbroglio. Nevertheless, there are important consequences within concepts of life and death for race and sexuality politics. Recently, Jasbir Puar has revisited questions of life and death while working along the lines of what she calls a "bio-necro" political analysis which "conceptually acknowledges [Foucauldian] biopower's direct activity in death, while remaining bound to the optimization of life, and [Mbembe's] necropolitics' nonchalance toward death even as it seeks out killing as a primary aim."[15] In this, she provides potent revising of the place of new homonormativities in geopolitical negotiations of biopolitics. Indeed, the givens of death are already racialized, sexualized, and, as I will argue, animated in specific biopolitical formations.

Since biopower as described by Michel Foucault is thought in two ways—at the level of government, and at the level of individual (human) subjects—how inanimate objects and nonhuman animals participate in the regimes of life (making live) and coerced death (killing) are integral to the effort to understand how biopower works and what its materials are.[16] I am drawn to the potent claims and articulations of biopolitics, given their extraordinary relevance to concerns with sexuality, illness, and racial "matters." Because of a lingering Eurocentrism within what is thought of as biopolitics—its implicit restriction to national bodies, for instance, as well as its species-centric bias that privileges discussions about human citizens—there are productive openings for transnational race, animal, and sexuality scholarship. This contested terrain also opens up new ways of thinking racially and sexually about biopolitics, particularly around governmentality, definitions of population, health regimes, and deathly life. What biopolitical story, for instance, could a discussion of enlivened toxins like transnational lead, their effectivity and affectivity in young white bodies, and their displacement of deathly black and contagious Asian bodies tell? At the least, a consideration of the animation of otherwise "dead" lead and its downstream effects and affects challenges and extends given notions of governmentality, health, and race beyond a national framework.

The anima, animus, animal, and animate are, I argue, not vagaries or templatic zones of undifferentiated matter, but in fact work as complexly racialized and indeed humanized notions. I also highlight what linguistic semantics has done with this concept and bring some of its productive peculiarities (such as the seemingly circular relation between life and death) into conversation with animacy's contemporary theoretical questions. If language normally and habitually distinguishes human and inhuman, live and dead, but then in certain circumstances wholly fails to do so, what might this tell us about the porosity of biopolitical logics themselves?

Animate Currents

The stakes of revisiting animacy are real and immediate, particularly as the coherence of "the body" is continually contested. What, for instance, is the line between the fetus (often categorized as "not yet living") and a rights-bearing infant-subject? How are those in persistent vegetative states deemed to be at, near, or beyond the threshold of death? Environmental toxicity and environmental degradation are figured as slow and dreadful threats to flesh, mind, home, and state. Myths of immunity are challenged, and sometimes dismantled, by transnationally figured communicable diseases, some of them apparently borne by nonhuman animals. Healthful or bodily recuperation looks to sophisticated prosthetic instruments, synthetic drugs, and nanotechnologies, yet such potent modifications potentially come with a mourning of the loss of purity and a concomitant expulsion of bodies marked as unworthy of such "repair."

7

Theoretically, too, the body's former fictions of integrity, autonomy, heterosexual alignment and containment, and wellness give way to critiques from discourse studies, performance studies, affect theory, medical anthropology, and disability theory. In view of such relevant breadth of disciplinary engagement, this book is indebted to, and thinks variously in terms of, philosophical considerations of life, care, and molecularity; linguistics considerations of the sociocritical pulses that radiate out from specific kinds of speech; security studies questions about how threats are articulated and ontologized; and animal studies questions about the links between animals or animalized humans and the human questions they are summoned to figuratively answer.

Among linguists, animacy's definition is unfixed (and, in standard dictionaries, absent). The cognitive linguist Mutsumi Yamamoto describes it as follows:

> The concept of "animacy" can be regarded as some kind of assumed cognitive scale extending from human through animal to inanimate. In addition to the life concept itself, concepts related to the life concept—such as locomotion, sentiency, etc.—can also be incorporated into the cognitive domain of "animacy." . . . A common reflection of "animacy" in a language is a distinction between animate and inanimate, and analogically between human and non-human in some measure. However, animacy is not simply a matter of the semantic feature [+–alive], and its linguistic manifestation is somewhat complicated. Our cognition of animacy and the extent to which we invest a certain body (or body of entities) with humanness or animateness influence various levels of human language a great deal.[17]

By writing that animacy "invest[s] a certain body . . . with humanness or animateness," she implicitly rejects the idea that there is a fixed assignment of animate values to things-in-the-world that is consistently reflected in our language, taking instead the cognitivist approach that the world around us animates according to what we humans make of it.

But Yamamoto also remarks on the complicity of some linguists with the apparent anthropocentricity of a hierarchical ordering of types of entities that positions humans at the top. She makes an observation regarding John Locke's *Essay Concerning Human Understanding*, written in 1694: "Locke argued that the identity of one animal or plant ('vegetable' in his word) lies in maintaining one and the same life, whilst the identity of one person is maintained through one and the same (continuous) consciousness. . . . [H]owever, how can it be proved that [one animal or plant] does not possess one continuous consciousness throughout its life, as a human being does?"[18] Here, Yamamoto clearly supports a broad definition of consciousness that seems quite in keeping with Aristotle's notion of animating principle, or "soul." In this book, I further the productive skepticism inherent in Yamamoto's more radical take on animacy, and move beyond the realm of linguistics to consider how animacy is implicated in political questions of power and the recognition of different subjects, as well as ostensible objects.

Animacy is conceptually slippery, even to its experts. In 2005, Radboud University in the Netherlands held an international linguistics workshop on animacy, noting that it both "surfaces in the grammar" and "plays a role in the background" and proposing that participants finally "pin down the importance of animacy in languages and grammar."[19] In the concluding words to her book, Yamamoto shifts away from analyzing data to appeal to the language of mysticism: "it is of significant interest to linguists to capture the extra-linguistic framework of the animacy concept, because, as it were, this concept *is a spell which strongly influences our mind* in the process of language use and a keystone which draws together miscellaneous structural and pragmatic factors across a wide range of languages in the world."[20] Animacy seems almost to flutter away from the proper grasp of linguistics, refusing to be "pinned down."

Thus, the very animate quality of the term itself is useful, not least because it has the potential to move among disciplines. Taking the flux of these animacies into account as I theorize various connectivities (for instance, subjects and their environments, queers and their kin, couches and their occupants, lives and their biopolitical formations), *Animacies* uncovers implicit mediations of human and inhuman in the transnationally conceived United States, not least through cultural, environmental, and political exchanges within and between the United States and Asia. I pace animacy through several different domains, including language and subjectivity; selected twentieth- and twenty-first-century film, popular culture, and visual media regarding racialized and queer animality; and contemporary environmental illness. Through these case studies, the book develops the idea of animacy as an often racialized and sexualized means of conceptual and affective mediation between human and inhuman, animate and inanimate, whether in language, rhetoric, or imagery.

I argue that animacy is especially current—and carries with it a kind of charge—given that environmental threats (even those that are apparently invisible) such as polluted air, poisoned food, and harmful materials are constantly being figured within contemporary culture in the United States. These purportedly unseen threats demand such figuration, yet also escape direct depiction and are usually represented associatively, in terms of animation, personification, nationalization, integrity, and immunity, as well as in relation to other threats. *Animacies* makes critical links between popular knowledges of environmental entities (which often gather around a few select objects of heightened concern) and the larger sociopolitical environments in which they are seated. This book builds on environmental justice work that tracks the subjects and objects of industrial capital and environmentalist movements that examine the implicit or explicit raced and classed components of toxic threats.[21] Yet I also inquire into the imputations of toxicity as an animated, active, and peculiarly queer agent.

Furthermore, political interest stokes public alarm toward "toxins." We must therefore understand the ways in which toxicity has been so enthusiastically taken up during times of economic instability and panic about transnational flow. *Animacies* demonstrates that interests in toxicity are particularly (if sometimes stealthily) raced and queered. Indeed, toxins participate vividly in the racial mattering of locations, human and nonhuman bodies, living and inert entities, and events such as disease threats. This book aims to offer ways of mapping and diagnosing the mutual imbrications of race, sexuality, ability, environment, and sovereign concern.

In addition, animal and science studies have offered tools through which we can rethink the significance of molecular, cellular, animal, vegetable, or nonhuman life.[22] *Animacies* not only takes into account the broadening field of nonhuman life as a proper object, but even more sensitively, the animateness or inanimateness of entities that are considered either "live" or "dead." Considering differential animacies becomes a particularly critical matter when "life" versus "death" binary oppositions fail to capture the affectively embodied ways that racializations of specific groups are differentially rendered. Sianne Ngai explores the affective meanings of the term *animatedness*, focusing on its manifestation as a property of Asianness and of blackness: "the affective state of being 'animated' seems to imply the most basic or minimal of all affective conditions: that of being, in one way or another, 'moved.' But, as we press harder on the affective meanings of animatedness, we shall see how the seemingly neutral state of 'being moved' becomes twisted into the image of the overemotional racialized subject."[23] Animacy has consequences for both able-bodiedness and ability, especially since a consideration of "inanimate life" imbues the discourses around environmental illness and toxicity. For instance, the constant interabsorption of animate and inanimate bodies in the case of airborne pollution must account for the physical nonintegrity of individual bodies and the merging of forms of "life" and "nonlife." This book seeks to trouble this binary of life and nonlife as it offers a different way to conceive of relationality and intersubjective exchange.

I detail an animacy that is in indirect conversation with historical vitalisms as well as Bennett's "vital materiality."[24] Yet this book focuses critically on an interest in the animal that hides in animacy, particularly in the interest of its attachment to things like sex, race, class, and dirt. That is, my purpose is not to reinvest certain materialities *with* life, but to remap live and dead zones away from those very terms, leveraging animacy toward a consideration of affect in its queered and raced formations. Throughout the book, my core sense of "queer" refers, as might be expected, to exceptions to the conventional ordering of sex, reproduction, and intimacy, though it at times also refers to animacy's veering-away from dominant ontologies and the normativities they promulgate. That is, I suggest that queering is immanent to animate transgressions, violating proper intimacies (including between humans and nonhuman things).

For the purposes of this book, I define affect without necessary restriction, that is, I include the notion that affect is something not necessarily corporeal and that it potentially engages many bodies at once, rather than (only) being contained as an emotion within a single body. Affect inheres in the capacity to affect and be affected. Yet I am also interested in the relatively subjective, individually held "emotion" or "feeling." While I prioritize the former, I also attend to the latter (with cautions about its true possessibility) precisely because, in the case of environmental illness or multiple chemical sensitivity, the entry of an exterior object not only influences the further affectivity of an intoxicated human body, but "emotions" that body: it lends it particular emotions or feelings as against others. I take my cue from Sara Ahmed's notion of "affective economies," in which specific emotions play roles in binding subjects and objects. She writes, "emotions involve subjects and objects, but without residing positively within them. Indeed, emotions may seem like a force of residence as an effect of a certain history, a history that may operate by concealing its own traces."[25] The traces I examine in this book are those of animate hierarchies. If affect includes affectivity—how one body affects another— then affect, in this book, becomes a study of the governmentality of animate hierarchies, an examination of how acts seem to operate with, or against, the order of things (to appropriate Foucault's phrasing for different purposes).[26]

Queer theory, building upon feminism's critique of gender difference, has been at the forefront of recalibrating many categories of difference, and it has further rewritten how we understand affect, especially with regard to trauma, death, mourning, shame, loss, impossibility, and intimacy (not least because of the impact of the HIV/AIDS crisis); key thinkers here include Ann Cvetkovich, Lauren Berlant, Heather Love, and Lee Edelman, among others.[27] As will be demonstrated, these are all terms that intersect in productive ways with animacy. Thus, this book fixes particular attention on queer theoretical questions of intimacy, sexuality, and connectivity; critical race work on the flexible zones of extension of race, the ways that raciality circulates transnationally, and the intersections of race and environment; the staging of animals to displace racial and sexual questions; disability studies questions about toxicity and recuperation; environmental justice connections between environmentally condemned marginalized communities and the toxins conferred upon them; and queer of color mappings of race and sexuality in "unlikely" places.

How the Chapters Move

The book is organized into three parts, with two chapters each: "Words," "Animals," and "Metals." These three parts each examine and track a feature of animacy in detail, along the lines of a focus: in "Words," language and figural dehumanization; in "Animals," queer animals and animality; and in "Metals," the toxic metal particles lead and mercury. Each pair attempts to investigate a question about kinds of animacy, and each exhibits, or performs, the result of letting its object *animate*, that is — considering that its etymological history still survives somewhere in its linguistic present — letting it breathe, gender itself, or enact "animus" in its negativity. For instance, in the "Words" part, the animacy of the word *queer* is unleashed to find new linguistic loci; later, in "Animals," the animal transubstantiates beyond the borders of our insistent human ontologies; and finally, toxic metals are let loose in the bloodstream of the text to queer its own affective regard.

In this sense, each chapter, while an animation in itself, is simultaneously an attempt to seek a transdisciplinary method forged through my background in cognitive linguistics and inflected by my commitments to queer of color, feminist, and disability scholarship. Thus, animacy is still identifiable, even if it leaves behind its epistemological pinnings. If these methodological efforts may seem eccentric, my hope is that they might, in their animate crossings and changing disciplinary intimacies, be plumbed for a certain kind of utility, particularly to the extent that each is engaged in some way with questions of race, sexuality, and disability.

Words

"Language and Mattering Humans," the first chapter, is framed by a consideration of language as animated, as a means of embodied condensation of social, cultural, and political life. Here I consider in detail a particular political grammar, what linguists call an *animacy hierarchy*, which conceptually arranges human life, disabled life, animal life, plant life, and forms of nonliving material in orders of value and priority. Animacy hierarchies have broad ramifications for issues of ecology and environment, since objects, animals, substances, and spaces are assigned constrained zones of possibility and agency by extant grammars of animacy. The chapter examines a seemingly exceptional form of linguistic usage to think through gradations of animacy and objectification: the insult, a move of representational injury that implicates language as capable of incurring damage. Linguistic insults vividly demonstrate that language acts to contain and order many kinds of matter, including lifeless matter; they also show that language users are "animate theorists" insofar as they deploy and rework such orders of matter. Furthermore, insults that refer to humans as abjected matter or as less than human — for instance, Senator George Allen's infamous "macaca" utterance from 2006—cannily assert human status as a requisite condition for securing nonhuman comparators, thereby rendering the idea of "dehumanization" paradoxical.

Chapter 2, "Queer Animation," then asks: if language helps to coerce certain figures into nonbeing, or to demote on an animacy hierarchy, then what are the modes of revival, return, or rejoinder? One popular social strategy has been to "reclaim" distressed objects as a move toward political agency, sometimes literalized in a discredited social label. Both subtle and explicit de-animations, therefore, may be responded to with plays at re-animation through linguistic reclaiming acts, not least with the act of speech itself, and I investigate this possibility by giving special consideration to the scholarly and political uptake of an identity reference and theoretical entity called *queer*, a term that seems semantically predestined to launch its own animations. Analyzing *queer*'s multiple senses with cognitive linguistics, I show how two conceptual forms emerged with two lexicalized forms, verb and noun: a re-animated queer verb and a de-animated queer noun, which open it to some critiques that queer politics have made the "wrong" turn to essentialization and identity politics. I suggest that Foucault's governmentality might be revisited in the linguistic notion of governance, especially concerning its sensitivity to the animacy hierarchy.

Animals

In chapter 3, "Queer Animality," I consider animality as a condensation of racialized animacy, taking up inquiries relating to the paradoxical morbidities and vibrancies of the queer figure and its potentiality for nonnormative subject formations. I locate queerness, in this chapter, in both wrong marriage and improper intimacy. Using performativity as a point of departure for a theoretical kinship frequently found between queerness and animality, I examine a signal argument in the work of the language philosopher J. L. Austin. Austin set up the example of a failed pronouncement of marriage: in this case, nonauthorized official speech by evoking "a marriage with a monkey." Here I read the "exemplary ridiculousness" of Austin's example as indicating a wider anxiety about the legitimacy of exchange between properly animated figures, teasing apart the combined intimations of sexual oddity with racial nonwhiteness and figural blackness. Moving then to a selection of visual media from the turn of the twentieth century, I assess the role that queerness, miscegenation, and comparative racisms play in rendering some bodies less animate, even when affective intensities surround them. Closely attending to this visual culture, I examine how controversies around citizenship in the United States at this time were displaced onto the figure of the "dumb" animal, which was both raced and sexed for rhetorical effect.

In chapter 4, "Animals, Sex, and Transsubstantiation," I ask what happens when the matter of gender, race, and sexuality itself shifts, either in our diagnostic ontologies or in its own figural actuality. I begin with biopolitical questions of animal—and human—neutering, asking how gender and family are queered in both normative and exceptional ways; here, I use "queer" to indicate challenges to the normativity of sex (sexing) that are sometimes biopolitically authorized. I then turn to an odd yet pervasive omission in cultural animal representations—that of the missing morphology of the genitalia suggesting that such a phenomenon could, instead of being seen as a trivial or expected circumstance, be thought in relation to the cultural production of animals. I ask what this missing morphology animates, whether due to notions of propriety; to the idea that skin and fur are treated as essentially sartorial, displacing but confirming an interior human; or to an attempt at symbolic neutering (since animals often serve as stand-ins for rampant sexuality) or transing. Questions of transgendering are put into conversation with this omission to ask after the valence of this kind of queer affectivity.

Metals

Turning to allegedly insensate—but nevertheless potent—particles, chapter 5, "Lead's Racial Matters," considers the Chinese lead toys panic in the United States in 2007 and its representation in mainstream media. Here, animacy becomes a property of lead, a highly mobile and poisonous substance that feeds anxieties about transgressors of permeable borders, whether of skin or country. The chapter traces the physical travels (animations) of lead as an industrial by-product, while simultaneously observing lead's critical role in the representation of national security concerns, interests in sovereignty, and racial and bodily integrity in the United States. I argue that the lead painted onto children's toys was animated and racialized as Chinese, whereas its potential victims were depicted as largely white. In the context of the interests of the United States, the phrase *Chinese lead* is consistently rendered not as a banal industrial product, but as an exogenous toxin painted onto the toys of innocent American children, and as the backhanded threat of a previously innocent boon of transnational labor whose exploitive realities are beginning to dawn on the popular subconscious of the United States. This lead scare shifted both its mythic origins and its mythic targets, effectively replacing domestic concerns about black and impoverished children and their exposures to environmental lead.

Finally, chapter 6, "Following Mercurial Affect," shifts the book's perspective from a theoretical examination of animacy to the biopolitical impact of environmental toxins on human bodies in the context of present-day emergent illnesses. Here the term *animacy* takes mobile, molecular form, as particles that both intoxicate a body into environmental illness and as particles that constantly threaten that body's fragile state. The chapter considers the ways in which environmental illness restages expected forms of sociality, rendering them as queer, disordered proximities in the case of molecular intimacies and orientations. Such altered sociality also evinces in the case of the often-different geographies of affective ties to animate and inanimate objects exhibited in autism (which in some views symptomatically overlap with environmental factors, rather than being determined by them). Such forms of sociality have the potential to trouble the alternative socialities offered by queer theory, as well as the thematics of negativity that recent queer theory takes up as a political question.

I conclude with an afterword, "The Spill and the Sea." It opens by pairing the oil spill in the Gulf of Mexico in April 2010 and the "killing" language summoned to commemorate its technological resolution with an unlikely partner: the human-wannabe-fish protagonist of the animated Hayao Miyazaki film *Ponyo*, released in 2008. These two different phenomena come together as an indication of the questions that continue to be raised by the affective politics surrounding both animate and inanimate things. Miyazaki's cosmology is imbued, I argue, with unexpected affectivity, which is part of his animation's magic. I end with a plea to revisit the possibility of "care" across the realm of animacy, considering it as a means of unlikely cross-affiliation, a politics that wanders in and out of mainstreams.

Disciplinary Animation, Shifting Archive

Fundamentally interdisciplinary in nature, *Animacies* traverses a number of intersecting fields. First, it comes out of, but is by no means limited to, my training as a queer feminist linguist with a heightened sensitivity to the political and disciplinary mobility of terms. My argument tracks how the notion of animacy implicitly figures within and reorients a range of theoretical constructions, from disability studies with its focus on redefining given conditions of bodily and mental life; to queer theory's considerations of feeling, sex, and death; to biosecurity studies with its mapping of the character of national obsessions about terrorism, ingestion, transmission, and infection. I build on the feminist insight that "nature" is a feminized counterpoint to masculinized "culture," but also approach "nature" as a complexly differentiated site, gendered, racialized, and sexualized in ways that are not consistent or predictable.[28] And in view of the place that a heteronormatively textured sovereignty takes in the national anxieties of the United States about disability and illness, such as the lead toy panic, it is instructive to turn to both disability theory and queer theory in the consideration of environmental illness. Here I am indebted to queer-disability theorists such as Eli Clare and Robert McRuer.[29]

I want to affirm, study, and reflect upon the monkey whose marriage to a human Austin dismissively refers to as a mockery in chapter 3, for this queer, potentially racialized, invalid marriage has much to say. That is, nonlife as life, and monkey as legitimate marrying subject, materialize, replenish, and trouble ideologies, sentiments, and ontologies of race, humanness, and security. I reside in this so-called negative zone, one of abjection, racial marking, toxic queerness, and illness, to think about the epistemic riches of possibility within. If this is not a recuperative project, it is nevertheless an affirmative one.

Thinking through the fluidities of either "life" or "death" that seem to run across borders of animate and inanimate, and through orders of state preference that (in large part due to the commodifying and virtualizing and abstracting processes of capitalism) disregard common understandings of "life" or "liveliness," I follow connectivities that animate before me, without a fore-given attachment to a "proper" or "consistent" object. The chapters of this book therefore interanimate, rather than organizing fully and completely with regard to one another.

Furthermore, *Animacies* steps out of and around disciplinary closure, particularly since my objects of concern seem to call for movement. Thus, I shift weight between interdisciplinary stresses of analysis, from linguistic to literary to phenomenological, alternately focusing on close readings of films, illustration, archival research, linguistic evidence, newspaper accounts, and popular media coverage. The concluding chapter, framed by personal narrative, performs a provocative and pointedly intimate invocation to rethink animacy in the reader's own terms.

Finally, a word about my shifting archive. This book uses several lenses to explore the rangy, somewhat unruly construct called animacy. In my view, a somewhat "feral" approach to disciplinarity naturally changes the identity of what might be the proper archives for one's scholarship. Nonetheless, my research is grounded in twentieth- and twenty-first-century cultural productions, ones that are often framed within transnational encounters between the United States and Asia, from Fu Manchu to the contemporary Chinese artist Xu Bing. As I shift from discussions of dehumanizing language (linguistics?) to animal genitality (cultural studies?) to health discourse (science studies?) to (in)human and queer sociality (queer theory?), it is my intention and design that the archives themselves feralize, giving up any idealization about their domestication, refusing to answer whether they constitute proper or complete coverage. At the same time, I take care to contextualize (whether temporally or geopolitically) the "thing" under discussion, since I have no interest in running roughshod over historical particularity.

Thinking and moving ferally constitutes a risk, both to the borders of disciplinarity and to the author who is metonymically feralized along with the text. Yet it is arguably also a necessary condition of examining animacy within disability, postcolonial, and queer studies. I venture, as well, that as surely as intersectionality "matters" lives and nonlives, animacy might ask of queer of color analysis, and other modes of analysis that rely upon intersectionality, that the seeming givens thought to centrally inform race, sexuality, and gender might bear further examination — that is, that animacy tugs the categories of race and sexuality out of their own homes. I refer to Roderick Ferguson's useful discussion of queer of color critique's potential to counter the obliquely intersecting racialization, gendering, sexualization, and classing that exist within national spaces. Notably, Ferguson describes queer of color critique itself as "a heterogeneous enterprise made up of women of color feminism, materialist analysis, poststructuralist theory, and queer critique."[30]

I use the word *feral* in direct conversation with the disability scholars Sharon Snyder and David Mitchell, who ask about the location of disability theory within disciplinary formations: "Is it possible to keep the freshness—the insight-driven 'wildness'—of the field in the midst of seeking a home base in the academy? Can disability studies sustain its productive 'feral' nature without being reduced to a lesser form of academic evolutionism or thoroughly domesticated as an academic endeavor?"[31]

The notion of feral also brings up ambivalent identifications with antihomes, since it both rejects the domicile and reinvigorates a notion of public shelter. As a moving target, the sign of the feral also invokes diaspora and its potential to naturalize nationalisms and capitalist geopolitics. Gayatri Gopinath's work on queer South Asian public cultures is useful here; Gopinath, reflecting on diaspora's simplest definition as "the dispersal and movement of populations from one particular national or geographic location to other disparate sites," provokes us to closely examine valences of queer "home" that interrupt and trouble diaspora's "dependence on a genealogical, implicitly heteronormative reproductive logic."[32] Indeed, the ambivalently homed feral figure also appears in my text as the sign of a biopolitical (nationalized) demand for population control.

I choose instead, here, to allow for the impression of a certain surfeit, and simultaneously to refuse to categorize humans, animals, objects as so very cleanly distinct from one another. To do this is to hope for a certain "wiliness" of the sort performed by the writer and queer critic Silviano Santiago, who in his essay "The Wily Homosexual" answers the implicit request posed by Western white queer conference-goers to provide "native" Brazilian knowledge by responding both vertically (as expected) and horizontally. That horizontality, which Santiago describes as a "supplement" rather than a clumsy inversion of the hierarchy of values implicit in the question, can be described as "elusive" only from an insistently typological drive to closure and hence leaves a certain trace of mystery and escape in the path of his text.[33] My hope is for that opening, insofar as it can be found in this book, to be inviting and productive. Animacy, after all, is an unstable terrain; this means that (and it is my belief that) its archives are not "pinnable." The various archives, which seem at first to be distinct, are surprisingly very much in conversation with each other and, beyond my attempts to "interarticulate" these connections, ring with one another's strange vitality.

As many scholars of illness have remarked, "living through illness" seems, at least at first, to confound the narrativized, temporalized imaginary of "one's human life," for it can constitute an undesired stopping point that is sporadically animated by frenzied attempts (to the extent one's energy permits) to resolve the abrupt transformations of illness that often feel in some way "against life." Some transformations suggest a suspension of time (productivity time, social time), and some involve the wearing of a deathly pallor or other visible registers of morbidity.[34] But for those with the privileges of food, care, and physical support, this pause can also become a meditation (if forced) on the conditions that underlie both illness and wellness, that is, the biopoliticized animacies that foretell what may become of a changing body, human or not, living or nonliving. For this, I am grateful for the pause that, even if it took me "out of life," gave me the matter that could animate this book.

PART I ✳ WORDS

1

Language and Mattering Humans

This chapter aims to recover the alchemical magic of language, whether benevolent or vicious, by demonstrating explicit ways that it animates humans, animals, and things in between. I suggest that this can be done in collusion with existing registers of citizenship, race, sex, ability, and sexuality, depending on the recurrent materializations of iterative power; and it might possibly be done without abandoning the nonhuman animal to the realm of the nonlinguistic (as dominant hierarchies foretell). Language's fundamental means, I suggest, is something called *animacy*, a concept most deeply explored in cognitive linguistics.

In what follows, I sketch a brief history of the study of animacy within linguistics, as I range beyond the borders of that discipline to think through how de-animation (by way of objectification) also proceeds through and within speech. I go directly to linguistics and ask after its own devices, beginning with the moment in anthropological linguistics where animacy hierarchies first appeared. Then I provisionally deploy a specific framework from the subfield of cognitive linguistics, insisting on the generally untold stories of conceptual mattering and materiality that lie there. I then turn to questions of objectification that have long circulated in critical race, feminist, and disability theory; for while, as I will demonstrate, objectification is a preeminent kind of mattering, its linguistic instance is far from a self-evident process. I pay special attention to how the "animal" is relentlessly recruited as the presumed field of rejection of and for the "human."

Introducing Animacy

For linguists, animacy is the quality of liveness, sentience, or humanness of a noun or noun phrase that has grammatical, often syntactic, consequences. Bernard Comrie calls animacy an "extralinguistic conceptual property" that manifests in "a range of formally quite different ways . . . in the structure of different languages."[1] Despite animacy's apparently extralinguistic character, however, it pushes forward again and again: Comrie explains that "the reason why animacy is of linguistic relevance is because essentially the same kinds of conceptual distinction are found to be of structural relevance across a wide range of languages."[2]

Mutsumi Yamamoto notes that, by necessity, no treatment of animacy can be limited to the linguistic, for animacy lies within and without. While animacy does not behave in a regular fashion in relation to language structures, it retains a consistent cross-linguistic *significance* that no other concept seems to address: "the same kind of conceptual distinction seems to be working as a dominant force in various different structural and pragmatic factors across a wide variety of languages in the world."[3] Furthermore, Comrie notes that even if animacy is not apparently structurally encoded in a language, it can influence the direction of language change, as in the case of Slavonic languages.[4] Even if language is in some sense tuned to animacy, animacy is clearly not obligated to it. Does animacy slip out of language's bounds, or does language slip out of animacy's bounds? In this book, the slippage of animacy in relation to its successive co-conspirators will be a repeating, and in my view most productive, refrain.

Many scholars credit animacy's first serious appearance in linguistics to Michael Silverstein's idea of an "animacy hierarchy," which appears in a comparative study of indigenous North American Chinookan, Australian Dyirbal, and other indigenous Australian languages published in 1976.[5] While most understandings of animacy today depart from Silverstein's binary-features account and his focus on finding an explanation for ergative languages, largely in first, second, and third personhood, his initial insights and formulations maintain relevance today in their close pairing of extralinguistic factors with linguistic structure.

Ergative languages (such as Basque) are distinguished from accusative languages (such as Japanese and English) by how their behavior is mapped in relation to transitive verbs (verbs that have a subject and direct object) and intransitive verbs (verbs with only one argument, a subject). How the subjects or objects of these two types of verbs receive "case marking," that is, a grammatical indicator of their semantic role in relation to the action of the verb, determines the overall language classification. In accusative systems, the *object* of a transitive verb (the lion ate *me*) can receive distinct marking, whereas the subject of a transitive verb (*I* ate the lion) and the subject of an intransitive verb (*I* panicked) are the same. In ergative systems, the *subject* of a transitive verb receives ergative case marking, unlike the object of the transitive verb or the subject of an intransitive verb. Such behavior, however, is not entirely fixed. Many ergative languages exhibit "split" behavior in which both ergative and accusative case markings are possible for certain subject or object arguments; that is, certain expressions can be rendered either way.

Silverstein explained this split by proposing a hierarchy of animacy. He claimed that many similar Australian languages appeared to show "splits of ergativity patterned with respect to a lexical hierarchy," locating the determining line of distinction between ergative and accusative markings in the characteristic semantics of nouns:[6]

> In this paper, I want to bring out the fact that "split" of case-marking is not random. At its most dramatic, it defines a hierarchy of what might be called "inherent lexical content" of noun phrases, first and second person as well as third person. This hierarchy expresses the semantic naturalness for a lexically-specified noun phrase to function as agent of a true transitive verb, and inversely the naturalness of functioning as patient of such. The noun phrases at the top of the hierarchy manifest nominative-accusative case-marking, while those at the bottom manifest ergative-absolutive case marking. Sometimes there is a middle ground which is a three-way system of O-A-S case markings. We can define the hierarchy independent of the facts of split ergativity by our usual notions of surface-category markedness.[7]

Silverstein observed that *less* animate subjects were *more* likely to receive special ergative marking, in a kind of communicative reassurance that such types of subjects could indeed possess the agentive or controlling capacities required to do the action provided by the verb.

More animate subjects did not need this marking and could receive regular nominative (unmarked) case. His observations resulted in a suggested "hierarchy of animacy" from inanimate to third, second, and first personhood: "So the case-marking system here seems to express a notion of the "naturalness" or unmarked character of the various noun phrases in different adjunct functions, particularly the transitive ones. It is most 'natural' in transitive constructions for first or second person to act on third, least 'natural' for third to act on first or second. Decomposed into constituent hierarchies, it is natural for third person to function as patient (O) and for first and second persons to function as agent (A), but not vice-versa. The marked cases, ergative and accusative, formally express the violations of these principles."[8]

First- and second-person animacies, all else being equal, tend to value higher in animacy than third-person ones. Later studies found that another major parameter of animacy is the individuation scale.[9] More easily individuated entities than those that are massified or "instances of a type" receive more animacy. Furthermore, Silverstein noted that the hierarchy was implicational: if a borderline entity behaved in a certain way, then those entities *below* its animacy level could not behave syntactically as if they were more animate. We can begin to see here how racism, stereotyping, and a lack of empathy can coconspire to construct deflated animacies for some humans (and, arguably, some nonhuman animals) in spite of biological equivalences.

Perhaps the broadest cross-linguistic study of animacy hierarchies was done by John Cherry.[10] Cherry's study, representing several language families and including Swahili, English, Navajo, Shona, Chinook, Algonquian, Hopi, Russian, Polish, and Breton, yielded a summary that roughly characterizes each station (with its own hierarchical orders) in an animacy hierarchy, and offered perhaps the most detailed summary of its kind:

> *Humans*:
> adult > nonadult; male/MASC gender > female/FEM gender; free > enslaved; able-bodied > disabled; linguistically intact > prelinguistic/linguistically impaired; familiar (kin/named) > unfamiliar (nonkin/unnamed); proximate (1p & 2p pronouns) > remote (3p pronouns).
> *Animals*:
> higher/larger animals > lower/smaller animals > insects; whole animal > body part;

Inanimates:

motile/active > nonmotile/nonactive; natural > manmade; count > mass;

Incorporeals:

abstract concepts, natural forces, states of affairs, states of being, emotions, qualities, activities, events, time periods, institutions, regions, diverse intellectual objects.[11]

This schema asserts that an adult male who is "free" (as opposed to enslaved), able-bodied, and with intact linguistic capacities, one who is also familiar, individual, and positioned nearby, stands at the top of the hierarchy as the most "animate" or active agent within grammars of ordering.[12] Lower down, and hence less agentive, would be, for example, a large, distant population of females. Lower still would be nonhuman animals (ranked by size). Near the bottom would be something like "sadness." Obviously, this conceptual ordering has profound ramifications for questions of gender and sexuality, species difference, disability, and race (though race as such is not broached on Cherry's list); the hierarchalizations written into these questions are explored in the following chapters. Cherry deems these hierarchalizations socially significant cognitive categories, but not others. To that extent, his work does not begin to contend with the social, political, and often colonial contexts that subtend these very categories. The merit of Cherry's work is that, for him, "animism" is a generalized perspective rather than a belief system proper only to "primitive societies." And he further cautions against taking the list as rigid.

Yet in a subtler vein, Cherry does seem to align "adult" taxonomies (in contrast with underdeveloped "child" taxonomies, which are considered rife with errors, full of anthropomorphizing slippages between animal, inanimate matter, and human) with more hierarchalized relations between elements, in the form of popular biological understandings that encode more expected horizontal and vertical relations among humans, nonhuman animals, and plants. Taking animacy variabilities seriously, and not just as a matter of child development, has consequences for possible resistance to what Cherry calls "adult" taxonomies. It further demonstrates the likelihood that language users will draw differing lines between what is "socially constructed" and what is "biological." The cross-linguistic consistencies among the data do not vitiate this possibility of variation, even if they might press us to contend with the notion that something widespread (even universal, that is to say, prevalent as a norm) about preferred manners of distinguishing things just might be going on. Why, after all, are person distinctions so common?

Studies of linguistic animacy tend to culminate in the idea that for all of animacy's many component features, their significance is collective: it is their derivation, or the contextual importance of some factors over others, that results in the most likely effector of the possible action denoted by the verb. Comrie tentatively wrote, "A high degree of animacy is necessary for a noun phrase to be interpreted as having a high degree of control or as an experiencer, but is not a sufficient condition."[13]

Yamamoto, the author of the most recent comprehensive study of linguistic animacy, has been even more salubriously tentative, writing that "in addition to the life concept itself, concepts related to the life concept—such as locomotion, sentiency, etc.—can also be incorporated into the cognitive domain of 'animacy.'"[14] That is, lifeliness in itself does not exhaust animacy. Even though animacy seems to be generally scalar, it is not monolithic, since it is sensitive to further distinctions; locomotion might trump sentience in one instance, whereas the relation is reversed in another instance. More importantly, animacy is realized in sometimes radically different ways both within and across languages. Yamamoto shows how many instances controvert what the generalized animacy hierarchy predicts, even when biological theories that contradict this hierarchy stand beside such "knowledge," whether because of early language conflations, fanciful imagination, or a remarkable cosmology. (She shows this even though she offers as examples the rather innocent ones of child language, profound companion animal horizontality, fictional conceit, and language representing decisions made by corporations.)[15] That abstractions tend to be placed at the bottom of animacy hierarchies belies the fact that they are easily gendered or personified; consider the conventionalized gendering in the United States of weather forces such as hurricanes.

Furthermore, animacy variations may be within languages or across them. For instance, within English, some language users may not make any distinctions in animacy with their dogs, while others do; whereas in Manam, an indigenous language spoken in Papua New Guinea, the dual and paucal grammatical forms are used only for humans and a select group of "domesticated dogs, birds (including fowls), and now domesticated goats, horses and other larger animals introduced quite recently into New Guinea," though not necessarily used for the same animals when they are wild.[16]

Given animacy's insistent presence, as well as its variation, it is compelling to consider where and how such hierarchies might be generated. For Cherry, animacy (which he calls *animism*) is a phenomenologically derived intuitive recognition of like kind on the basis of one's own *embodiment, purposiveness,* and *activity,* which is installed early in development: "We are necessarily oriented to other entities in the very terms implicit in our orientation to our own selves. Phenomenologically, the first figure against the background of the world is always oneself."[17] This "like kind" recognition is similar to what Ronald Langacker calls an *empathy hierarchy.*[18] Yamamoto also attributes animacy's very hierarchical nature to anthropocentric human cognition, but pointedly asks, "why [are] *Homo sapiens* supposed to be much more 'animate' than, say, amoebae?"[19] Further, she points out that linguists themselves, beholden to human supremacy, have often unthinkingly made the error of substituting "human/nonhuman" distinctions for "animate/inanimate." The degree of anthropocentricity most certainly varies, is arguably more cultural than universal, and helps us to see how certain animate hierarchies or animate variants become privileged in one group or another.

If animacy not only works in different ways for different cultures but indicates different hierarchalizations of matter, then it is critical to distinguish between relatively dominant formulations of animacy hierarchies and relatively subordinated ones, a project that seems all too vital for studies that reify the place in "nature" of non-Western or subordinated cosmologies.[20] (If we were to assume that nonhuman animals themselves had animacy hierarchies as part of their ontology, then we could count nonhuman animacy hierarchies as also subordinated.) There is thus good cause for either serious consideration of subordinated animacy realizations or—as is my project here—mapping the coercivities and leakages of the dominant ones.

The rest of this book focuses on this conceptual hierarchy in the context of the recent United States, while retaining a grasp on the renderings of it presented here. While I consider the animacy hierarchy as linguists do, as a prevalent conceptual structure and ordering that might possibly come out of understandings of lifeliness, sentience, agency, ability, and mobility in a richly textured world, I actively contextualize this hierarchy as a politically dominant one, one potentially affected and shaped by the spread of Christian cosmologies, capitalism, and the colonial orders of things. In this way, I depart from Yamamoto, Cherry, and Comrie, since my understanding of grammar expands beyond linguistic coercion to broader strokes of biopolitical governance.

That is to say, I read this hierarchy, treated by linguists as an avowedly *conceptual* organization of worldly and abstract things with grammatical consequence, as naturally also an ontology of *affect*: for animacy hierarchies are precisely about which things can or cannot affect—or be affected by—which other things within a specific scheme of possible action (with the added delimitation within linguistics that the hierarchy is, with reference to a culturally shared order of things, a field of reference whose shared usage facilitates communicating). Finally, I take a rather uncommon linguistic approach of studying not this dominant animacy hierarchy's norms, but its failings—as I call them, its leakages, its "ambivalent grammaticalities"—to map the ways in which such a conceptual hierarchy cannot but fail, the ways in which it must continually interanimate in spite of its apparent fixedness. Above all, I claim that animacy is political, shaped by what or who counts as human, and what or who does not.

Making Macaca

Animacy underlies language and serves in specific ways to inform words and their affective potency. Utilizing linguistic theory and cognitive linguistics to both *follow* and *imagine* language—at the same time paying attention to the fault lines of these fields and their workings—I am interested in tracing how animacy is defined, tested, and configured via its ostensible opposite: the inanimate, deadness, lowness, nonhuman animals (rendered as insensate), the abject, the object. In what follows, I examine how the semantics and pragmatics of objectification and dehumanization work through and within systems of race, animality, and sexuality. Insults, shaming language, slurs, and injurious speech can be thought of as tools of objectification, but these also, in crucial ways, paradoxically rely on animacy as they objectify, thereby providing possibilities for reanimation.[21]

Both objectification and dehumanization are central notions within critical theory; in my view, these terms cannot operate without close

I. Senator George Allen pointing to S. R. Sidarth,
"this fellow here . . . macaca." Still from YouTube
video, uploaded August 14, 2006.

attention to animacy. I begin with two recent examples of insulting language to consider how de-animation functions, in particular how insults utilize complex social and political devices that hinge on animacy. I then turn to summarize how both dehumanization and objectification have historically been theorized, considering a range of thinkers, including Karl Marx and Frantz Fanon, to investigate how these terms have been deployed.

On August 11, 2006, U.S. Senator George Allen, a Republican from Virginia, at a rally related to his candidacy for reelection to the Senate, was being videorecorded by a Virginian of South Asian heritage, Shekar Ramanuja (S. R.) Sidarth, who was a volunteer for the opposing Democratic campaign of James Webb. Sidarth was the only nonwhite person present. Allen pointed to Sidarth (figure 1), saying: "This fellow here, over here with the yellow shirt, macaca, or whatever his name is. He's with my opponent. He's following us around everywhere. And it's just great. . . . Let's give a welcome to macaca, here. Welcome to America and the real world of Virginia."[22] Allen's gesture of pointing straight at Sidarth's camera lens also had the effect of pointing directly at the viewers of the video, viewers who thereby potentially became implicated (or even hailed) in this exchange.

Whether Allen was attempting to neutralize the felt threat of an opponent's videotaping of the event, or capitalizing on what he read as an opportunity to emphasize the demographic and ideological differences between him and Webb, the means he chose to do so were unmistakably vicious (and apparently fatal, in the case of his candidacy). This condensed utterance, when unpacked, suggests at the very least a tacky commingling of racialized signifiers and negative insinuations: "yellowness" as a signifier of Asianness; the lack of a proper (Americanized) name; being unworthy of a title (Allen was a Californian import to Virginia and may have missed that eliding the honorific "Mr." is generally unacceptable in Southern politeness norms); the double social meanings of "following" (suggesting a dependent child); the exogeneity to the United States implied by "Welcome to America" and a peripheral relationship to the authenticity and authority of Virginia as a state and as a place; and the presence of apparent Tunisian slang for "monkey" or "macaque," often used in racist ways to refer to darker-skinned Tunisians, some of whom are referred to in Tunisia as "blacks." If objectification works by a concert of language, address, and gesture, are these some of the linguistic conditions of dehumanization? Does dehumanization benefit—or is its process made baldly transparent—by the explicitness of an animal direct comparator against which the human is measured (such as a macaca)?

Within hours, Sidarth had reported the event to his supervisors. The video of the event was eventually made public, timed carefully by Webb's campaign. While Allen initially denied that he had anything to apologize for, the video's presence ballooned on the Internet. Its viewing in all parts of the United States effectively forced Allen to eventually make an official apology. The incident was ultimately credited with Allen's downfall; he lost his election bid to Webb. Though Allen's words functioned as "hate speech," the responses to his outburst did not exactly follow the expected juridical or litigious routes, for Sidarth did not sue or bring charges (as Wendy Brown has argued, efforts to regulate such "injurious" language end up further legitimizing the State).[23] Instead, an inchoate collective public shaming was aimed back at Allen. Mari Matsuda in 1989 wrote of the juridical treatments of hate speech, "The choice of public sanction, enforced by the state, is a significant one. The kinds of injuries and harms historically left to private individuals to absorb and resist through private means is no accident."[24] In this case, the viral potency of the video demonstrated the publicity of the uptake of Allen's act—particularly as politicians are considered "public figures" rather than private citizens—and worked outside the strict auspices of the State.

Animacy figures in this event in several senses, from the animality implied by the insult itself, to the "viral" nature of the incident's clip on the Internet, which took on (as is said about such widely dispersed videos) a life of its own. The Allen campaign's first explanation was that the word "sounded like" *mohawk*, in recognition of Sidarth's hairstyle, a curious deflection toward another racialized figure (the Native American). Sidarth said, however, that though the sides of his head were shaved, he was sporting more of a "mullet," yet another racialized (white) and markedly classed hairstyle. Having long seemed to minimize or conceal his heritage, Allen had reason not to acknowledge the possible provenance of such a racial insult in the Tunisian French of his own immigrant mother; when this fact was revealed, Allen accused the questioning reporter of making "slights" against him and his mother. A pointing gesture, for its part, can index phenotypic components of the structure of race and the scopic aspect of show, example, and display. Allen's accusatory pointing finger recalls Frantz Fanon's discussion of the utterance "Look, a black man!" while "macaca" recalls Fanon's uncertain equivocation between whether he had been hailed as a "black man" or, in fact, an "animal."[25] In Fanon's oft-discussed scene, the narrator is surrounded by whites at an Algerian train station and is pointed to by a frightened child:

> "Look, a Negro!" It was an external stimulus that flicked over me as I passed by. I made a tight smile. "Look, a Negro!" It was true. It amused me. "Look, a Negro!" The circle was drawing a bit tighter. I made no secret of my amusement. "Mama, see the Negro! I'm frightened!" Frightened! Frightened! Now they were beginning to be afraid of me. I made up my mind to laugh myself to tears, but laughter had become impossible. . . . My body was given back to me sprawled out, distorted, recolored, clad in mourning in that white winter day. The Negro is an animal, the Negro is bad.[26]

Fanon notes that that racist spectacle, in which the pointing is both verbal and gestural, not only directs attention to a shared focus, but it renders the (black) body into an object of consciousness; in its subjectivity, it nevertheless becomes an object and is forced to cultivate a "third-person consciousness," to be an objectified subject, one that in its objectivity becomes interchangeable with an animal. (I return to Fanon later in this chapter.)

Media coverage of Allen's "macaca" slur was comprehensive. In the *New York Times*, Frank Rich wrote, "His defense in the macaca incident was that he had no idea that the word, the term for a genus of monkey, had any racial connotation. But even if he were telling the truth—even if Mr. Allen were not a racist—his non-macaca words were just as damning."[27] In *Salon*, Michael Scherer retold the story: "Over the next week, people consult dictionaries in several languages. They find that the word 'macaca' is a term for monkey, used in some places around the world as a racial epithet."[28] Finally, in its "Person of the Year: You" issue (subtitled "Yes, you. You control the Information Age. Welcome to your world," echoing Allen's welcome to Sidarth), *Time* profiled several individuals representing the new "digital democracy," among them Sidarth, in an implicit reference to the democratically styled viral video "activism" he initiated. In the profile's only reference to race, Sidarth says, "He'd never addressed me before, and then to do so in this context, it was humiliating. That it was in a racial context made it worse."[29]

For all its facets, this very brief interchange precisely hinged on the *racial politics of animality*, yet the complex historicity of racialized animality was quickly glanced over by the major news media covering the event. All of these accounts referred to the use of "macaca" as a racial epithet without elaboration, perhaps, in the elision, demonstrating that the notion that calling someone a monkey is racist should be self-evident. Frank Rich's writing asserted the common assumption that one either is or is not a racist, rather than that one is woven into and situated within specific discourses of racism. He did correctly identify the "damning" racializing of immigration in Allen's other utterances: it was while *looking at* Sidarth and indexing his physical and social position for others that Allen could utter "welcome to the real America."

There is no need to credit Allen with the inheritance of an exogenous form of racism to explain its racial content (as Scherer did: "used in some places around the world"). Allen only needed to have a reference to contemporary American architectures of racism; for instance, a simian imputation for a human being readily invokes theories of evolution that place monkeys and apes at earlier, "primitive" stages of evolution or development than the "higher" humans being compared to them. Many nuances of racism, while in some ways articulated around "race," are themselves built upon many complex animacy hierarchies (animality being one), each of which can potentially implicate directly the charge of racial abjection without reference to race itself. Though Allen did not provide the equation between "race" and "simian" as Fanon did, his surrounding speech and gesture, enabled by an animacy hierarchy, made that equation evident.

For his part, Sidarth summed up the dense interchange with Allen by addressing the salience of the nonhuman animal at its center: he submitted a three-word "essay" to a selective seminar at the University of Virginia: "I am macaca." (He did not write "I am Macaca," which would have the effect of individuating the type into a proper name.) This declarative statement, referring to a positive identification with a previous nomination that became a public event, an identification that confronts its racist deployment while being categorically false, gets simultaneously at the dizzying is-and-is-not politics of the reclaiming of insults, as well as at the shared taxonomic heritage of humans and macaques. It also invites us to reconsider the structures that make that simple equation either work or falter.

Turtle's Eggs and Other Nonhumans

I turn now to another example to further illustrate how dehumanizing insults hinge on the salient invocation of the nonhuman animal. In 1994, Jimmy Lai, the founder of the major Asian clothing brand Giordano, who as a child had emigrated out of China to Hong Kong, launched an in-print diatribe against Chinese state repression which culminated in a highly personal insult against then Chinese Premier Li Peng. This railing was the latest of a series of outspoken criticisms by Lai of Chinese nondemocratic policy: Lai had long been promoting the importance of democratic principles such as free speech and freedom of the press within China. In an editorial in his Hong Kong news magazine *Next Weekly*, he referred to Li Peng, the official who had given final orders for the murderous response to the Tiananmen student prodemocracy demonstrations in 1989, this way: "Not only are you a *wang bak dan* [turtle's egg], you are a *wang bak dan* with zero IQ Goodbye."[30]

The "turtle's egg" is an insult that implies a bastard provenance of a human addressee. It was a patently absurd (hence, sacrilegious) representation; it yielded a reading of defiant insult; and it was taken very seriously. Chinese authorities shut down Giordano stores and factories in China and Lai was forced to sell his interest in Giordano, relinquishing control of the company by 1996. The event's transnational character had many faces. At the time of Lai's writing, Hong Kong was in the midst of cultural identity politics in relation to China as it ramped up for a handover to Chinese supervision planned for 1997. At the time, Hong Kong remained a British colony with a degree of independence and a critical lens toward Chinese policy. The IQ measure is its own transnational phenomenon, originating out of the psychometrics movements in Europe and the United States, which were informed by eugenics.[31] An attribution of "zero IQ" is in a sense more precise than "stupid": focusing on intelligence measures, it signifies a scientifically authorized diagnosis of severe cognitive disability, as well as a dearth of a particular *kind* of intelligence or competence that might be characterized as "Western." At the zero IQ limit, however, Lai might be suggesting something about human disability's *own* seeming limit: a radical lack of subjectivity, of capacity for judgment; in American terms, a "vegetable."

In the following diagram, I visually map Lai's utterance (figure 2). As with any diagram, some explanation of terms is in order. With the exception of the turtle egg image, the orbs each represent "possible worlds," not in the philosophical sense (as a series of ontological conditions related to the "real" world that could be true or false), but in a cognitive sense, where everything is conceptualized (some of which is in relation to one's material setting, for instance) and "reality" is only that which enjoys maximal epistemic value. Loosely based on the schematics of Giles Fauconnier and Mark Turner's conceptual integration theory, each orb is a field of meaning, including like or experientially related elements, the characteristics of each element, and the relationships between elements.[32] Each element can itself be a world, just as bodies themselves are arguably cohesive entities internally structured. Between the turtle egg and the son of a turtle egg is a link, a kinship relation of filiality and biological reproduction.

In cognitive terms, each circle is a conceptual "space." In this view of language, as prompts are received as conceptual directives by way of language's precise grammatical forms, conceptualizers manipulate spaces according to the conventions of those linguistic forms, adding elements to them, forming connections, changing configurations

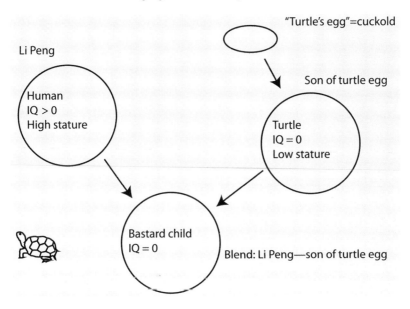

2. A cognitive linguistic mapping of Li Peng's utterance. Diagram by the author.

of elements: in essence, *animating* them. This conceptual "mattering" is ontologizing in the sense that it has a relation (which is however sometimes nonidentical) to considered "reality" and is hence eminently consequential. Note that while the diagram suggests an invitation to imagine how things proceed, it is nothing like a *representation* of language or of meaning; rather, according to Fauconnier and Turner, it simply "corresponds" to interpretive possibilities of language processing.[33]

In effectively being urged by Lai (or the citation of Lai) to consider Li Peng the "son of a turtle egg with zero IQ," a conceptualizer (regardless of desire) is prompted to reconcile the two, that is, to form a cognitive *blend* between "Li Peng" and the conceptualization prompted by the noun phrase "son of a turtle egg with zero IQ." These are the suturing and coercive functions of linguistic address and, more generally, of language used indexically; as Denise Riley writes, "if there is linguistic love which is drawn outward to listen, there's also linguistic hatred, felt by its object as drawn inward. A kind of 'extimacy' prevails in both cases."[34] While there are many interpretive possibilities for the "son of a turtle egg" (is it a son of a "bastard," a diminutive bastard, a really tiny egg?), key to interpreting this event is its paradoxical dehumanization: at once, Li Peng is reaffirmed as human, while simultaneously, in some interpretations, made part turtle. The violence of the insult is located in the *simultaneity* of Li Peng's human and nonhuman animal conceptualization (again, is-and-is-not), and in the sexual politics by which "bastards" are stigmatized. Without assuming any actual psychic injury to Li Peng himself, the insult revealed that his administration perceived his political image as somewhat vulnerable and therefore undertook recriminatory measures.

A Note on Diagrams

Within linguistics, diagrams are used as methods to spatialize or render visual more abstract concepts. As Fauconnier and Turner write, "While this static way of illustrating conceptual integration is convenient for us, such a diagram is really just a snapshot of an imaginative and complicated process that can involve deactivating previous connections, reframing previous spaces, and other actions."[35] Here I take a brief detour, or explanatory digression, to think through my own use of the diagram—a very particular kind of image—within this book. Viewed as suspect in its association with positivist science, or at best eccentric, and understood as comparatively coercive, final in intent, and static in meaning, the diagram occupies a peculiar place (or a no-place) in contemporary written discourses of philosophy and critical theory (much more fraught than the photograph or illustration); as a two-dimensional medium, it seems to stand for complete certainty, or a lack of interpretive flexibility. Once an occasional-to-frequent accompanist to textual argumentation (for instance, the illustrations of gendered signage accompanying Lacan's famous discussion of "urinary segregation"),[36] it is now to be almost superstitiously avoided, if conversations with my colleagues in the humanities over the years are any indication.

When the diagram does inch into the genres of science studies, it does so with a telling ambivalence. Donna Haraway, for instance, offers an "apologetics of the table." When announcing a ten-page table on biological kinship in the twentieth century, she writes, "Claiming to be troubled by clear and distinct categories, I will nonetheless nervously work with a wordy chart, a crude taxonomic device to keep my columns neatly divided and my rows suggestively linked."[37] Recognizing that the appearance of diagrams in this kind of text is "nervous," or at the very least somewhat unusual, it is my hope that they are viewed as an invitation to *play*, to take up alternative means of apprehending the offerings of a text.

Far from being positivist accounts of the workings of a mind (and no self-respecting scientist would believe in a diagram's ontological veridicality), the diagrams are meant to be taken as further mediators of knowledge production. Without bowing to the final superiority of either word or image, a diagram thus grants the polyvocalities that texts offer. But as any art historian can also tell us, an image, whether an elaborated photograph or a denuded line drawing, need (should) not be taken at face value. For instance, though Deleuze and Guattari write in *A Thousand Plateaus* that "a diagram has neither substance nor form, neither content nor expression," they include several line drawings (including one that charts "the center of the signifier") that could be categorized as diagrams.[38] They attempt to debunk the diagram's undeserved attribution of perfectionism and its apparent aspiration to truth status. Following Deleuze and Guattari, for me diagrams function to animate thinking, and to prompt new configurations of analysis.

The diagram mentioned earlier is no exception to my invitation to play, the immediate evidence being the random placement of the turtle. Anna Tsing uses both a diagram and an image representation of an acronym and meditates on the meaning of "play" in reference to the "oversimplified" diagram she uses: "I name each of the three scale-making projects I discuss in a self-consciously joking manner. Yet the playfulness is also a serious attempt to *focus attention* on the specificity and process of articulation."[39] That is, diagrams focus attention, as do texts; they simultaneously perform and suggest apparent condensations and connectivities of knowledge structures. Furthermore, and I know I generalize here, the resolute alignments against diagrams (within the humanities) and for them (within the social sciences) further displace these respective sectors toward or away from certain thinking types, or cognitive styles. Importantly, these are styles that can be understood as gendered and ableized.

Being Vegetable: Animate Subjects and Abject Objects

There are very basic questions about animality, objectification, and humanity embedded within the examples of George Allen and Jimmy Lai. What is "macaca"? What is "I"? What, finally, is it to be "human"?

How do these categorizations, and the elisions as well as the segregations between them, work? On what principles of division and identity are they coded? And how do codes shift for different bodies? These questions begin to get at the complexities of many structures of inequality, not least sexism, homophobia, and ableism. Further, if racism is the hierarchalization of power and privilege across lines of race, then its reliance on the construction of a fragile *humanity* is one of its most profound dependencies.

We have seen two examples of dehumanization by way of juxtaposition and blending with relatively animate and (arguably) inanimate substances, a macaca and a turtle's egg (which contains within it only the future *potential* of lifeliness). While each of these close readings may make local sense, a question remains: what background assumptions or structures must be present, or serve as support, for these dehumanizations to do their imaginative work? At the least, what seems almost certainly operative in both these cases is a reference cline (a graded linear scale) resembling a "great chain of being," an ordered hierarchy from inanimate object to plant to nonhuman animal to human, by which subject properties are differentially distributed (with humans possessing maximal and optimal subjectivity at the top). When humans are blended with objects along this cline, they are effectively "dehumanized," and simultaneously de-subjectified and objectified.

The insults *macaca* and *turtle's egg with zero IQ* may well be examples of "abject subjects": a subject aware of its abjection; a clashing embodiment of dignity as well as of shame. This paradox of the simultaneity of abjection and subjectivity is particularly emphasized in Julia Kristeva's articulation of the abjection of self: "If it be true that the abject simultaneously beseeches and pulverizes the subject, one can understand that it is experienced at the peak of its strength when that subject, weary of fruitless attempts to identify with something on the outside, finds the impossible within; when it finds that the impossible constitutes its very *being*, that it *is* none other than abject."[40] The examples are, far from merely propositional, deeply imbued with affect: in the coincidence of high stature and base animality, the blendings embody an intensity, a fraught collision between humanity and "zeroness."

What does it mean to exist at the level of the zero, moving away from humanness down the animacy hierarchy? Take the phrase "I just don't want to be a vegetable," uttered by a person who fears a loss of mental capacities. This sentence simply does not make sense unless it is understood as a disavowal of the next relevant position on a cline, a position to which one could slide if deprived of certain subjective properties. Between vegetable and animal lies a notable conventional difference in mentality, if we can call it that: the presence of an entity called the brain, which is commonly afforded the locus of thought. *"I just don't want to be a stone" (recalling Aristotle's soul-less body), however, seems to go too far within this dominant hierarchy (and thus receives a linguist's mark for ungrammaticality or unacceptability, the asterisk); some kind of animacy, some kind of thriving and sensitivity, must be preserved for the person's denial to highlight the major locus of difference between what is desired and what is undesired. The varying acceptability of these phrases reiterates that subjective properties are assigned to various stations on that cline, running from human, to animal, to vegetable, to inanimate stone.

If we ask further what lies beyond the strict material positionality of an object, what the object may have been *affectively* invested with—in a sense, this is to acknowledge that vegetality may be defined as more than simply not being able to think, but a failure of lifeliness, of ability to act upon others—we find something like *animacy*. The question then becomes: Who are the proper mediums of affect? Are they humans? Humans and animals? Vegetables? Or inanimate entities, such as the incorporeal blend or a "dead" but warming and comforting piece of furniture?

"I just don't want to be a vegetable," while seemingly an imaginative fancy, also informs, microcosmically and iteratively, of what proper humanity resembles—nonvegetables—and, further, that humans *could* in some way become vegetables. Further, it describes what discredited human subjects are like: vegetables. Indeed, vegetables, believed to be living, are not at the bottom of the animacy hierarchy, as stones seem to be; for instance, when humans and nonhuman animals eat them, they have specific effects and can be either nourishing or toxic to bodily systems. As Jane Bennett cogently notes, food itself is an "actant."[41] Using a term like *persistent vegetative state* potentially, again microcosmically, informs us of how we should understand vegetables themselves: vegetables cannot think; they are passive; they merely survive; they are dependent, not freestanding plants, but partaking of plants' nutrients. In this way, the "vegetality" (constructed between the medicalized language of "persistent vegetative state" and the lay expression "she's a vegetable") of Terri Schiavo, whose non-speaking body became the subject of contentious national, legal, and interfamilial debate for seven years, culminating in the court-ordered removal of her feeding tube in 2005, became a politicized *linguistic* event as well as a politicized discussion about life and death.[42] Indeed, Lennard Davis has pointed out that had Terri Schiavo been considered a "severely disabled woman" rather than a "vegetable," different politics—even different legal consequences—would have ensued.[43] As many scholars and activists have made clear, disability politics is a consistently unacknowledged and erased partner to right-to-die bioethical considerations; everyone loses by not thinking deeply enough about their underlying connections.

To the insistence of disability rights on the legitimacy of such lives as Schiavo's and the need for serious consideration of what is so dismissively dubbed vegetality, we might add an unlikely consideration by N. Katherine Hayles, who takes seriously the lessons of information architectures that distribute subjectivities among bodies and technologies, thereby threatening conventional definitions of human consciousness: "Shift the seat of identity from brain to cell or from neocortex to brainstem, and the nature of the subject radically changes. . . . Conscious mind can be hijacked, cut off by mutinous cells, absorbed into an artificial consciousness, or back-propagated through flawed memory. . . . Whether consciousness is seen as a precious evolutionary achievement that we should fight to preserve . . . or as an isolation room whose limits we are ready to outgrow, we can no longer simply assume that consciousness guarantees the existence of the self. In this sense, the posthuman subject is also a postconscious subject."[44] It is in such embroiled contexts that, given the conceptual resources that are loosely called animacy structures, language users of all kinds (including institutions and collectivities) not only contain or break the proper domain of vegetables, be they vegetal or human. Language users use animacy hierarchies to manipulate, affirm, and shift the ontologies that matter the world.

Dehumanization and Objectification

How are objectification and dehumanization positioned in relation to animacy? The two are not synonyms, but they do exist within overlapping spheres of meaning; and, I argue, they come to mean in a similar way in the brutal hierarchies of sentience in which only some privileged humans are granted the status of thinking subject. I examine both terms, sometimes unearthing quite specific meanings (Marxian objectification, for instance, which bleeds into dehumanization), but cognizant of the ways that the terms sometimes diverge; throughout, I gloss them as responding to or logically relying upon underlying animacy hierarchies.

What, after all, does it mean to dehumanize? In present times, certainly the animalizations and dehumanizations of suspected "terrorists"—discernible in extrajudicial complexes of cages and discourses of "barbaric" practices and militarized hunts (for instance, the presidential candidate John Kerry's comment in a debate: "I will hunt them down, and we'll kill them")—implicitly invoke economies within the animacy hierarchy. If dehumanization often involves a positive (that is, active) force, then what acts work to do so? One form of what is understood as dehumanization involves the *removal* of qualities especially cherished as human; at other times, dehumanization involves the more active *making* of an object.[45]

Indeed, perhaps the most unsparing dehumanization is an approximation toward death. Critical disability and feminist studies have raised biopolitical questions about certain living states of being that have been marked as equivalent to death: death was one of the many "bleak" futures prescribed by strangers, doctors, and fellow patients to the critical disability theorist Alison Kafer upon apprehending her body.[46] There are, too, conditions of illness so profoundly altering that categories of life, death, object, and subject are powerfully rewritten.

Susan Schweik points to the ways in which disability has proven to be a rubric by which people are dehumanized within regulating regimes of public law in the United States in her book *The Ugly Laws: Disability in Public*. She describes a Chicago city ordinance from 1881 which sought to "abolish all street obstructions," written in language that "makes it sound at first as if the 'ugliness' in question concerned inanimate objects, such as 'piles of bricks.' But the street obstructions turned out to be humans."[47] The coincident relation between legalistic abstraction (obstruction), inanimacy (piles of bricks), and certain humans (the targets of the ugly laws in this case) speaks of a stunning (if quiet) suturing of animacy terrains to public sentiment, legal bodies, and notions of propriety, a suturing to which people with visible disabilities are regularly subjected.

Consider another instance that involves the deathly recategorization of otherwise "live" embryos. Charis Thompson writes of clinics for assisted reproductive technology which develop two categories of embryo, the "good" embryos and the "bad" embryos, whose definition may flex with the growing privatization of assisted reproductive technology:

> There are thus only certain conditional outcomes by which embryos become waste, all of which involve conditions that cannot be known about before they occur, even if it is necessary to plan for their possibility. These conditions include the undesired but almost entirely uncontested "medical" reasons, where embryos die or a technician judges them abnormal after fertilization, division, or thawing. This category may grow, granting waste immunity to a wider range of embryos, as preimplantation genetic diagnosis becomes more widespread and reveals more abnormalities in apparently normal embryos. . . . The largely private questions on the status of embryos in the clinic may well not be containable if stem-cell and other biomedical technologies break the tight fit that I described as a monopoly of desperation where physicians, patients, activists, and drug companies have managed to forge collective interests through interacting spheres of privacy.[48]

Thompson points to the contingency of the life and death of embryos in the biopolitical futures of assisted reproductive clinics, where a more sensitized mapping of "abnormalities" (read as, for instance, disabilities or undesired conditions) broadens zones of terminability. Her savvy term *waste immunity* points to the resilient untouchability of a thing that has been declared as waste and its deployment by rapidly privatizing interests.

A second form of dehumanization is transformation (or, indeed, imaginative transmogrification: the transformation into a grotesque or fantastic appearance, which I consider in the "Animals" part of this book), though each form (removal of qualities and active transformation) readily imputes the other in the extended analysis. The figurative substitution of a human with an animal figure often accomplishes both of these things and constitutes a displacement to lower levels of the animacy hierarchy. The two types, indeed, have been equated by various feminisms, studies of colonialism, and Marxist approaches. A brief overview of the historical claims of these discourses, which continue to inform contemporary theory, can demonstrate how animacy hierarchies have been long used to reason. Generally, discussions of dehumanization and objectification depict persons actively subordinated to structures of authority: in the criticism, these may include laborers in a capitalist economy, women within patriarchal structures, medicalized and de-subjectified disabled persons, persons of color subjected to racist psychologies, and persons exposed to the effects, or aftereffects, of economies put into effect during colonization. Above and beyond the possibility of dehumanization, objectification is often also understood to deprive people of their proper humanist freedoms and rights.

In Marxist discourse, two objectifications are of note. With industrialization's introduction of capital, private property, and the economic and social relations that result, there emerges an investment of value in the objects produced by labor (the reification of the commodity object as a fetish) and concomitantly an estrangement of the workers who perform that labor (hence, their commodification). Of objectification, particularly the relations between the objectification of labor, labor's products, and the animality of laborers themselves, Marx writes, in "The Estrangement of Labor":

> We shall begin from a present-day economic fact. The worker becomes poorer the more wealth he produces, the more his production increases in power and extent. The worker becomes an ever cheaper commodity the more goods he produces. The devaluation of the human world grows in direct proportion to the increase in value of the world of things. Labour not only produces commodities; it also produces itself and the workers as a commodity, and indeed in the same proportion as it produces commodities in general. . . . Finally, the external character of labour for the worker is demonstrated by the fact that it belongs not to him but to another, and that in it he belongs not to himself but to another. . . . The result is that man (the worker) feels that he is acting freely only in his animal functions—eating, drinking, and procreating, or at most in his dwelling and adornment—while in his human functions, he is nothing more than animal. It is true that eating, drinking, and procreating, etc., are also genuine human functions. However, when abstracted from other aspects of human activity, and turned into final and exclusive ends, they are animal.[49]

Marx reasons capitalism's deprivations using notions of estrangement, barbarity, animal life, possessibility, and control relationships.

For Marx, the creation of an alienated laborer depends on a concerted interplay of factors, including the unequal distribution of capital, the enhanced nature of "things" as opposed to the "human world," the identification of a laborer with the labor it produces, and the dependency of a laborer on that labor. One consequence of this transformation of social and economic relations is the loss of a laborer's connection to its once-elaborate *human nature* (presumably civilization and the enjoyment of other "higher" forms of social relation), leaving it in the world of the "*animal* functions." Furthermore, self-possession is no longer the laborer's right, since the laborer belongs to the labor on which it depends for its livelihood. Commodification impels the laborer away from what makes it distinctively human and toward the circumscribed and limited lives of animals: "they are animal."

I pause here to note that in such invocations not only is the animal caught on the wrong side of a species boundary, but theorizing has caught itself up in a contradiction of downward deferral that cannot quite succeed. Hence, perhaps the most significant, and most commented-upon, "leak" within animacy hierarchies: Human self-representation's original "error," if such a determination could be ventured, was in attempting to essentially provoke an unhappy wresting of animacy in order to apply it "above" the level of the animal itself (a simple class to which humans certainly belong), to the realm of the (rationalized) subject. In domains of taxonomic dependence, the is-and-is-not complex rises again here, affectively intense in its contradiction.

There are consequences for this precarious design, co-conspiring as it must with prelapsarian fantasies of mirthful animality, precivilized and innocent. For the "human," feeling must then be forever in battle with rationality, and as humanity's categorical guarantor, rationality had every time to win out as the exclusive and primary property of humans. The responsibilities of feeling then fell to lower places on the hierarchy—women, animals, racialized men, disabled people, and incorporeals such as devils or demons. The theory of the subject thus had consequences that had everything to do with animacy and mattering, given the distribution of ontological castings down along the hierarchy. Marx hinges the human struggle with alienation precisely against "the animal," almost backhandedly leaving an illusory vitality to the animal itself (since otherwise it would just be a commodity).

Marx's theorizations of objectification raise questions retrospectively: how did such qualities become collectively available to him in the context and era in which he did his work? More precisely, what informed Marx's vision of the process which objectifies and alienates the worker? And further, what led him to populate this vision with the elements that form the consequential relationships? What is the nature of the substance that is lost in the process he describes? Marx partook of a long philosophical tradition harking back at least to Aristotle, one which carefully segregated humans from, and reasoning via, nonhuman animals (thus defined as simply "animals"), in which a condition of human animality (or barbarity) represents the simultaneous legitimation of enslavement, a relative lack of philosophical awareness other than recognition of one's need to be ruled, and a dispossession of right to self-determination (hence, justified enslavement).

Marx also emphasizes objectification as the insidious concealment of labor in the creation of products, products which carry with them or are animated by another displaced form of value, in the form of commodity fetishism. In Marx, we already begin to see the associative indictments that might befall a victim of perhaps other kinds of objectification, animalization, or dispossession. What gave Marx access to these associations was, of course, in some part his innovation; but we might further imagine that he was also relying on an animacy-inflected economy of humans, animals, and objects as his own referential field.

In the past few decades, feminist theory has also detailed ways in which women can be or have been objectified by representational practices. Laura Mulvey's classic text from 1975, "Visual Pleasure and Narrative Cinema," examined psychoanalytic aspects of the contemporary cinematic conventions of Hollywood, particularly male heterosexual pleasure and fetishistic desire.[50] In such a view, women are thus posed as visual object, staged against a socially cultivated union between the *perceiving* and *acting* male subject, a kind of condensed object-making which has borne significant discussion not only in feminist film theory and feminist theories of race and transnationality (for instance, Trinh T. Minh-ha's indictment of Western anthropological discourses' selectively voyeuristic gaze),[51] but also in relation to pornography, which is a particularly polarizing topic for feminist debate.[52]

Some feminists believe that pornography unambiguously denigrates women, as its images treat women as immovable or inanimate property, "like chattel." The title of Andrea Dworkin's antiporn study written in 1981 summarizes this view: *Pornography: Men Possessing Women.*[53] What is more, Dworkin occasionally turns to animals as metaphors for objectification, for instance, writing about the derogatory use of the term *beaver* to describe both a woman and her genitals. (Indeed, nonhuman animals figure prominently in arguments about female objectification.[54] Carol J. Adams, in her book *The Sexual Politics of Meat*, polemically argues that the treatment of women is much like the treatment of meat for human consumption.[55]) Catharine MacKinnon defines pornography as "graphic sexually explicit materials that subordinate women through pictures or words,"[56] though this understanding does not allow for a great range of positionalities (with regard to sexuality, gender, and race) of readers of the images that might impact how they are situated within these discourses. Radical queer thinkers such as Gayle Rubin, writing against Dworkin and MacKinnon, emphasize that objectification should not be monolithically condemned and point to the many shades of desirable objectification in sexual erotics both explicit and subterranean.[57] Mulvey's work, too, has been taken to task by black feminists like bell hooks for its inattention to resistant gazes and nondominant subjects of looking.[58]

Disability theory forthrightly confronts the complexities of the objectifications inherent in staring.[59] It has also offered some provocative and important responses to mainstream feminist denouncements of (women's) human objectification. For these denouncements of objectification can easily come attached to a logic in which objectification *is* disability and, as a disability, must be overcome. Susan Wendell, responding to the implicit ableism of feminisms (for instance, Iris Marion Young's definition of women under patriarchy as physically handicapped), suggests, "Until feminists criticize our own body ideals and confront the weak, suffering, and uncontrollable body in our theorizing and practice, women with disabilities and illnesses are likely to feel that we are embarrassments to feminism."[60]

In Alison Kafer's "Compulsory Bodies: Reflections on Heterosexuality and Able-Bodiedness," which studies Adrienne Rich's signal essay for feminism and queer theory, she traces the linking of Rich's lesbian subject to an elaborated position of implicit able-bodiedness and discusses Rich's single invocation of the word *disabling*, which is used metaphorically to signal a state that should not be tolerated for women: "Disability only appears as the negative other."[61] Furthermore, disability theorists suggest that there are alternatives to the othering closure of the spectacle: as Sarah Chinn shows us, it is within a multisensory economy and a disability framework that Audre Lorde, in her biomythography *Zami*, "replaces struggles over 'objectification' and 'sexual freedom' with a sexual language that represents lesbian bodies as sacred, communicative, instrumental, textured, difficult."[62]

Hoping to add more philosophical nuance to feminist debates about objectification, Martha Nussbaum, in her essay "Objectification," identifies seven ways of "seeing and/or treating of someone as an object," including *instrumentality, denial of autonomy, inertness, fungibility, violability/breakability, ownership,* and *denial of subjectivity.*[63] Through her analyses of a few classic literary texts of sexual objectification that she takes as "morally assessable," she attempts to rescue the previously totalizing readings of sexual objectification from the likes of MacKinnon, suggesting that "some features of objectification . . . may be either necessary or wonderful features of sexual life."[64] Linguistic objectification can indeed bring pleasures, sexual or otherwise: evidence the use of terms of endearment such as *my little pumpkin, my dear heart,* even *honey.* Between these extremes, of course, is the cognitive process of mundane object-rendering as the result of everyday cognizing and discourse: the very act of naming, pointing, indicating, discussing other people, beings, and objects. Yet it is important to recognize that linguistic objectification is framed by historical, national, and social configurations of power, and is not always able to be recuperated into realms of pleasure.

Theorists of colonialism have examined the ways that colonization affects the self-determination of a subordinated people, particularly the ways in which colonization presses both "colonizer" and "colonized" into mutual psychological entanglement, compromising any renewal or nascency of national identity and leaving effects long after any formal establishment of independence. Given that colonial expansion in Western Europe was driven in part by an abiding scientific racism that drew on the framings of Enlightenment thought, subjects of the colonies posed an apt exercise for the emphatic reiteration of the relative humanity of European colonizers as compared to the animality or "objectness" of the colonized.[65] The process of colonization has in fact been referred to by Aimé Césaire as *thingification.*[66]

Emphasizing the anxious psychology of the colonial interaction, Frantz Fanon, in *The Wretched of the Earth*, writes, "When we consider

the efforts made to carry out the cultural estrangement so characteristic of the colonial epoch, we realize that nothing has been left to
chance and that the total result looked for by colonial domination was
indeed to convince the natives that colonialism came to lighten their
darkness. The effect consciously sought by colonialism was to drive
into the natives' heads the idea that if the settlers were to leave, they
would at once fall back into barbarism, degradation and bestiality."[67]
Because a process of economic and territorial domination in the history of European colonialism has inevitably summoned forms of
psychological support in one domain or another, colonial subjects are
often understood to be represented and treated as in some way "less"
than fully human subjects, less than fully self-possessed, readily "subject to subjugation," and further, potentially pressed to see themselves
in such terms. Fanon points to, on the part of colonized subjects, the
approximation of "barbarism, degradation and bestiality" (that is, a
felt closeness and a recent occupation) made evident in the fear of
return. Here is a further kind of objectification: a dispossession of
humanist self-determination, self-definition, and agency. Colonialism
was, and continues to be, driven by capitalism and hence invested in
the management of domains of private ownership. In the context of
an analysis of the cultural logic of capitalism, critical race theory has
examined the durative rendering of slaves in the United States as legal
property rather than citizen-subjects proper, particularly the historical weaving of enslaved African and Caribbean bodies into U.S. property law. This important work not only examines the contemporary
legal ramifications of an early rendering of slaves as property but further examines the legacy of such a bifurcation of citizen-subjectivity
and objects of property.[68]

As this excursus details, many of the theoretical discussions about
objectification invoke inanimate or less-animate matter as well as animals as generalized standards of comparison, often rendering the distinctions between these categories as simplified and even templatic.
In fact, many contemporary discourses continue to disavow, if not
simply ignore, the possibility of significant horizontal relations between humans, other animals, and other objects. Within such discourses, the category "animal" often comes with a segregating frame
that categorically opposes "human" to "animal"; any symmetries between humans and other animals tend to emerge as marked, as in the
phrase *the human animal*.

Thought and Cognition

One of the ironies made evident in Sidarth's essay-statement "I am macaca" is that at the same moment that it claims a macaca identity, it simultaneously must preserve the speaker's human capacity for language, for articulation. That is, a macaque is simply unlikely to speak those words (at least, let us say, these exact words), for we would ask a language of it that is apparently not its own. This is indeed one of the ironies of the general use of language to dehumanize: while (human) language is being used to impute a nonhuman animality to a human, it is also already viewed as a unique quality of humans.

To return to the linguistic mattering that opened this chapter, I refute the recent moves to evacuate substance from language, for instance, the notion that language is simply dematerialized; one of the outcomes of this belief, it seems to me, is that language discussions seem to disappear in the theorizing of new materialisms. The concern about language's absent materiality has in part to do with what are, in my view, misconceptions regarding the role of thought and mentality in general, which language is understood primarily to register. For all the attention paid to nonverbal communication, it is true that much scholarship about language renders it proximate to *thought*, which is a dangerous territory for those attempting to move away from "the subject" and its philosophical trappings.[69] For some theorists, language is dependent upon or issuing from thought and intentionality, so that nonhuman animals which appear to use complex communication but which do not exhibit complex cognition or do not clearly evidence communicative intent are thereby discredited. Yet what is understood as "thought" continues to expand in contemporary social sciences and humanities, particularly among cognitive scientists and philosophers; associated notions such as "judgment," "decision," and "comparison" have gradually shed their humanist accoutrements and augmented, for instance, their neurological and sensory correlates, opening to the possibility of their capacity in other creatures than human.

The idea that language structure is intimately tied to thought structure—that is, linguistic relativity—reaches back to Benjamin Lee Whorf's "strong" linguistic determinist theories concerning the relationships among language, thought, and culture; according to Whorf, language structure has a determinative effect, a constraining effect, on what could be habitually thought or imagined by its speakers.[70] Later theories of weak linguistic relativity, which were more widely taken up by linguists, discuss a less rigid version of determinism, allowing for a nonabsolute relationship between language and thought, that is, language did not necessarily have a say on what would be conceptualizable for its speakers.

The cognitive linguist Dan Slobin, suggesting "thinking for speaking" as an activity-specific corrective to the vagaries of linguistic relativity (such as about what exactly constitutes "thought," or even "habitual thought"), describes the ways that linguistic and cognitive structures must be engaged for speaking to happen: "there is a special kind of thinking that is intimately tied to language — namely, thinking that is carried out, on-line, in the process of speaking."[71] Here I must make a special note of sign language, for which the grammatical complexity and level of sophistication of gesture takes center stage (whereas it is deemphasized for many spoken language users, especially those for whom gesture is less necessary for communication to be satisfying). It is in signing that language's materiality becomes particularly apparent, though the spatial iconicity of ASL (to take one sign language) is by no means a simplistic mapping, and it indeed seems to be mediated by certain cognitive preferences among signers.[72]

Two cognitive linguists, Ronald Langacker and Gilles Fauconnier, developed theories (Cognitive Grammar and Mental Space Theory, respectively) in which language — that is, spoken, written, gestural language — is a multimodal series of conceptual *directives*, meant to alert and enliven the conceptual imaginary in order to build, elaborate, and indeed *animate* cognitive entities (and such conceptualization is presumably not unique to human language users).[73] Thus, rather than juxtapose or oppose thought and language, cognitive linguists and cognitive anthropologists imagine an ontological confluence between them. Under this view, conventions of "semantics" provide for the templatic readiness of conceptual elements, while conventions of "grammar" provide for the templatic conceptual manipulation of those elements.

Thus, in a cognitive rendering of listening between speakers or seeing between signers, the "processing" of language — for all the formalistic computation such a term as processing suggests — simply amounts to bringing a listener's unique conceptualization to bear, via "blending," on structures or parts of structures alerted by specific linguistic features such as gestural articulation or location (affecting the spatial relationality of the indicated element to the rest of the structure being constructed), paralinguistic features such as facial expression (adding affectivity), or in the case of spoken grammar, locative prefixation (affecting the spatial relationality of an element to the rest of the structure), nominalization (staticizing and substantivizing an otherwise more dynamic element), adjectivization (modifying an existing substantive element with properties), and adverbials (modifying and shaping a dynamic event).

Thus, it is due to both semantics and grammar that a phrase such as Allen's "this fellow here . . . macaca" objectifies. Or, to take a different example, "those queers over there" could be said to quadruply objectify a group of humans. This utterance (1) collectivizes a number of individuals as a group, which in linguistic terms constitutes a shift down the animacy hierarchy, all else being equal (particularly for contexts in which individualist social norms are maintained); (2) distantiates them by use of the distant demonstrative deictic "those"; (3) marshals the distant locative deictic "there," which prompts a conceptualizer to render an element as distant rather than proximate from the reference point of "here"; and (4) invokes the nominal (non-)use of *queer*, which, thanks at least in part to the nominalizing will of queer identity politics, continues to do the iterative—even *de-animating*—work of substantivizing the still predominantly adjectival *queer*.

Language is as much alive as it is dead, and it is certainly material. For humans and others, spoken and signed speech can involve the tongue, vocal tract, breath, lips, hands, eyes, and shoulders. It is a corporeal, sensual, embodied act. It is, by definition, animated. But in spite of, or because of, the so-called linguistic turn (which occurred outside of the social-science discipline of linguistics, largely in the humanities) and the influence of poststructuralist thought, language in theory has in many ways steadily become bleached of its quality to be anything *but* referential, or structural, or performative. Some attempts at theorizing language have been labeled shallow "linguisticisms" that fail to recognize, or include, the vast materialities that set up the conditions under which language might even begin to be spoken. As Judith Butler has stated, "the point has never been that 'everything is discursively constructed'; that point, when and where it is made, belongs to a kind of discursive monism or linguisticism that refuses the constitutive force of exclusion, erasure, violent foreclosure, abjection, and its disruptive return within the very terms of discursive legitimacy."[74]

Words more than signify; they affect and effect. Whether read or heard, they complexly pulse through bodies (live or dead), rendering their effects in feeling and active response. They are a first level of animation, one in which we deeply linguistic creatures attached to our own language are caught, but not the last. Indeed, language is but one discourse among many in a cacophony of anti-, re-, and mis-coordinations between objects, things, and beings. It sometimes only sees itself; if it sees outside of itself, it sometimes responds only with itself; and it sometimes must be left altogether, perishing in the nonlanguage the moment demands. If we think only about insult and effect, injury and response, then language, for all its special investments, cannot suffice as the final agent or medium by which any of these is actuated.

George Allen lost his campaign by an animation not only of language but also of image and technology: the video of his social and political infractions "went viral." It was recognized as potentially damaging by his opponent's campaign, which released it strategically, but precisely who and how many viewed it could not have been planned. That is, the video bore a kind of animate liveness in its collectivity, as well as in the unpredictability of the precise paths of that uptake: hence, a rhizomatic virality. Jimmy Lai suffered retribution in the similarly *anti*-viral actions taken by investors of his publishing company after 1997, when China reacquired Hong Kong as a special administrative region: they feared that if they remained attached, retribution could be eventually taken on their media enterprises, and so disassociated from Lai's company before it was too late.

Ultimately, animacy remains an unfixed notion. Linguists' humility before this elusiveness speaks to both disciplinarity's hopeful possibility (since exhaustive attempts still remain humble before the possibility of other disciplinary studies) and the failure of disciplinarity (to achieve the final mastery of its objects, if and when it ever hopes to do so). Animacy's slipperiness here is beneficial for another reason: it serves as a reminder of the transformative importance of transnationality and migration. Consider that number can play a part in determining animacy. Fortunate mismatches can occur for second-language English speakers who might not give a damn about whether proper number marking (singular or plural) or proper pronominal gender has been applied (as has been the case with my Chinese immigrant parents), and animacy's effects need not have anything to do with intentionality either. In this transnational case, ontologies are interrupted, faced with their own instability, since sentience, agency, and control relations are thus remapped, vitalizing some linguistic referents and devitalizing others. Animacy's slipperiness in such circumstances suggests, from a new direction, the troubled consolidation of the (Western) subject.

Resorting to questions of universality is not my interest here; it suffices to note that animacy seems to be *around*, pressing itself into linguistic materiality (and in this hesitant validation I am no different from various linguists who are still wondering what it is, even if it "stays around"). Rather, the question is: why—or rather, how—does animacy *matter*, both in the critical and political sense? And, perhaps, what are the limits (analogical or otherwise) of a linguistic analysis? The shortest answer is that if animacy gradations have linguistic consequences and linguistic consequences are always also political ones, then animacy gradations are inextricably political. Language tells us of shared priorities (cognitive or not) and material-linguistic economies, in which some "stuff" emerges and other "stuff" remains ineffable, unmaterialized. The sentience of a noun phrase has linguistic and grammatical consequences, and these consequences are never merely grammatical and linguistic, but also deeply political.

This was a chapter primarily about language and its role in insults, involving combinations of animality and objectification, as well as an account of what might enliven and give language its force: animacy. Animacy is a craft of the senses; it endows our surroundings with life, death, and things in between. In the chapter that follows, I continue my investigation of the linguistic notion of animacy to consider in-depth the term *queer* as it has migrated over time through various parts of speech; in doing so, I ask how its animacy has been figured and redeployed.

2

Queer Animation

How might a term *cast off* its dehumanization? That is, how might a historically objectifying slur like *queer* be reanimated? And to open the question well beyond identitarian resistive actions such as reclaiming, why are some people (including academics) still using *queer* with regularity? Though *queer* was highly controversial and its linguistics were hotly debated for many years, it appears in many ways to have settled. Still, it bears asking how this word has traveled in various linguistic economies since its wary entry into the spheres of academic and political discourse twenty years ago. I examine this question from a cognitive-linguistic perspective, one explicitly attentive to animacy, to shed new light on these debates.

This chapter—the second half of a part on words—thus stays in the realm of language, engaging animacy as it concerns the circulation of *queer* as a political and sexual, and now guardedly institutional, term. *Queer*'s institutionality can be found singly in titled academic programs (for example, "queer studies") or as part of such programs (for example, LGBTQ), as well as in a proliferation of conferences and talk series, in colleges and universities. It is also used today to name some political organizations (Queers Against War). In academic practice, it is found in humanities scholarship less as a name that designates an identity or group than as an analytic and method; indeed, throughout this book I use the word *queer* as such. The most telling sign of *queer*'s institutionalization is the current circulation of terms like *postqueer* in discussions of the "after of sex" and the "after" of identity, though this also signals skepticism toward the strictures that even a seemingly broad category such as queer can impose. Hoping to revise the term's historical dependence on "totalizing" notions of subjectivity, Carla Freccero advocates for, "rather than an after of sex, . . . a return to questions of subjectivity and desire, to a postqueer theoretical critical analysis of subjectivity that brings together . . . psychoanalysis and other analytics and objects of study."[1]

Twenty years after the institutional embrace of *queer* by way of signal conferences and publications naming "queer theory" and "queer performativity," this chapter assesses *queer*'s political uptake as a *linguistic* object, specifically with regard to its being understood as "reclaimed," simultaneously the object and means of political transformation. My discussion investigates its semantic and grammatical proliferation, plumbing the relationship between *queer*'s particular and changing semantics, its social and political forms, and the productive terms of its animacy. I argue that in micro- and macropolitical worlds in the United States, *queer* has followed the two contradictory paths of *re-animation* (beautiful collectivity/assemblage/reengagement of self with animate force) and *de-animation*, which might help to explain the widespread fatigue with queer identity politics and internal racisms.

I do so by focusing not on the politics of a monolithic *queer*, but rather on the politics of *polyvalence* that are instituted in part by the "bleeding" of *queer* into diffuse parts of speech, as well as by examining the social technologies of those parts of speech in fine detail. By focusing on animacy, I wish to veer away from simply repeating the almost glibly reproduced, yet generally underinvestigated, story that there are many people of color who reject the term *queer* because of the term's racism and false promise of intersectionality. This is not to deny that such conditions have existed—indeed, the political leveraging of *queer* in certain contexts and not in others followed quite predictable paths of exclusion—but to think more precisely about the linguistic conditions that helped this be so.

A Queer Word

To begin, we have to ask whence the *queer* that *got* "reclaimed." This is relevant not only because there are those who claim that a word's historicity has direct bearing on its current affectivity (consider Judith Butler's discussion of *queer*'s iterability in and through its traumatic history),[2] but because its future efflorescences do not emerge randomly. Stories of *queer*'s origins vary. Many documentations of the word yield—in that circular way that majoritarian terms, forces, and normativities reproduce themselves—primarily dominant and even somewhat exclusive (hence, their own homonormative) histories of *queer*. Despite the performative possibility that these histories may reiterate dominant traces, I cautiously use these histories as a starting point, because they revealingly tell of the undeniably privileged process of *queer*'s reclamation. But I also, somewhat forgivingly, ask what might productively remain of today's *queer*'s enduring potencies, not least of which is the growing institutionalization of queer of color scholarship, which might be said to save *queer* from its own willful mobilities.

I take advisedly the words of E. Patrick Johnson, who writes of the failure of dominant forms of *queer* (and queer theorizing) to contend with cultural positionality, particularly that of race and class privilege. Johnson suggests drawing from African American vernacular *quare*, not to provide yet another queering of the queer, but rather to relink it to certain priorities, for instance, to restore a materialist sensibility to the term and its scholarship.[3] Compared to *queer*, published linguistic histories of African American *quare* are nearly nonexistent; indeed, in a seeming acknowledgment of this, Johnson brilliantly patches together an etymological entry specific to African American usage that both acknowledges the *Oxford English Dictionary*'s elision of African American *quare* (it mentions only the Irish English *quare*) and affirms "curious" links with "black" Irish and the "blackness" of the Irish.[4] Instead of the tack Johnson takes, one that might be described as "an alternative lexical investment" that comes with its own correctives, I confront *queer* directly and work from there.

There are two majoritarian stories of the English-language *queer*'s (re-)emergence: First, there is that of the *Oxford English Dictionary*, which relies on documented written use (and, hence, casts out entire histories of oral forms of documenting) and can only paint broad outlines of the political arbitrators of its semantics. Second, there are also more specific political-linguistic histories drawn by queer scholarship, which—even as or because so many of these cite the OED in a convention of the defining genre—frequently leave behind linguistic detail in the interest of privileging *queer*'s masterly slipperiness, its aporetic quandaries. In the hope of bridging this gap, I instead extend and expound on a word now so commonly voiced that it threatens to dissolve into background noise.

For centuries in English usage, the word *queer* did not seem to exist consistently as a noun before the turn of the twentieth century (specific dates are inconclusive). According to the OED, at least in the significantly widespread English senses that it tracks, where *queer* existed adjectivally, there were two main adjectival lexemes. Its primary adjective modified an object to mean "strange, odd, peculiar, eccentric, in appearance or character. Also, of questionable character, suspicious, dubious"; secondarily, "Out of sorts; unwell; faint, giddy. Formerly also (slang): drunk (obs.)." Note though that besides the still-extant nonsexualized or gendered verbal use of *queer*, which according to the *American Heritage Dictionary of the English Language* means to "spoil or ruin" or to "put someone in a hopeless or disadvantageous position," we also find contemporary crystallizations of both adjectival and verbal forms of the earlier sense of *queer* in the idiomatic British phrases *queer street*, meaning "where the debtors live," and *queer the pitch*, meaning "ruin the plan" or "spoil the chances of success."[5] Debra Burrington patches together the senses of *Queer Street* (not yet understood as involving debtors) as "an imaginary street where people in difficulties are supposed to reside" and as "strange, odd," the first sense of the primary adjectival lexeme.[6] Its third sense, now apparently dominant in a way that renders the other senses obsolete, indicates homosexuality:[7]

> colloq. (orig. US) Of a person: homosexual. Hence: of or relating to homosexuals or homosexuality. Although originally chiefly derogatory (and still widely considered offensive, esp. when used by heterosexual people), from the late 1980s it began to be used as a neutral or positive term (originally of self-reference, by some homosexuals; cf. QUEER NATION n. and also quot. 1952 at QUEER n. 2) in place of gay or homosexual, without regard to, or in implicit denial of, its negative connotations. In some academic contexts it is the preferred adjective in the study of issues relating to homosexuality (cf. queer theory n. at Special uses 2); it is also sometimes used of sexual lifestyles that do not conform to conventional heterosexual behaviour, such as bisexuality or transgenderism.[8]

Such uses have been recorded since the beginning of the twentieth century. The second *queer* is restricted to the qualifying rubric "criminals' slang" and it included the now-obsolete (mid-sixteenth century through the mid-nineteenth) adjectival sense "bad; contemptible, worthless; untrustworthy; disreputable." It came with a cautionary note that mentions the otherwise obvious fact that "the exact sense varies with the noun to which the adjective refers." This second sense is followed in prominence by the adjectival "of coins or banknotes: counterfeit, forged," followed by the nominal "forged or counterfeit money. Also in extended use."

The segregation of *queer* into two lexemes suggests that lexicologists consider these as homophones or otherwise semantically remote senses, rather than as a single polysemous *queer*, raising questions about the social, ontological, and interpretive gaps between normative language and "criminals' slang" on the one hand, and normative language users and criminals on the other. (Did homosexual criminals not have a slang term for themselves? Were homosexuals already unimaginable to criminals who were already in some sense queer?)[9] Not waiting for a lexicological resolution or simply ignoring the judgment of homophony, queer theorists have had good fun with the play between the notions of fraudulent capital and illegitimate sexual bodies.[10]

In the 1910s and 1920s, according to the historian George Chauncey, gay men generally resisted *queer*'s effeminizing connotations in the larger culture of the United States, choosing instead *fairy* to denote the same and permitting the self-identificatory *queer* to align with masculinity.[11] Then, owing in part to nationalist impulses existing from the crisis of the stock-market crash in 1929 through the alarmist and paranoid McCarthy era, in which heteronormativity was held up as a necessary condition for national strength and survival, *queer* narrowed in a number of contexts—not abandoning the "former" sense, but existing beside it—to mean sexually nonnormative, whether in behavior, affect, or biology.[12] This narrowed use was indeed negative and hence tended not to be used among gays or lesbians; for men at least, *gay* was the new preferred term.

By the 1970s, perhaps incited by the increased interest in recognition by the wider public, the word *queer* began to be used again, self-referentially, by some gay men. The AIDS political activism of the 1980s and 1990s led to a newly urgent push for gay visibility; linguistically, this meant that striking, compact, and confrontational slogans and images were politically foregrounded. The AIDS crisis accelerated the strategic use of the word *queer* to encompass a broad and multifaceted population.[13] The linguistic politics of Queer Nation and ACT

3. Queer Nation in action at the inauguration of the California governor
Pete Wilson, 1991. Photo by Marc Geller.

UP echoed its resistance to compromise and complacency: consider
the oft-cited slogan "We're Here! We're Queer! Get Used to It!" A
photo from a Queer Nation rally in 1991 shows a racially diverse group
of gay men wielding such a sign, some of them clad in T-shirts embla-
zoned with other contested slang, such as *dyke* and *fag* (figure 3). Such
an image is an important reminder that the history of *queer*, while
today understood by scholarship as particularly laden with exclusions,
has also been a significant rallying cry and point of coalition building,
one that both summoned and ironized the "nation" as the primary site
of shared affinity.[14]

Early consumer-capitalist forays inside some gay male communities led to a humorous offshoot, somewhat ignorant of its own
class politics: "We're Here! We're Queer! Let's Go Shopping!"[15] Discussions about queers' relationship to capital are ongoing, recently
most densely around the notion of "homonormativity."[16] Lisa Duggan's sense of homonormativity refers to a neoliberalism that has the
ability to absorb and indeed deploy homosexuality for its purposes.
Within this framework, queer consumer capitalism falls neatly in line
with (neo-)liberal ideologies and subject formations.[17] Queer activist groups contesting the normativization and prioritizations of gay

capital have formed and remain active today, for example, the group Queers for Economic Justice. Today, *queer*'s generic adjectival meaning of "strange" continues, albeit in limited discourses, alongside the "sexual" meaning, which is presently conversant with gay, lesbian, bisexual, transgender, and other nonnormative sexual identities. There are now increased *nominal* senses of *queer*: uses like "all the young queers" are not only grammatically acceptable but widespread.

Fraught Institutionalizations, Fraught Reclamations

Within the United States, the term *queer* has been cautiously accommodated in the academy as queer studies has, in some regards, solidified into a field, though it remains very much a rangy, interdisciplinary nexus of interests, objects, and methodologies. There are now queer studies programs, minors, and fellowships at institutions throughout the country. It has partially displaced "lesbian and gay studies," which has been a rubric since at least the early 1970s; the first courses in queer studies were taught at the San Francisco City College in 1972. This efflorescence of *queer*'s uptake in academia, and the concomitant institutionalization it signals, is in part due to the cross-fertilization of activism and academic intellectual concerns.

A brief examination of the history of the moniker *queer studies* indicates that not everyone has equally embraced the term. In her book *Borderlands/La Frontera: The New Mestiza*, published in 1987, Gloria Anzaldúa explicitly refused to separate queerness from race, preferring *mestiza queer*. She had an incisive critique of the term's relations: both *queer* and *mestiza(je)* are crossroads, but *queer* can erase race.[18]

Anzaldúa's important and somewhat less salubrious observation about queerness, that it was threatened not, for instance, by inspecificity, but by whiteness itself, was an early caution that did not see significant recognition until much later. Even then, she did not reject the term altogether; she used it in a way that was prescient of later coalitional queer politics. In her earlier poem "La Prieta," published in 1981 in *This Bridge Called My Back*, she defined *queer* as operating intersectionally and well beyond sexuality: "We are the queer groups, the people that don't belong anywhere, not in the dominant world nor completely within our own respective cultures. Combined we cover so many oppressions. But the overwhelming oppression is the collective fact that we do not fit, and because we do not fit we are a threat.

Not all of us have the same oppressions, but we empathize and identify with each other's oppressions. We do not share the same ideology,
nor do we derive similar solutions."[19]

Four years later, as follow-up to a conference in 1990 in which she
discussed the interruptions of the term, Teresa de Lauretis edited a
special issue of the feminist journal *differences* that signaled one shift
from *lesbian and gay* to *queer*; its title, *Queer Theory: Lesbian and Gay Sexualities*, is often mentioned as a proposition for a field, a turning point in
the history of "queer theory."[20] Anzaldúa's texts are not hailed as key
origin points in this history,[21] though they predate de Lauretis's text,
a historicizing which some critics attribute to the invisible operations
of whiteness. In the history of queer theorizing, these three textual
moments could indeed serve as examples of the hesitant lag time of
the mainstream adoption within queer theory of enterprises of queer
theory by people of color.

In her article "Critically Queer," which appeared in the premiere
issue of GLQ: *A Journal of Lesbian and Gay Studies* and placed "queer" at
the center of a journal whose very name reiterated the importance of
maintaining the terms *gay* and *lesbian*, Judith Butler examined some of
the currents within contemporary politics and theory that gave this
term its critical purchase.[22] The early 1990s in particular was a time
when terms like *queer* were cautiously embraced as "more than just
new labels for old boxes"; for academics such as Duggan, writing in
1992, the designations of Queer Nation and Queer Theory "carry with
them the promise of new meanings, new ways of thinking and acting
politically—a promise sometimes realized, sometimes not."[23] In 1993,
Michael Warner wrote an assessment that feels dated in its wonder-
ment but reiterates current mystifications of *queer*'s indeterminacy,
commenting on the word's purchase but also its potential difficulty:
"The preference for 'queer' represents, among other things, an aggressive impulse of generalization; it rejects a minoritizing logic of tol-
eration or simple political interest/representation in favor of a more
thorough resistance to regimes of the normal . . . its brilliance as a
naming strategy lies in combining resistance on [the] broad social terrain with more specific resistance on the terrains of phobia and queer-
bashing, on one hand, or of pleasure, on the other. 'Queer' therefore
also suggests the difficulty in defining the population whose interests
are at stake in queer politics."[24]

Finally, in 1993, Eve Kosofsky Sedgwick evocatively depicted *queer*
as "fraught": "A word so fraught as 'queer' with so many social and

personal histories of exclusion, violence, defiance, excitement . . . never can only denote; nor can it only connote; a part of its experimental force as a speech act is the way in which it dramatizes locutionary position itself."[25] Thus, Sedgwick alleged that *queer's* denotative meaning cannot simply be treated independently of its many connotations (what she calls "social and personal histories of exclusion, violence, defiance, excitement"). It is worth noting that for some women, the recent use of *queer* to refer to all genders (as well as a spectrum of sexualities that includes bisexuality) is seen as a problematic erasure of the specificity of lesbianism akin to the false neutrality of using the word *man* as an ostensible generic for all humans. Some also feel that women are erased when *gay* is no longer used alongside its usual companion phrase, *and lesbian*, and is used a singular, gender-inclusive term.[26]

Given this complexity, to say that *queer* was "reclaimed" (as one might say in an introductory queer studies or sociolinguistics course), regardless of its status in either institution or populace, is not only somewhat reductive; it is to promulgate a certain kind of linguistic politics. It raises the questions: what event denotes the achievement of that reclamation? Its first attempts? Its widespread use by younger generations of a group? The quality of its affectivity? Its use by the largest possible population beyond the group's borders? For such questions, turning to existing scholarship on racial and ethnic reclamation can be informative. *Black*, for instance, has been held up by some (but not all) linguists as a premier example of successful reclamation, because it can now be used referentially, without risk of insult or self-abnegation. In 1977, the linguist Geneva Smitherman wrote that "the term 'black' had achieved widespread usage and acceptance by both blacks and whites," though she acknowledged that "there are some blacks, especially older ones, who do a double flinch at being called 'black.' You see, they remember when black was not so beautiful."[27] Yet we must also note that by this account of reclaiming, it would seem that the goal of reclaiming is a deflated neutrality, essentially a loss of the word's affective valences. According to the linguist Hans Hock:

> Just as with tabooed words, the response until recently consisted in a constant turnover in the words designating Afro-Americans, ranging from "Ethyopian," "African," "Colored," "Negro," "Afro-American" to the six-letter obscenity still commonly used as a term of insult.

This linguistic turnover was in the nineteen-seventies brought to a halt by a conscious and deliberate redefinition of the word "black": Where previously this word had negative and derogatory connotations, even among Afro-Americans, it was now redefined by the "Black-Power Movement" as a word with neutral or even positive connotations, completely on a par with the word "white" which had traditionally been employed in reference to Americans of European origin. And since then it has replaced all its predecessors, including Afro-American, as the most commonly used, neutral term for Americans of African descent.[28]

Such a view comes closest to an idealized assimilationist perspective, more along the lines of "civil rights" inclusion than, in fact, Black Power's antiestablishment aims (in this schema, the reclamation of *nigger* or *nigga* would seem far less promising).

In light of the linguistic possibilities for assimilation and neutralization, I am interested in queer liberalism's own schema, similar to that of civil rights, and its regulation of affect in debates on gay marriage as a way to probe *queer*'s place in the terrain of politics in the United States. David Eng writes that "under the banner of freedom and progress, queer liberalism . . . becomes linked to a politics of good citizenship, the conjugal marital couple, and the heteronormative family."[29] He further argues that queer liberalism deploys race while erasing its traces. If queer could be reclaimed to the point that it is fully absorbed and assimilated, then what would a neutral queer look, feel, sound, or taste like? Or—to indulge a bit further—a *neutered* queer? I cannot ignore here the common understanding of animal neutering, perhaps made baldly obvious by the liberties taken in its behavioristic approach to animals, that neutering is motivated in part by a pet owner's desire to flatten and redirect animal affect (though I should note also that no holds were barred for intellectually disabled and poor black women subjected to sterilization). When performed on pets, neutering is commonly understood to level temperamental swings in relation to mating drives, thus helpfully neutralizing sexualized affect (I will more extensively address animal neutering and its gendered and biopolitical complexities in chapter 4). For all that marriage is understood to organize and even encourage (private) reproductive sexuality, gay marriage curiously conceives of itself as having a gaping, inactive lacuna in sexuality's place, exaggerating the invisibilizing proprieties of straight marriage.

66

It is notable that though there are many self-identified "queers" who would like to get married, perhaps in view of the continuing "rub" of *queer* and its failure to denote compliance or the templatic, "unadulterated" extension of rights, many same-sex marriage advocates—in mainstream organizations especially—have shunned trans and intersex folks and other radical queers, as well as gays, lesbians, and other queers of color.[30] So do neutered queers become gays? If only it were so simple. For neoliberal gayness has its own ghosts: in an unambiguous indication of the perceived whiteness of homosexuality (or the racism of neoliberal gayness),[31] African Americans were largely blamed by political liberals for the passage of Proposition 8 in California, which banned same-sex marriage, though religion was found to have played the determining role in the proposition's outcome.[32] *Queer* is found nowhere in the slogans "Marriage Equality," "Freedom to Marry," "Gay Marriage"; and only good neoliberal gay and lesbian subjects "just like you," mostly white, coupled, and with children, are viewed on television ads in states where marriage laws are in contention. Hardly visible are the childless sex radicals, interracial threesomes, and leather queers. Is this perhaps because *queer* animates too much, exacerbates rather than contains frisson, soars beyond its bounds? Is an untamed *queer*—linguistic or embodied—still beyond the ken of either sympathetic heteronormativities or neoliberal homonormativities? Beyond noting the heightened contradictions it comprises, how might we assess its affectivity?

Lexical Acts

Against such flattening aspirations—the hope for a conclusory stage of the past participial "reclaimed" to describe the linguistic neutering success of an entire population—the linguist Arnold Zwicky productively prompts, "For which speakers, in which contexts, and for which purposes has the word been reclaimed?" making it clear that for lexicographers it is the many, often contested *senses* of a word that must be documented.[33] Thus, for instance, when we say that "queer is an adjective," we either neglect its occasional use as a noun or simply mean to mark its predominant sense. Linguistic creativity drives semantic language change, and nearly *any* lexical item, unless especially constrained as a delimited grammatical operator, is likely to have multiple senses, some of which may fall into different parts of speech. What could look like linguistic creativity to some reads as "failure" or misunderstanding to others; but it is hard to tell the difference be tween these two, and indeed the ubiquity of the language innovation that emerges from linguistic mixing suggests that they not be differentiated. Even the preposition *over*, something commonly thought of as a simple grammatical operator, has many different senses, some of which contradict each other. In "the house over the bridge," *over* scans an imagined trajectory and is hence qualitatively different from its positional sense in "the bee hovers over the flower," which in turn differs from the gravitational wrapping sense of "I draped it over the dining table."[34] This sense multiplicity cannot be any less true of *queer* and, even more interestingly, its mythical opposite, *straight*.

If we talk about primary senses, or shifts in the strength of one sense versus another, then still another specification must be made: the population of language users for whom these shifts are relevant. What is, after all, a queer "community"? Contemporary self-identifying queer "communities" grew at least partly out of gay and lesbian coalitions in the 1980s who began self-referring as queer. Since the early 1990s, queer communities are touted to include all forms of sexual minority: homosexual men, lesbian women, bisexuals, transvestites, transsexuals, transgender folk, BDSM/leatherfolk, and others who simply identify with nonnormative sexual practices or interests.

Queer theory and activism of course profoundly informed how *queer* was meant politically. Ideally, queer identity is inclusive of those who continue to fall "in between" majoritarian, heteronormative categories of identity, particularly interstitial sexualities and genders. Within the narrower confines of queer writing in academia, *queer* is cannily understood (or, according to a number of dissenters, only aspires to be understood) as probing beyond the bounds of normativity, taking on the load of rejection, resistance, negativity, indiscretion, quirkiness, and marginalization. For instance, Sedgwick suggests, "Queer can refer to: the open mesh of possibilities, gaps, overlaps, dissonances and resonances, lapses and excesses of meaning when the constituent elements of anyone's gender, of anyone's sexuality aren't made (or can't be made) to signify monolithically."[35]

Continuing Sedgwick's compendium of interstitial possibilities, David M. Halperin writes, "Queer is by definition whatever is at odds with the normal, the legitimate, the dominant. There is nothing in particular to which it necessarily refers. It is an identity without an essence."[36] Though "identity without an essence" could describe any distinctive adjective, when considered in queer theoretical terms, this seems a lovely formulation. For all practical purposes, we could say that identities are by and large *nominal* (that is, they are referred to using nouns or noun phrases). For instance, one cannot use a verb to identify, unless it is nominalized: "I am a lo*ver*, not a figh*ter*." One might translate Halperin's formulation in linguistic terms to mean that *queer* is something like "an adjective without a noun to modify, disguised as a noun." In such a view, *queer* launches into perpetuity with its very own linguistic identity crisis, compelling its readers to epistemological vagaries in a "not-yet" that suspends both ontological conviction and the possibility of proper legibility. If this is so, then not only are the identificatory signifiers mobile, but the subjects who pronounce them are too: in this idealized view, subject positions are up for grabs.

In linguistic terms, we might say that adjectival *queer*'s function is to modify an attached (implicit or explicit) noun concept, in particular, to select the peripheral aspects of meaning of, say, concepts such as heterosexuality or sexuality.[37] Adjectival *queer* therefore acts to shift meaning to the side of a normative interpretation, away from meanings associated with the notional center. Besides its "denotatively perverting" meaning, *queer*'s apparent mobility of meaning benefits further from its more prevalent grammatical use as an adjective rather than a noun. Adjectival *queer* is hence a *function*. If, for Halperin, *queer* is an identity, then it is this function which has been refigured into an identity. While queer theory's questioning of what is "natural" resembles, and likely inherits from, feminist inquiries about what is considered "natural" about women (and the ways in which women themselves are produced *as* "nature") it also departs from dominant feminisms in the United States (which remain attached to the category of "woman") in its refusal, by promulgation, if not in action, to advocate or politically favor any particular category other than the (sexually) nonnormative.

Indeed, many queer theorists reject the "nonessentialist" or "antiessentialist" postures of queer politics, suggesting that it is just as essentialist as any other since it poses an essential and identificational "queer" against an implicitly essential "heterosexual."[38] Thus, queer theory has been perceived to shift between the positions that "we are all queer/nonnormal/perverse" and the stance that heteronormativity is false, pervasive, and oppressive. But looking further into the linguistic nature of *queer*, we see that its animacy—insofar as it is deployed, with some contestation, as a noun—opens into a much more complex situation than this binary model suggests.

Tracking Queer Animacies

If certain words are deemed proper to only certain users, *queer* has for many been historically associated with a proper user of only injurious intent. I earlier noted that today, under certain circumstances, explicit identificatory statements such as *they're queer* or *I didn't know I was talking to a queer* have been used in ways that refer to the generalized queer identity without an apparent affective impulse (derogation, intensity, or clearly negative or positive value). Furthermore, these uses have not necessarily been delivered ironically or used to make salient political statements.

We can further note that the use of *queer* as a noun rather than an adjective is characteristic of another trend: the de-adjectival nominalization of the sexual-identity sense of *queer*. The nominalization of *queer* as a member of an (identity) group is also accompanied by the relatively widespread appearance of the *verbal* use of *queer*, especially but not limited to queer scholarship, with meanings that pointedly refer to sexuality and gender. Examples began to proliferate in the early 1990s; for instance, Jonathan Goldberg's methodologically representative words in the introduction to his anthology *Queering the Renaissance*, published in 1993, in which he comments that the essays seek to "queer the renaissance . . . in the recognition that queer identity is far less easily regulated or defined in advance than legislatures and courts imagine, and that literary texts are far more available to queer readings than most critics would allow or acknowledge."[39] Outside of academia, the Canadian "Queers United Against Kapitalism" claims, "We seek to queer the radical community and to radicalize the queer community"; *queer* becomes at once a noun and an adjective here, as well as an action verb. If *queer* was previously understood to be a "dehumanizing" slur figuring its subjects as abject or "lesser than," this formerly "objectifying" term has taken a life of its own, with the power to *animate* some other object. Here this is meant quite literally, since grammatically speaking an action verb sets the object of the sentence into motion, engages its capacity to be affected. Arguably, the word in some vital ways is thus deobjectified.

If these observations are evidence of a referential and linguistically diversifying trend within queer groups by now well known, this trend simultaneously signals at least a partial attenuation of *queer*'s derogatory force. At the same time that queer theorists use the word freely in all manner of institutional contexts, statistics from the National School Climate Survey in 2009, compiled by an advocacy network of queer educators and their allies, reports that *queer* still carries a sting for many, especially in middle and high schools in the United States, where nearly 85 percent of all self-declared lesbian, gay, bisexual, and transgender students report being verbally harassed by their peers, with over 40 percent physically harassed because of sexual orientation. *Queer* (along with *dyke* and *fag*) is still widely mobilized as a popular, and stinging, insult among youths.[40] We have a mass of senses and a mass of affects: how to apprehend these denotative, connotative, and affective contradictions, short of throwing up our hands and saying "everything's contested" or ignoring them altogether?

At this point, I turn to cognitive linguistics to provide an analysis of the uneven status — reclaimed or not — of *queer*, an analysis of its different grammatical use-functions and their divergent paths. I suggest that the observations made by queers/gays/lesbians of color that queer identity and nomination tended toward white essentialisms can be substantiated from a cognitive-grammar perspective that considers closely not only the failures of linguistic representation and reference, but more centrally how linguistic usage manifests and innovates in direct relationship to *grammar*.

Since *queer* now appears in different word classes, particularly as a verb, adjective, and noun, it is useful to first examine cognitive-linguistic characterizations of generic word classes. While it is fairly obvious that the availability of such a diversity of meanings for *queer*, such as "different from normal," "to change," and "sexually identified person," is a result of *queer*'s proliferation in contemporary discourses, it is less obvious how these senses are structured linguistically as adjective, verb, and noun. For one thing, they possess radically different temporalities. By and large, *verbs* are defined as processes, that is, they are structured on some *time* relation (since things are dynamic: change is inherent to a verb). On the other hand, nouns, adjectives, adverbs, prepositions, and more are considered *atemporal* relations (they describe fixed states or nonchanging operations). Furthermore, when *predications* — the semantic structures corresponding to expressions —

are *relational*, they involve the profiling (salience, emphasis) of inter-connections; when they are *nominal*, they involve the profiling of a given conceptual region.

One implication this has for language use is that words used according to certain grammatical conventions will inspire conceptualizations that have some slant or another, depending upon that convention: for example, an expression that raised the ire of many a second-wave feminist, "who gives this woman away?" In it, the placement of a marriageable woman ("this woman") in a grammatical position as object for the verb *give* effectively prescribes a processual operation on a conceptual region: that is, it casts the referent of *woman* statically, as both a notional object and in objective perspective, as the target of a dynamic "giving" process. This sounds much like objectification, though it is of course just a microcosm of the ceremony; the gender of the woman's future spouse, for instance, may confer contradictory subjectivity in other grammatical formations during the ceremony. From another angle, using the same word in both the verbal position ("queer the Renaissance") and as a noun ("a Renaissance queer") poses strongly different constraints for how it can be conceptualized in relation to action, agent, and animacy.

The lesson of both kinds of examples is that though some degree of linguistic creativity is always possible between two speakers—including in my view the very salutary second-language and dialectal "violations" of standardized grammar—many basic grammatical conventions are very difficult to violate while still being "understood": precisely because they are so conventional, they are likely to be taken for granted. While for humanities scholars sometimes the most interesting thing about language is that its constraints are not hermetic and can thus be "failed" by "bad linguistic subjects," I wish here to demonstrate the creativity that works within and around such compelling constraints. *Animate theorists*—my term for creative language users—work within and around a set of given normativized targets, much like José Esteban Muñoz's rubric of disidentification.[41] It is therefore in relation to these targets—not with abandon—that *queer* can enliven and animate itself; for all its self-identification as nonnormative, there is nothing magical about *queer* that releases it from trucking with the conventions and norms of language itself. What I want to show is that some of these conventions and norms are precisely *grammatical*: I can then elucidate what is the substance of *queer*'s artful innovation in its political context in the United States and also show where it missed grammar to undercut its own twisty aims.

Queer has been animated—and continues to animate (to more or less effect, as I show later)—across a range of meanings, especially in the context of its participation in a political movement. Political movements whose strategies include institutionalization or institutional recognition are generally hard pressed to avoid collective nomination entirely. As long as one must articulate a political demand on the basis of a group of persons, a "we" (whether in the form of "we want," "we demand," or the often problematic "for them") in some way entitles itself, particularly in the rights frameworks of liberal democratic politics. That "we" claims to have some characteristic that, under some generalized cultural frame of rights and privileges, relates it to another a group that already enjoys legitimation or privilege. The linguist and cultural theorist Geneva Smitherman, in the context of her important work about black language, has written about the cultural valences of the naming of "African Americans" in the era after the civil rights movement as a way of enlivening a "we" that politically aligns with, and hence joins, a network of either multicultural ethnic or transnational immigrant groups.[42] John Baugh discusses the linguistic strategies in the changing adoption patterns of the adjectives *black* and *African American*, especially with regard to self-reference in the dynamic racial landscape of the United States.[43] Both Smitherman's and Baugh's findings address the political utility of the terms of choice for their speakers and the understood promise of the political demands they can achieve, which sometimes depends on their semantic distance from the feckless terrain of abjection.

In the case of *queer*, naming a perhaps previously inchoate group of individuals as a collective body (that is, creating a noun to contain *and* welcome), while announcing who is to be welcome, is a preeminent substantiation that puts a group materially on the terrain of politics and, in one fell swoop, seems to *make* an identity, one that becomes available for conceptual partaking by individuals. This making-on-the-go, rather than a sober reflection of who *is*, runs from the optimistic to the utopian. I will say more on this later, along the lines of the collectivizing politics of nominalization.

Politicized group descriptions—that is, descriptions in part leveraged for political engagement—are also under pressure to be linguistically economical (for example, as in a "sound bite" or a "motto").

Hence, one is likely at some point or another to name persons, whether individuals or groups, by the descriptive adjectives used to characterize that group or its political assertions. How is this done? In formal terms, naming occurs by nominalization, which is defined as a shift, with minimal change in form or conceptual characterization, toward noun status from another word class, or by a combination of any set of word forms to form a composite noun.

There are, in addition, purely linguistic pressures, that is, pressures outside of specific cultural or political demands, for noun forms to be innovated. These demands of expression range from the relative articulatory expediency of a single noun form (*queer*) over adjective-noun combinations (as in *queer person*), to the relative subcategorizational independence of a noun over other word classes (transitive verbs subcategorize for, and hence "seek" for their completion grammatical subjects and objects; adjectives and adverbs subcategorize for, and hence "need," nouns and verbs respectively; and so on). Nominalizations will function to fix, stabilize, and, most crucially, enable bounding, especially for countable nouns. The fixing and stabilizing normally comes from deverbalization. If a noun transposes from a verbal form in particular, then basic dynamism—the verbal temporal aspect—is removed by dropping the verb's inherent time relationships, because that noun can then no longer be a process. Thus, to use a word in such a way that befits nominal grammatical status (*the queers*, or even, probably much more likely, noun phrases that include the adjectival form of *queer*, as in "Queers for Christ") is to encourage a bounded reading of the concept's content, and hence—this is no minor consequence—to render identities finite.

It is further, in cases of deverbal nominalization, to detemporalize a form so that it refuses a dynamic reading. To the extent that nouns can serve as identities, that is, to the extent that nouns invoke conceptualizations that a person may identify with ("a bunch of queers"), subordinating oneself to that identity is, I would argue, subjecting oneself to the loss of dynamism, as well as to the boundedness of that noun. While that person's "self" cannot be but a blend between that person's acquired identity—the prepackaged, sometimes stereotyped identity—and the rest of their sense of self, to identify with such an identity seems to me a genuine risk, for it is not clear which aspect of self depends on which other. If noun meanings are less mobile, I contend that they are arguably less "alive"; as notionally bounded substantives, they have less capacity to animate elsewhere than to be acted upon. At the same time, nouns are agents of action that "govern" the grammar of a sentence; as we have seen, however, according to animacy hierarchies' inherent reasoning, some have less capacity to do this than others.

It is worth noting further that verbs and adjectives can quite easily be nominalized, either through innovation or through long-term development. For instance, the verb *move* may be bounded as a deverbal nominalization: *Trent's move went smoothly*. *Queer* may be "fixed" (opaquely, because it shows no phonological modification, and hence betrays no cues toward its own modified meaning) in at least two ways: first, the modifying adjectival *queer* can be nominalized by the metonymic naming of the thing modified by *queer* with the modifier itself, which is a common process (consider, for instance, calling women *blondes*); second, the verbal *queer* (which may in itself be formed by de-adjectival verbalization, as in *beautify* or even *yellow*: paint yellows when it ages) can undergo nominalization, as in "the one who queers," often realized phonologically by suffixation with *-er* ("the eater.") Its nominal fixing can be compounded by pluralizations, such as *queers*.

Queer's Many Senses, or Grammars of Forgetting

In the diagrams that follow, figures 4(a) through 4(e) represent various instantiations of *queer*. In most cases, these are relational concepts, except for 4(b), verbal *queer*, which is a process comprising developments of relations along a time path. In cases 4(b) and 4(c), the landmark (lm) of a relation is that entity that is "being queered" by the trajector. In cases 4(d) and 4(e), the landmark is an implicit "queered" category; the trajector is a member of the category, situated nonnormatively in relation to the landmark.

We can define the images as follows. Figure 4(a) represents a prototypical use of the adjectival *queer*, as in *queer theory*. As an adjective, it is a dependent structure in the sense that it requires a noun to modify. The two concentric circles of the image suggest that the adjective "selects" everything but the center of the noun category that it grammatically modifies. In 4(b), the queer-theory verbal use, as in *queer the academy*, shows a process: the trajector is the agent of the process, for instance, the queer theorists; the landmark, "the academy,"

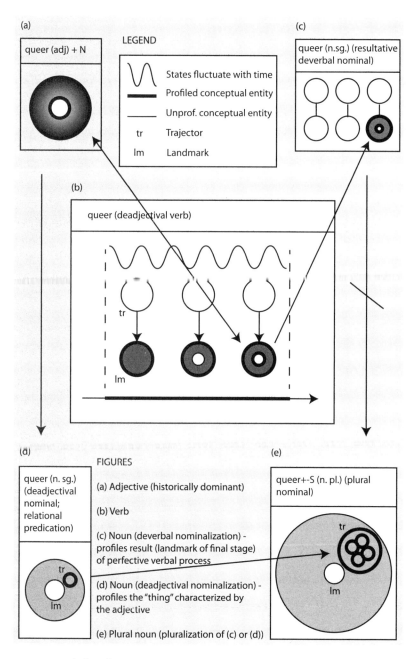

(a)

queer (adj) + N

LEGEND

States fluctuate with time

Profiled conceptual entity

Unprof. conceptual entity

tr   Trajector

lm   Landmark

(c)

queer (n.sg.) (resultative deverbal nominal)

(b)

queer (deadjectival verb)

tr

lm

(d)

queer (n. sg.) (deadjectival nominal; relational predication)

tr

lm

FIGURES

(a) Adjective (historically dominant)

(b) Verb

(c) Noun (deverbal nominalization) - profiles result (landmark of final stage) of perfective verbal process

(d) Noun (deadjectival nominalization) - profiles the "thing" characterized by the adjective

(e) Plural noun (pluralization of (c) or (d))

(e)

queer+-S (n. pl.) (plural nominal)

tr

lm

4. *Queer*'s many contemporary senses. Diagram by the author.

is "queered" with time: in the central relation, its normative center is excised; in the rightmost relation, the "new," peripheral region is selected and made cognitively salient. Figure 4(c) shows the "resultative" deverbal nominal, the noun that can be made out of the landmark after its undergoing the verbal process of 4(b).

The interpretation, however, for 4(c), given that it conventionally stands for the identity and not "academia" or some other concept, is that the trajectors that have operated on that landmark through the queering process have been *the self*, in case a queer casts his or her sexuality as a matter of choice, or some external concept like *society*, in case a queer chooses to describe oneself as having been "perverted" by outside forces. Note that 4(c) has lost its dynamic quality; it is fixed, timeless. Figure 4(d) is another noun that can result by making a nominal form directly out of the adjective. This is also a timeless relation. Here, *queer* is a trajector who stands in a peripheral relation to the landmark normative center. In 4(e), this de-adjectival nominal is pluralized: *queers*. All stand again in a peripheral relation to the central landmark.

Something has been missing in the account up to this point: the preceding diagrams are somewhat utopian, representing an idealized version of the meanings of *queer*, one perfectly in line with the intentions of queer politics. They are optimistic, in particular, about the presence of kinds of memory needed to "know" what *queer* means in the way it is intended. As cultural terms, instances of the use of *queer* invoke intracultural (and, hence, eccentric in many public or outgroup domains) frames of reference which may not, for all queers— or in all contexts in which queers may appear—be so easily accessed; and in their place other, more normative cultural frames may get invoked. One of these normative, cultural frames, which plays some part (even if a contested one) in seemingly all identities formed in the United States, is that of the neoliberal self: an entity that is autonomous (hence, nondependent) as well as responsibly self-authored, and one that owes no sense of its formation to a past trace in time.

Hence, it is in the public discourse (which again, is the risk of any movement which reaches for the public word) that the atemporality of a noun, and the atemporality of identities in the United States, collude quite insidiously to cut identities off from their roots. This atemporality might in fact be seen as itself bound up in queer ways of understanding time, historicity, and the discontinuities of the past within the present.[44] There are many forces that make this so, of course; I do not wish to be reductive, but I believe the quieter workings of linguistic structure are less noticeable and, as such, certainly less available to intervention. There is a further risk for the adjectival *queer* alone: the very condition for its definition, that it be defined *in relation to the norm*, is easily made opaque by a renormalization of the category *queer* itself, which is that it too must have a center and a periphery. The brilliance of political movements that have enforced center-periphery structures on such complex entities as *the nation*, *the people*, and so on has been that they take advantage by making implicit appeal to one folk structure of categories: the belief that any given category is simplistically structured by an essence.[45]

According to cognitive-linguistic findings, nearly all categories seem to be arranged according to a center and periphery, or some kind of radiality, with better or worse examples, to be played out in context.[46] In any category subject to this kind of structure, its presumed center-periphery character can be easily exploited as a basis for implicit reasoning. For instance, it is easy to assume, unreflectively, that one who is talking about the "center" of any given concept is perfectly justified in doing so. So it is, in figure 5, that the population of *queers*, under construal as a category, can easily slip from 5(a) to 5(b), "losing" their relationality, or, more dramatically but no less plausibly, from 5(a) to 5(c), reinfused with dimensions of center and periphery.

Here, too, is a case where, for humans who use language conventionally, a nominal category can seem to "forget" its history, particularly when there are not adequate supporting models (as in, for example, a surrounding culture infused with queer sensibilities that would support the revisionary meanings of reclaimed *queer*). There is, in other words, a way that the partiality of queer materiality has effects of forgetting. While it first seems that restorative "forgetting"—the spontaneous imputation of normative category structure—could happen at any time, and that there is an apparent ignorance of the other signifiers present, it ultimately becomes clear that the surrounding social and cultural context has everything to do with the affordances and effectivities of semantic change.

The imputation of reclaiming to a group presupposes that the group has been disempowered in some way and has an investment in regaining agency. In *Excitable Speech*, Butler writes about linguistic "restaging" and "appropriation," with an emphasis on a broader set of structures that necessarily circumscribe subjectivity and agency.[47] Butler's

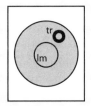

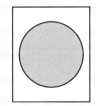

(a) queers (tr) as vs. general populace; normosexuals (lm) serve as landmark

(b) queers, non-relational predication; relationality is "forgotten", history made opaque

(c) queers, non-relational predication; imputed center-periphery (folk) category structure

5. Renormalization of category *queer*. Diagram by the author.

argument turns on the Freudian notion of *repetition-compulsion*. For Freud, a subject who has undergone trauma continues to experience a sequence of unconscious-driven reenactments of that injury (or rather, its condensed or displaced symbol). These reenactments are called repetition-compulsions, or "repetition with a difference." It is only through psychoanalytic work that the subject can bring the trauma out of the unconscious, by "remembering, repeating, and working-through" (to cite the title of Freud's relevant essay) the injury to identify the original trauma, bringing it into consciousness and thereby securing recovery from it.[48] In engaging this Freudian concept, Butler suggests we see reclaiming, or its wider phenomenon (the repetition of "recited and restaged" injurious words), as a necessity: "Indeed, their repetition is necessary (in court, as testimony; in psychoanalysis, as traumatic emblems; in aesthetic modes, as a cultural working-through) in order to enter them as objects of another discourse."[49] Butler suggests that reclaiming is part of a broader, ongoing resignification over which participating subjects cannot have sovereign control, and in which they cannot be fully aware of the terms of resignification.

If queers are poised to "reclaim," there is something to be reclaimed, regained. We are thus invited to construe the group of queers as dispossessed, lacking, or associated in some way with loss.[50] In queer studies, loss's associated categories of Freudian (processual and recoverable) mourning and (suspended) melancholia, trauma, disenfranchisement, and bodily alienation have all been addressed from perspectives of queer life and death (not least of all in consideration of the impact of AIDS) and liberal political life.[51] To the extent that members of the group "inherit" its grammatical character as identities, this is a loss which is hardly chosen. In the case of the term *black*, the ready associations of the color black, with all the flying signifiers of darkness, death, and mourning, not to mention the racist logic of associative qualities such as poverty, dirt, and crime, means that the word *black* is, while not necessarily tabooed, in a position to have to wrestle with imposed abjection. Both *queer* and *black*, in many circumstances, further permit negative loads, which, as already suggested, continue today. And due in part to norms of politeness and the fear of linguistic contagion, items with negative loads are only pronounceable in certain restricted conditions, for instance, in self-descriptions or when outward insult is intended. That is, if saying "queer" is like having public sex, then linguistic contagion is very much at stake.

But there are ways that we also cannot treat *black* and *queer* similarly, just as we cannot treat their related discourses of race and sexuality the same way. Notwithstanding the insistence that many (sub-)groups appear to be practically and effectively left out by the identity label *queer*, the label is *itself* rather queer. As a relatively recently constituted category of social identity (at least, in the present form that is not gender-specific), and as a category which only recently got a name, *queer* may not enjoy "material" existence to the degree that, say, racial categories do or the two dominant gender identities do. In other words, the degree to which queerness has been woven into mainstream schemas of materiality is still relatively minor.

There are a number of perspectives from which the category *queer* may be understood to have an uncertain materiality. One is that its pronouncement or textual appearance has some responsibility for reifying it *as* a category; as both structuralist and poststructuralist thinkers would agree, language is a singular device by which categories become "real." If the frequency with which a term such as *queer* appears in everyday speech and in prevalent media forms borders on the insignificant, it would seem that the infrequent act of naming a category *for which there are no other names* consigns it to a reduced existence, a reduced cognitive salience. In a cognitive linguistics perspective, there are direct relations between the possibility of *lexicalization* (the engendering of a relationship between a phonological form and a cognitive entity or concept in a linguistics community) and the degree of cognitive *entrenchment* (the strength of a concept, as determined by its frequency of invocation).[52] Lexicalization is a collectively shared cognitive entrenchment (hence, a conventionalization) into an explicit linguistic form. The pairing of lexicalization and entrenchment is one means by which a concept achieves social strength as a thinkable thing.

Furthermore, what is the nature of the elements that are iterated? If we put a naive meaning of materiality in conversation with notions of presence, then the utterance of a name—as a manifestation of a concept—may have significant import in queer contexts. Given the non-self-evident membership of *queer*-citing queers in the United States, it is worth asking whether "queerness" may well be constituted as more individuated, more verbal, and more on-line ("live") than other kinds of identity whose utility as a "prepackaged"—entrenched, standard—social resource is more immediate.[53] This near, or tremulous, materiality does not seem to be easily explained away and has a curious resonance with the "criminal's slang" meaning of fraudulence or falsity, now declared obsolete. Indeed, "queerness's" own celebrated queer conditions of existence, which at first seem unique, are similarly present and operative in other cases, but simply remain quiet or backgrounded: for instance, fluctuating membership and unclear satisfying conditions for membership. (What, after all, is "nonnormative" sexual behavior?)

But *queer*'s semantics are both more and less complex than this, as can be seen when we look to places other than where English is spoken (as well as linguistic economies in which English plays only a small part).[54] For instance, the closest word for *queer* in communist China is *tongzhi*, which is the combination of two morphemes, one meaning "same" (like the English prefixal *homo-*) and the other "intent." This word ironically reappropriates—perhaps not only in a cynical way—its earlier communist meaning of "comrade." The Chinese *tongzhi* thus requires that we take another look at our articulation of homonationalisms or homonormativities—as Duggan and Puar do, in different registers—as only a product of late-capitalist modernities, as the next stage of incorporation of affective nationalist heteronormativities by gays and lesbians.[55] To take another example, in Deaf communities in the United States, American Sign Language signs for *queer* have shifted and changed along with political movements. For instance, the derogatory sign for *gay* (the hand gesture for the letter *g* made while touching the chin) is often defiantly avoided by queer Deaf subcultures, who instead preferred to finger spell either *gay* or *queer*.[56] What is more, a sign for *transgender* was quite recently invented, in concert with a growing political community of deaf transgender folks. The professional signer and queer artist Ric Owen reports that some transgendered Deaf groups came together and, in recognition of the paucity of sign language to capture trans life, innovated their own sign: "In the past, ASL didn't really have specific signs for transgender and transsexual. Quite often one sign was confusingly used for both groups. As the Deaf transgendered community became empowered and more organized, they held meetings and workshops to address their concerns and issues. It was at one of these gatherings that the members of the community discussed and created a new sign to mean 'transgender.' The sign roughly looks like a flower closing on the chest and while voiced as 'transgender,' its visual meaning is 'to accept all parts of myself.'"[57] "Transgender" has been taken up in a widespread manner as an innovated sign by Deaf transfolks; it would hence be dangerous to assume that the time of queer linguistic creation is over, as if it mirrored the "death" of the linguistic turn in the humanities. Innovations of sign, gesture, or word remain, of course, a vital part of community formations and retain their power as trajectors of meaning that not only illustrate but animate.

Governing Queer Animacy

Recall that with the "criminals' slang" second variant of *queer*, the OED lexicographers deemed it necessary to remind its readers, even though it is true by definition of all adjectives, that "the exact sense varies with the noun to which the adjective refers." Why? I propose that both senses of *queer*'s animacy inspired a rich exchange and a reactive repetition of the rules by which language items *should be* bound. The riddle assumes closure in the annals of the OED: Q: When must an adjective behave as an adjective? A: When the exact sense varies with the noun to which the adjective refers.

Queer, by its own mettle, both is and is not bound by such rules. It has been both re-animated and de-animated. While it continually re-animates in new formations—thanks particularly to queer of color, transnational, disability, and trans scholarship—it has also achieved nominal fame as an identity; but it has simultaneously coalesced, gotten sticky, inertial, lost its animation and its drive in the context of the

United States. Its nominal terminus along certain semantic paths has led it to an atemporal staticization, a lack of cognitive dynamism, an essential death, and a future imaginable only according to its modification by something else. At the same time, its essence is present by fiat and too often lives as the body of its most audible or legible or entitled asserters; transnationally it is subject to, and subjects others to, the fixed temporality and identitarian U.S. centrism of what Paola Bacchetta calls a "from-Stonewall-diffusion-fantasy."[58] In some ways, then, de-animated *queer* seems to invoke white morbidity, coming with the decreased vitality and increased objectification and alienation of bourgeois capital (following Marx), and the vacuity of neoliberal or neoliberal Left politics (following Duggan). Who would want this sort of de-animated, defanged, or depoliticized *queer* (but homonormative aspirants)? Certainly, its vitality can change entirely—even in its noun form—in the altered subcategorizational linguistic biopolitics of mixed language spaces. But its terms are difficult to predict.

One wonders, for example, at the possibility of the contribution of a borrowing of *queer* for China's linguistic territory of sexual identity terms; indeed, Beijing's Queer Film Festival was in its early years canceled by the authorities. According to Chou Wah-shan, *tongzhi* ("comrade," itself appropriated in 1989) already secures a collectivity by "taking the most sacred [communist] title from the mainstream culture," affirming rather than rejecting a certain familial proximity (as Chou claims is true of *queer*). Yet *tongzhi* (already) has queerlike effects, since it "connotes an entire range of alternative sexual practices and sensitivities in a way that 'lesbian,' 'gay,' or 'bisexual' does not."[59] Transnationally, *queer*'s linguistic expropriation and importation is subject to the subcategorizing requirements of its new host language, while simultaneously being accountable for the temporal politics of its claim, borne by the United States, to the status of the "modern" in progressivist narratives of the globalizing gay.

However, within the deadening identity politics of the United States, it is entirely healthful—part of a salutary technology of self—that some queers of color reject the term *queer* as an identity. E. Patrick Johnson was trenchant in obliquely referring to the Irish *quare* in generating his own etymology for African American *quare*. Indeed, the "lost" sense in the OED, which is rarely mentioned, is precisely what has been eclipsed in queer genealogies of *queer*: it is defined as an intensifier ("b. Sc. and Irish English. As an intensifier: = QUARE adj. 2."), lending intensity to that to which it is grammatically attached. This is a linguistic governance entirely defined by animation, whereby a lifely quality of animacy is magically transferred to another object in its local instantiation.

How do we comprehend "dead nouns," taking into consideration the fact that work on linguistic animacy shows that the sentience of a noun phrase in some sense has some control relation over the rest of the utterance? *Government* is a linguistic term that refers to sub-categorization of the templatic needs that a specific word requires (or requests) for the rest of the utterance. The verb *queer*, for instance, because it codes a direct action, "subcategorizes for," or requires a grammatical subject and a noun phrase direct object. It is useful to turn here to Foucauldian governmentality, which he considered alongside the key terms of *security* and *population* in his theorization of the biopolitical. For Foucault, governmentality functioned as a rela-tion between the technologies of self and technologies of domination and was an exploration of the techniques of biopower; it was histori-cized as a salient concern and rapidly materializing European phe-nomenon in the sixteenth century.[60]

With the "government" of language, I wish to meditate not only about dual meanings of the linguistic "subject" and the social-critical "subject," as has been commonly done in the humanities complica-tions of the long-time central term *subject* (consider Emile Benveniste, for instance, who located in the grammatical subject a foundation for subjectivity),[61] but also about the control relations of elements of lan-guage in relation to the rest of an utterance. This allows us to move away from subject and subjectivity as a question with (humanist, rationalizing) restrictions and toward *sentience*—again, broadly con-strued—as a decisive factor in the architecture of language. Though governmentality has been carefully taken up by critical discourse theorists such as Norman Fairclough,[62] Foucauldian governmentality has to my knowledge not been considered in relation to the strict sub-categorizational governance of language, most relevant here to the extent that I have studied *queer*'s emergence into parts of speech. The verb form of *queer*, notably, does not subcategorize for either a high-animacy subject or a high-animacy direct object; this is apparent in its academic uses in a world of theoretical abstraction ("the prevalence of alternative sexual formations queers heteronormative schemes"), but was already present in earlier histories of the word ("queer the pitch").

When animacy hierarchies are implicated, as they inevitably are, we can say that an everyday biopolitics takes place, a biopolitics that perpetually resituates, recombines, and rearticulates the matter of life—and potentially its very own ecologies—in the particularized bodies of its animals, objects, humans. Even further, *queer*'s biopolitics, the biopolitics of queerness, are (re-)animated in its every use: In their anthology *Queering the Non/Human*, published in 2008, Noreen Giffney and Myra Hird temptingly note without elaborating that the encounter of "human" with "posthuman" is facilitated partly by the fact that the term *queer* appears in the anthology "variously as a noun, adjective, verb and adverb."[63] Considering that the noun status of *queer* remains in flux, their comment can be expanded to mean that *queer*'s profusion into various parts of speech, combined with its uncertain nouniness, sets its users up for a suitably messy governance, even an antigovernance.

I want to end by insisting on *queer* beyond its affectively neutralized—neutered—senses. What are the possibilities of rejoinder, or revitalization, for this contested term if it still has the capacity to galvanize but also to damage? And who or what is given the power to do such a speaking-back-to? A person who is considered a nonsubject, a subject who is abject, a person who does not communicate normatively, an animal who doesn't humanly speak, indeed perhaps even a couch might not respond in expected terms. While the next chapter's task is to focus on the racialized complexities of nonhuman animal representation and its intersectional relation to queer and gender theory dialogues, I do not attempt to address questions of response, interactivity, and affective negotiation until the final chapter, where the possibility of interanimate engagement with inanimate objects is again broached.

This chapter examined how the term *queer* moves linguistically through and beyond the concept of animacy, and how its coercive grammatical inheritances are leveraged and manipulated in reactive and regenerative forms of linguistic governance. It was intended to provide a concrete, figural example of the kinds of animacy that language both puts and fails to put into motion, while retaining language's precise relevance for concerns of governmentality. These concerns, I argue, are sensitive to the complex gradations of animacy. The next chapter also begins with language, as it considers, in turn, the exclusion of nonhuman animals from (human) language and a racialized counterexample by the language theorist J. L. Austin in his theorizing of the linguistic performative.

PART II ✳ ANIMALS

3

Queer Animality

What happens when animals appear on human landscapes? In spite of their regular co-occurrence with humans, nonhuman animals are typologically situated elsewhere from humans, as in the linguistic concept of an animacy hierarchy, a scale of relative sentience that places humans at the very top. This presumed superiority of humans is itself duratively supported and legitimated by "modern" states in a transnational system of (agricultural) capital. Yet to consider the biopolitical ramifications wrought by these separated categories is extremely complex, since "humans" are not all treated one way and "animals" are not uniformly treated another way. This is why the statement that someone "treated me like a dog" is one of liberal humanism's fictions: some dogs are treated quite well, and many humans suffer in conditions of profound indignity.[1]

Considering animacy hierarchies as ecologies (with interrelations between types), and also as ontological propositions (with divisions between types), this chapter asks in what ways they are regularly, sometimes unwittingly, forsworn, disregarded, or overstepped by their very users. I choose "ecology" here to suggest an *imagined* system, not an actual, self-regulating one. What ecologies do such separations between human and animal rely upon and potentially transform? This chapter considers in particular how animality, the "stuff" of animal nature that sometimes sticks to animals, sometimes bleeds back onto textures of humanness. This fibrillation and indeterminacy is perhaps not surprising, given the radicality of the founding segregation. I suggest that thinking critically about animality has important consequences for queered and racialized notions of animacy; for it is animality that has been treated as a primary mediator, or crux (though not the only one), for the definition of "human," and, at the same moment, of "animal."

This chapter takes a specific tack: first, attending to questions of language, I ask after the politics of the exclusion of animals from language and assess the legitimacy, scientific and otherwise, of the stacked deck that it represents. Then I move to examine a signal moment within the work of language philosopher J. L. Austin from the viewpoint of racialized animality. While the passage by Austin is frequently glossed in queer scholarship, Austin's peculiar constellation of race, animality, and sexuality is here explored in depth. Following this, I look at historical visual culture that triangulates these terms, including a foundational text of Asian American studies, the fictional character of Fu Manchu, to rediscover and stage Fu's animality. In a coda, I look at a recent, somewhat spectacularized example, the story of a chimp named Travis, in order to pose questions about current, possibly queer, kinship formations between animals and humans and what they reveal of the unsteadiness of categorical hierarchies and the legitimacy afforded to some of their leakages. Throughout, I reconsider the persistent ways in which animals are overdetermined within human imaginaries.

Animal Language

Given the segregating terms of linguistic animacy, it is important to understand *how* the sentience of animals is assessed, especially with regard to its primary criteria: language and methods of communication. For instance, Derrida's famous essay "And Say the Animal Responded?" explores the possibility of nonhuman-animal "response" as distinguished from "reaction" by hermeneutically approaching the gap between the two; he levels a critique at the very use of language as a loaded criterion of division between humans and animals, offering the nonsingular, and animating, *animot* in *animal*'s stead. If he notes animals' exclusion from language within humanist traditions, he nevertheless does not explore the possibility of animals' own languages.[2] Akira Mizuta Lippit's work on animal figurations, too, expressly excludes animals from language, without attempting to think what language is or could be: "Animals are linked to humanity through mythic, fabulous, allegorical, and symbolic associations, but not through the shared possession of language as such. Without language one cannot participate in the world of human beings."[3] Neither of these writers is concerned, however, with the findings of linguistic research about animal communication, which finds ample intelligent language use in many species, not all of which are understood as taxonomically or intellectually proximate to humans.

Language's status among creatures, human and not human, continues to be hotly debated among humans, for as a register of intelligence, judgment, and subjectivity it is a key criterion by which lay, religious, and expertly scientific humans afford subjectivity—and sentience—to animate beings both within and beyond the human border. Who and what are considered to possess "language," and the qualities afforded to it within that location, are factors that influence how identification, kinship, codes of morality, and rights are articulated, and how affection and rights themselves are distributed; and hence how ranges of human-nonhuman discourses such as disability, racialized kinship, industrial agriculture, pet ownership, and "nature" itself are arbitrated.

Language is arguably a major criterion (or even the defining attribute) that separates humans from animals, even among theorists who decry the fact of the segregation. Aristotle's notion that language critically separated humans from animals becomes an evident legacy in Martin Heidegger's postulation: "Where there is no language, as in the being of stone, plant, and animal, there is also no openness either of that which is not and of the empty."[4] While all kinds of "behavior" (the primordial stuff of psychology, a particularly powerful humanist-scientific discourse in Western history) are richly elaborated (for instance, the marvelous capacities of various animate beings, including mammals and invertebrates, many of which seem to far outshine human capacity), it is *language's* degree of elaboration that seems to spike prominently and uniquely for humans. Of course, this is to the advantage of humans: the linguistic criteria are established prominently and immutably in humans' terms, establishing human preeminence before the debates about the linguistic placement of humans' animal subordinates even begin. Yet the exclusion of animals from the realm of language is, historically, a relatively recent and uneven phenomenon; as Giorgio Agamben comments, "Up until the eighteenth century, language—which would become man's identifying characteristic par excellence—jumps across orders and classes, for it is suspected that even birds can talk."[5] Agamben considers how the consolidation of the category *Homo sapiens*, as created through Linnaeus and his taxonomies, "is neither a clearly defined species nor a substance; it is, rather, a machine or device for producing the recognition of the human."[6]

Cary Wolfe describes the consequences of the liberal philosophical tradition's "self-serving abstraction of the subject of freedom" for animal-human ontologies, writing, "while the category of the subject was formally empty in the liberal tradition, it remained materially full of asymmetries and inequalities in the social sphere, so that theorizing the subject as 'nothing in particular' could easily look like just another sign of the very privilege and mobility enjoyed by those who were quite locatable indeed on the social ladder—namely, at the top."[7] This move follows earlier critiques of the ways that the abstracted subjects of liberalism simply installed, rather than removed, unmarked privileges among white, male humans in terms of gender and race.

One central task, I believe, is to be careful about conflating human ideas about an animal with the actual animal itself, a caution somewhat distinct from Derrida's concern that we are crafting a universal category of "the animal" by our use of the very word. This is a hard habit to break, given the species burden that an individual animal bears in the view of humans and the conflation of referent, even for us theorists, with actuality (which of course often leads to actual changes to that effect or in that direction). Simultaneously, we should not use the "actual" animal reflexively as a necessary ontological or epistemological pressure back onto human understanding, but should hold the two (or three or four) in a productive, self-aware epistemological tension.

As my investment in language within this book is primarily concerned with its material economies, I am less interested in tangling too extensively here with the precise question of "animal language" in terms of either the possibility of an epistemological meeting-ground or a philosophical disarticulation of the upper end of the animacy hierarchy; others have admirably waded through the complexities of this domain. Yet I am also reluctant to abandon the possibility of alternative foci of investigation (aside from language) into questions of what nonhuman and human animals are and what they share, since, as we know, difference does not collapse even when we wish it away.

To the extent that resolving the question of an epistemological meeting-ground could relieve some of the condescension that the profusion of human domains of research on and writing about animals (in terms that are clearly not theirs) would seem to enact, I suggest that, separately from questions of language, we be prepared to ask not only whether nonhuman animals might also possess something like a "hierarchy of animacy," but even more deeply, to ask after a register of sentience, broadly construed. The scientific study of perception certainly suggests the beginnings of some intimation of this "registry of sentience," whereby, on the one hand, the distinction between perception and cognition is being methodically worn down (see, for instance, the work of Louise Barrett)[8] and, on the other hand, there is the awareness that motion perception is very similar among nonhuman animals and human animals, including the presence of mirror neurons in great apes. Maxine Sheets-Johnstone's *The Primacy of Movement* extends animacy perception to all animate beings, arguing that movement is central to this understanding of animacy; she further makes the case that mind-body segregations continue to distortionary levels among cognitive scientists and neuroscientists.[9]

Thinking—and feeling—through sentience promises a revising of dominant animacy hierarchies, through its allowance of a broad range of interanimation and uncognized recognition. But sentience is also not without its problems, particularly if it is either restricted to what could be discoverable (and falsifiable) through experimental research or conceived in terms of the presence of pain and pleasure (the foundation for claims within animal rights). I return to these questions of sentience, subjectivity and objectivity, and transcorporeality at the end of the book.

Austin's Marriage, Revisited

Let us consider the animality of one originary moment in what is called "theory." Recently, a number of works have studied and critiqued the deployment of animal figures in theoretical argumentation. Indeed, theory itself has deployed the raced animal figure perhaps more than has been noticed, in this case precisely in a domain that attempts to struggle with questions of language as it "materializes": that is, within and through notions of the performative. In 1955, the British language philosopher J. L. Austin put forward a theory of language and action in a book called *How to Do Things with Words*, consisting of a series of transcribed and edited lectures.[10] As the lectures progressed, Austin developed the concept of the performative, from a simple class of utterances characterized by special main verbs in finite form, to a more complex tripartite typology of *acts* that involve not merely the special verbs but all utterances: locutionary (speech) content, illocutionary (conventional) content, and perlocutionary (effective) content. In an early lecture, Austin was working off the simple definition of the performative, one he would later break down, such as in the example "I thee wed" in a marriage ceremony.

Stating that a performative could not succeed without supporting conditions, Austin wrote, "Suppose we try first to state schematically . . . some at least of the things which are necessary for the smooth or 'happy' functioning of a performative (or at least of a highly developed explicit performative)."[11] He went on to list a number of ordered features, among them "a1. There must exist an accepted conventional procedure having a certain conventional effect, that procedure to include the uttering of certain words by certain persons in certain circumstances, and further, a2. the particular persons and circumstances in a given case must be appropriate for the invocation of the particular procedure invoked."[12]

Austin's model was also premised on the assumption that communication is "normally" goodwilled and relies on the proper positioning of that person delivering the performative. He wrote, "One might . . . say that, where there is not even a pretence of *capacity* or a *colourable* claim to it, then there is no accepted conventional procedure; it is a *mockery, like a marriage with a monkey*"[13] (my emphasis). Proper capacity and goodwill were critical to the success of Austin's performative, and these conditions remained, if somewhat sublimated, through developments of the language scheme. In the moment of defining a critical aspect of the successful performative, Austin turned to marriage; at other key moments in the text, marriage again emerged as a central exemplar. Eve Sedgwick has discussed this pattern's appearance in a flood of examples that curiously themselves tend to fail as performatives, either as counterexamples (how not to do) or simply as *examples*, which cannot therefore function as executing marriage.[14] Sedgwick does not, however, note that one of the dramatic flourishes

Austin recruits to seal the illegitimacy of an unauthorized marriage is the figure of a monkey. In addition, it is interesting that if a claim to capacity must exist, then it must have a kind of substance: it must be, in Austin's words, *colourable*. I read this as a suggestive provocation regarding "color" as an intensifier, one that is imbricated with questions of legitimacy and the force of the law under which utterances are enacted.

What does Austin's marriage with a monkey suggest, and on what does it rely to make any kind of sense? While Austin's articulation of "mockery, like a marriage with a monkey," seems mundane in the sense that monkey invocations often function as normative dismissals, we can look more closely at the significance of its collocations. More specifically, we can consider what a queer reading might offer: "A mockery, like a marriage with a monkey" equates a particular kind of animal with the performative's excess (and, perhaps, an affective excess inappropriate to the encounter), that which must be sloughed off for the performative to work efficiently and effectively.

But what of the monkey? Here the "monkey" stands in for something: a creature with limited, superficial identifiability, grammatically determined only by the indefinite article *a*; simile's backgrounded comparator (showing it to be even further expelled); a presumably language-less, cognitively reduced beast; and finally, the example which serves as an example precisely because it is self-evidently extreme. As existing scholarship tells us from many different disciplinary sites and, indeed, as everyday language practices also confirm, vivid links, whether live or long-standing, continue to be drawn between immigrants, people of color, laborers and working-class subjects, colonial subjects, women, queer subjects, disabled people, and *animals*, meaning, not the class of creatures that includes humans but quite the converse, the class against which the (often rational) human with inviolate and full subjectivity is defined.[15] This latter characterization exposes why animals have been so useful as figures, since they stand in for the intermediary zone between human and nonhuman status, and for the field of debate about the appropriateness of humane and inhumane treatment.

Shoshana Felman marks the monkey example as a "monstrous marriage" (the other, also in the text, being "bigamy") and evidence of the "black humor" of Austin's text, remarking on the function of the "triviality of the witty example."[16] While the example is surely witty, and while it might be said to evoke parallel planes of serious theory on the one hand and humor on the other, I wonder *what kind* of humor this provokes for its readers: is it really, or always, pleasurable, particularly if we critically examine the value of that monkey?

Marking this phrase as trivial humor is certain to foreclose an examination of its precise bite and of the quirky ontological logic of *negative* mattering, a mattering that, ultimately, matters. Felman considers the "witty example," which is in her view common for Austin, as distinct from the business of substantiation or of theory, claiming that it belongs to another stage entirely, one that is constructed as humorous and hence rubs up against the straight-faced realm of theory. But Austin's text should also be assessed against its own genre: that of ordinary language philosophy, which structured itself broadly around pointedly simple (silly?) examples. For instance, John Weightman's book on "language and the absurd" considers as its signature, titular case the ever-unraveling phrase "the cat sat on the mat."[17] As Derrida pointed out in his essay "Signature Event Context," "one will no longer be able to exclude, as Austin wishes, the 'non-serious' . . . from 'ordinary' language."[18] It becomes more difficult to determine what is trivial and what is not.

Read "seriously" enough to assess its textual value as simultaneously nontrivial, Austin's structural dismissal of the animal monkey and his matter-of-fact exclusion of the monkey from the institution of marriage together consign the marrying monkey to queer life.[19] I would assert that, in citing a particular kind of marriage just as he asserts its invalidity, however humorously, Austin is responding to a sensed threat. Someone's heteronormative and righteous marriage must be protected against the mockeries of marriage; and we might imagine that someone's righteous and heteronormative speech must be protected against the mockery of performative improprieties, which for all practical purposes are open to convenient definition. Arguably, then, it is not just marrying monkeys, but those who occupy proximal category membership, that is, those who *approximate* marrying monkeys, who are consigned to queer life.

What might have most registered as a threat or worthy of exclusion? Austin wrote these lectures in Britain in the mid-1950s, a period of intensive societal and legal flux in which both heterosexuality and racial purity were being actively shored up. In the 1950s, British police commenced a widely publicized purge of homosexuals, leading to the ar-

rests of many high-profile men who were convicted of "deviant" behavior. Parallel to the Cold War "lavender scare" in the United States,
the British Home Secretary Sir David Maxwell-Fyfe promised to rid
England of the "plague" of homosexuality, a promise he made good
on by prosecuting hundreds of men.[20]

Austin was also writing at a time in which immigrants from formally decolonized sites were arriving in greater numbers, as Britain
went through the intensified strains of postcolonial revision.[21] The
year 1948 saw the first group of West Indian immigrants enter Britain from sites in the Commonwealth, having been granted citizenship through the British Nationality Act. Violence and discrimination against the immigrants grew in the 1950s, resulting in restrictive
Commonwealth Immigrants Act of 1962 (the year of publication of
How to Do Things with Words).

Austin's monkey need not be innocent of this more generalized
context. Already circulating was a long history of British and European associations of apes and monkeys with African subjects, fed and
conditioned by the imperialist culture of colonial relations. These
were underlain by an abiding evolutionary mapping which temporally projected non-European peoples and nonwhite racialized groups
onto earlier stages of human evolution; this is part and parcel of what
Nicole Shukin has called "the productive ambivalence of the colonial
stereotype and the animal sign."[22]

The powerfully racialized undertones of "mockery" have been
theorized by thinkers such as Homi Bhabha, who opens his essay "Of
Mimicry and Man: On the Ambivalence of Colonial Discourse" with
a citation from Sir Edward Cust's "Reflections on West African Affairs
. . . Addressed to the Colonial Office" (Hatchard, London, 1839): "To
give the colony the forms of independence is a mockery."[23] Thus, we
might say that a racial—as well as freakishly gendered—body haunts
Austin's monkey, just as British whiteness may haunt Austin's authorized speaker. Once again, a colonial past might lurk inside a presumably "innocent" cultural form that seems to deploy a presentist—or
timeless—animal figure. Austin was working in a specific social and
political context, and to tease out the undertones of his language is
also to explore the contemporary hauntings or habits of epistemological projection with regard to animality, sex, and race. We might
also use this example to understand some linguistic animal figures as
racialized and sexualized before the fact, especially if used in contexts

where race has a history of social or cultural presence. The "monkey" is a powerfully loaded trope, but not always (or necessarily) negative; in his study of black vernacular language in African American literary works, Henry Louis Gates Jr. discusses how the "Signifying Monkey" is also, within African American culture, a critical trickster figure that self-reflexively speaks back to language.[24] Other monkey figures, such as the Hindu Hanuman and the Chinese mythical Monkey King, have culturally valued trickster ways.

Still, so many apparently innocuous conjurings of animal-human relating—as in the absurd mockery of marriage to a monkey—are underlain or counterpointed by far-from-innocent global histories whose legacies continue through animal-human mappings. For this, we can credit not only early classificatory divisions of Greek philosophers that included congruences between animals and slaves and between animals (nature) and women, but more-recent centuries of shifting borders to facilitate colonial animalization.

But how are each of these categories—animality, sexuality, race, ability—stationed in regard to one another? Again, animality cannot but mediate and interrupt simplistic analogies, even those in which it is involved. This present alteration in itself might properly be dubbed *queer*, in light of queer's own mutative animacy. In other words, within terms of animacy hierarchies, might we have a way to think about queer animality as a genre of queer animacy, as a modulation of life force? It is my contention that animacy can *itself* be queer, for animacy can work to blur the tenuous hierarchy of human-animal-vegetable-mineral with which it is associated. Recentering on animality (or the animals who face humans) tugs at the ontological cohesion of "the human," stretching it out and revealing the contingent striations in its springy taffy: it is then that entities as variant as disability, womanhood, sexuality, emotion, the vegetal, and the inanimate become more salient, more palpable as having been rendered proximate to the human, though they have always subtended the human by propping it up.

Animal Theories

Austin was not alone in his recourse to the animal as a metaphoric crux within theories of language and the law. Animals bear the burden of symbolic weight, not least within contemporary cultural criticism. At levels linguistic and gestural, political and theatrical, ritual and scientific, representations abound that implicitly or explicitly invoke animals and humans in complex relations. Animal studies is a multidisciplinary field, reaching across environmental studies, science and technology studies, psychoanalysis, ecocriticism, and literary and cultural studies. This growing field of makes clear the profound interconstitution of animal and human identities. At the same time, "the animal" stands in to melancholically symbolize what is being lost as a consequence ("natural" or not) of human dominance over the earth it occupies. Certainly, animal representations can remain symbolically tied to human anxieties about the extinct status of their real-life counterparts, as Ursula Heise found true of the fictional animals (regenerated dinosaurs, virtual animals, and electronic animals) in several works from the late twentieth century.[25] Made "freakish" by the technological innovations required to make them, they are often spectacularized as modern-day *lusus naturae*,[26] or, in the case of Heise's analysis of *Do Androids Dream of Electric Sheep?*, fetishized and commodified as pets.

Perhaps because it has served for the human as such a rich comparative repository—because it is kept significatorily empty—there is play in the animal: what the animal means, what it does, what kind of sex it has, what it wants. Such play yields a vast range of imagistic, affective, and economic projections, from images of bourgeois leisure in the park, to formal calculations of agricultural labor on the farm, to military might in the form of cultivated horses. At the same time, symbologies of freely romping or well-trained and valued animals are shadowed by the converse. They are also sources of reference for frighteningly indefinable or disallowable sexual practices (such as "beastly" rape or unctuous, multilimbed octopus sex), and they are the registers of the very disposability of life, where animal status yields death, such as when war legitimates dehumanizations or animalizations of state enemies. In Christian traditions, animals are further vested (or weighted) with a frolicking, prelapsarian innocence of Creation. What would it mean to take this variance of animal play seriously by exploring the ways in which racialities, animalities, and sexualities *interplay*, and are affectively rich, delightful, illusory, toxic, abject, innocent, dark, light, natural, and artificial?

This attraction-repulsion is not unprecedented. The human engagement with both nonanimals and with "technologies" predates by millennia such interabsorption of categories; consider Aristotle's discussion of slavery, which states that "there is little or no difference between the uses of domestic animals and slaves."[27] Indeed, it is not actually clear how we might diagnose this collapsing of animal, human, and machine as unique in terms of some greater speed or intensity of conceptual conflation. Rather, stubborn axes of human difference are imposed on the bodies of animals, and those of animal difference are thrust onto the bodies of humans, differences which repeat and repeat, calling on any narrative of utopian merging to account for itself.

When many axes of human difference collide, the stakes heighten; if the animal figure mediates many of these axes, then it becomes a condensed and explosive discursive site. These crises of humanity-with-animality are concerned with borders and attractions. And it is in fact not surprising that "even" in an era of biotechnology, racisms attain, for this would be to suggest that "innovation," at the leading edge of futurity, is also at the height of sociopolitical advancement. As Sarah Franklin has suggested in her book *Dolly Mixtures*, such charged drives toward unindictable advancement do not go unaccompanied by their affective underside: there are simultaneous concerns about biotechnology conditioned and fed precisely by the fear of what is yet to be known.[28]

Over and again, the animal, cited specifically as "animal" (in categorial contrast to "human"), thus survives in representation. Animals rematerialize here and there as multilingual, interdisciplinary beings, sometimes just themselves, sometimes vitalizing fictive monsters, facing humans. Other zones of encounter include zoos and exotic or domesticated pet ownership, each site with its own discursive terms; pets, for instance, bear the dizzying simultaneity of being named, individualized, and "kinned" while remaining special and distinct precisely for being nonhuman.[29] In a way, animals serve as objects of almost fetishistic recuperation, recruited as signifiers of "nature," or "the real," and used to stand in for a sometimes conflicting array of other cultural meanings (including fear, discipline, sexuality, purity, wisdom, and so on).

This special status applied to the animal is part of the "new economy of being" of modernity; as Lippit notes, "It is a cliché of modernity: human advancement always coincides with a recession of nature and its figures—wildlife, wilderness, human nature."[30] Lippit claims that animals constitute a third term, an "essential epistemological category" (mediating between scientific thought on the one hand and artistic representation on the other). However, in an interview, Donna Haraway voices frustration with the humanism subtending the singular conception of "the animal": "[T]he animal is every bit as much a humanist abstraction, a universal, an empty, a misplaced concreteness issue, but it's worse than that. It's stripped of all particularity and reality and most of all, from my view, stripped of relationality."[31] Haraway here refers to the regular forfeiture of particular knowledge about nonhuman animals, one that turns them into a "universal" abstraction and ignores the fact that the very category of "animal" might be so overly generalized that it threatens to collapse. Knowing what this category consists of with any particularity is made impossible not only by recourse to a pancategory like *animal*, but also by humans' ignorance, which scoops all that is nonhuman and animate into one fold (unless one is in a position to cultivate more specialized understanding, such as veterinary or breed-specific knowledge).

Haraway reminds us, too, that actual animals often bear little if any resemblance to the signifiers and discourses used to reference them. Though the difference between symbolic and actual is easily observed, the *quality* of this difference between a symbolic and actual animal is important. Critics of animal studies might interject that one fault of animal representation is that it appears to ignore the "real" lives of animals. Such a conflation takes too easily as given the indelible link between an animal signifier and its referents, as well as the purity of the natural "real." Because animal signifiers are so deeply bound up with human cultural, political, and social meaning, one can never assume these are one and the same. Rather, the connection they share is that *of reference*, a relation that is sometimes invoked, but all too often not. Haraway diagnoses the extraordinary significatory powers given to an entity called "the animal" as characterized by "misplaced concreteness."

Amid the fluctuations of animals' lives, "the animal" *as* animal sustains, while humans project the vexed peculiarities that are the consequences of interested humans' psychic fibrillations onto the specters and accomplices of animal representations. Certain kinds of animality are racialized not through nature's or modernity's melancholy but through another temporalized map: that of pseudo-Darwinian evolutionary discourses tied to colonialist strategy and pedagogy that superimposed phylogenetic maps onto synchronic human racial typologies, yielding simplistic promulgating equations of "primitive" peoples with prehuman stages of evolution. It is this discursive template that informs the contemporary discourse "on Africa," which, as Achille Mbembe writes in *On the Postcolony*,

> is almost always deployed in the framework (or in the fringes) of a meta-text about the *animal*—to be exact, about the *beast*: its experience, its world, and its spectacle. In this meta-text, the life of Africans unfolds under two signs. First is the sign of the strange and the monstrous. . . . [T]he other sign, in the discourse of our times, under which African life is interpreted is that of intimacy. It is assumed that, although the African has a self-referring structure that makes him or her close to being "human," he or she belongs, up to a point, to a world we cannot penetrate. At bottom, he/she is familiar to us. We can give an account of him/her in the same way we can understand the psychic life of the *beast*. We can even, through a process of domestication and training, bring the African to where she or he can enjoy a fully human life.[32]

Such a discursive mapping has had the effect of both temporalizing race and relegating the fields of barbarism, animality, and primitivism to yet another past, quite beyond the recession of animals under the sign of modernity. I am interested in exploring the means by which animal figures, in their epistemological duties as "third terms," frequently also serve as zones of attraction for racial, sexual, or abled otherness, often simultaneously. Mining sometimes disparate cultural works for these collocations reveals the more complex psychic investments of a whiteness triple-dipped in heteronormativity, ableism, and speciesism and tells of the precise quality of the animacies in which it is invested.

Animacy Theory

While it would be false to equate the two, relations between the two epistemological regions of *queer* and *animal* abound. The animal has long been an analogical source of understanding for human sexuality: since the beginning of European and American sexology in the nineteenth century, during which scientific forays into sexuality were made, homosexuality has served both as a limit case for establishing the scientific zone of the sexual "normal"[33] and, more recently, as a positive validation for "naturalness" (in which what nature maps is fail-safe to the nonhuman animal, as opposed to the messy interventions of culture in the human animal).[34] Such coincidences are by no means a tale of the past. A durable Enlightenment calculus, uplifting rationality and retaining its gendering as masculine, solidified the believed proximity or belonging of women to nature, and in some cases additionally imputed women's categorial attraction to animality. Such partnerings are intensified or provoked by marks of race and class, albeit unpredictably.

One key early scholar of queer animal studies, Jennifer Terry, has examined ways in which "animals provide models for scientists seeking a biological substrate of sexual orientation";[35] in addition, the popular equation of sexuality *as* evidence of one's animality or "animal nature" is oddly inverted. Under certain circumstances, the animal itself *becomes* sexuality, to the extent that the biological material of nonhuman animals (including but not limited to DNA) is used in human-directed reproductive research such as stem cell technology and that animal by-products and hormones are used to increase human sex drives.[36] Likewise, consumer-driven campaigns link young children's premature puberty with hormones in the cow's milk and chicken that they consume (concerns that are often racialized, as in the widely publicized case of the "epidemic" of accelerated sexual development in Puerto Rico).[37] In such "new natures," animals are not a third term; instead, humans and nonhuman animals recombine sexually within the same ontological fold in which they are sometimes admitted to belong.

While earlier works have understood scientific investments in terms of "homosexuality," more recent threads of scholarship have mapped the lessons of a more wide-ranging queer theory to the region of mediation between human and nonhuman animal. Thus, the sometimes resolutely materialized "animal" and the sometimes resolutely immaterial "queer" make for an intriguing conversation, one that may not promise resolution. The feat of animal-human connections has much to do with such ontologizing work.

There currently exists a range of work about queer animals, sexualized human animality, and animal racialization, although there remains some hesitation for some scholars to flesh out race or sex where it also appears. For instance, in an excellent recent book containing queer animal studies scholarship, *Queering the Non/Human*, one finds just a trace of work that deals substantively with the question of race.[38] To consider that categories of sexuality are not colorblind—as queer of color scholarship asserts—is to take intersectionality seriously, even when work seems to go far afield into the realm of the animal. Given the insistent racializations of animals, we can then study the tricky, multivalent contours of a communalism that includes both human animals and nonhuman animals, the border between which remains today intense, politically charged, and of material consequence, and run through and through with race, sometimes even in its most extreme manifestations. It is therefore increasingly apt to explore the insistent collisions of race, animality, sexuality, and ability, and to probe the syntaxes of their transnational formations.

Categories of animality are not innocent of race, as is gestured to in some queer of color scholarship; both David Eng and Siobhan Somerville study early psychoanalysis and early sexology's reliance on racial difference while also noting their interest in tying ontogeny (individual development) to phylogeny (evolutionary history), thereby loosely mapping animality to early developmental stages.[39] Still, "the animal" figure here is at best a haunting overlay. In my attempt to bridge the methodological and epistemological gaps among queer of color scholarship, linguistics, ethnic studies, and white queer studies, I propose an optic—or, rather, a sensibility—that seeks to make consistently available the animalities that live together with race and with queerness, the animalities that we might say have crawled into the woodwork and await recognition, and, concurrently, the racialized animalities already here. What, for instance, of the queerness of some human racialized animalities? What of the animality residing in human racialized queerness?

To extend my argument from the previous chapter, I do not imagine *queer* or *queerness* to merely indicate embodied sexual contact among subjects identified as gay and lesbian, as occurs via naive translations of *queer* as the simple chronological continuation or epistemological condensation of a gay and lesbian identitarian project. Rather, I think more in terms of the social and cultural formations of "improper affiliation," so that queerness might well describe an array of subjectivities, intimacies, beings, and spaces located outside of the heteronormative. Similarly, I consider *animality* not a matter of the creatures that we "know" to be nonhuman (for instance, the accepted logics of pets or agricultural livestock and our stewardship of them), so much as a flexible rubric that collides with and undoes any rigid understanding of animacy. This is a paradoxical space about which we both claim to know much and yet very little, that resists unbinding from its humanist formulation and from its strange admixture between science and racist imperialism.

Recently, some mainstream posthumanist subcultures have not only engaged machinic intimacies or affections but also embraced queer or trans animal affinities that are based in targeted, and somewhat partial, slides down the animacy hierarchy. These are found, for instance, in furries cultures, or "furry fandom." The sexual subcultures of "furries" (those who are turned on by dressing as animals or having sex with someone dressed as an animal) and "plushies" (those with erotic attachments to stuffed animals) are combinations of objecthood and animality that work despite patently false or even cartoon-styled costumes. These furry subcultures can be charted on a shared path with some BDSM subcultures insofar as both can engage in enriched animal figuration—what performance studies scholar Marla Carlson calls "theatrical animality"—without generally pursuing perfect animal representation or embodiment.[40] Yet, just as BDSM practices can deploy accoutrements of animalness—dog chains, dog bowls—to engage in elaborated relations of power, the hybrid creatures that furries represent seem to cultivate a sensualized sense of animacy embedded within animality that the costumes partially enable. The utopian relationality that furriness seems to represent is put into relief by Carlson's sad conclusion to her personal account of Stalking Cat, a biohuman who has undergone multiple surgeries to felinize himself over many years. Despite finding the promise of community among furries, there were limits to the possibility of multiple cohabitation: as Carlson carefully writes, "because expenses and dynamics became unworkable for this interesting household, Cat was asked to move out later that summer," reminding me of the ambition, the economics, the friction, and the intensity that so often occurs within human-identified queer subcultural collective households.

Furries cultures are characterizable perhaps as having a "multianimalist" utopian vision ("multianimalist" here is meant to play on "multiculturalist," particularly in its peremptory claim to egalitarian distributions of power). There appears to be nothing potentially harmful or exploitive, for example, about saying, "I'm a fluffy rabbit and I like carrots, want to do me?" The overwhelmingly cute, indeed aestheticized, vigor of this subculture—observable, for instance, in a quick survey of the self-nominations of furries—seems to come in line with its seemingly predictable paths of recourse to animal becoming. The popular furries figures are much more based on rabbits, cats, and dogs than on, say, lizards, eagles, and centipedes. As Deleuze and Guattari ask, "Are there Oedipal animals with which one can 'play Oedipus,' play family, my little dog, my little cat, and then other animals that by contrast draw us into an irresistible becoming?"[41] Furthermore, the animalized racialities that inevitably intervene into such subcultures (that, for instance, accompany "evil" animals and "good" animals, that is, the innocent whiteness of bunnies) seem to go uncritiqued.

I wish to assert that limiting ourselves to reworking the philosophies of animal-human dependencies, or the ethological studies of a particular animal, or this or that human-animal relationship, carries certain risks: namely, the importing of historical racializations and queerings (or, indeed, imperial tropes) that subtend the very humans and animals under discussion, despite all the bracketing we may be cautioned to do of Aristotle's reasoning about slavery on the basis of animality, the Westernism of Derrida's animal thinking, and so on. These frequently participate in a larger ecology called an animacy hierarchy; and the animal position within this hierarchy is difficult or impossible to fix. The animal figures—whether fictional or actual—that appear are themselves animate, mobile. The hierarchy slips not only because it iteratively renews itself; I suggest its slippage subtends its very fixture, and it calls for us to detect the ways it does so. I use this moment to call for, not animal theory, but *animacy theory*.

Sights of Queer Animality

Up to this point, I have largely been theorizing animacy in terms of language. But I am equally interested in other domains in which animacy might figure. In this section, I turn to historical visual cultures, offering animacy theory as an optic to apprehend them, an optic that applies as much to visualities as to language. Animacy theory is a fertile means of apprehending such slippery figures as a mobile simian figuration and an animalized human character, particularly, I suggest, in the context of the history of race relations in the United States. I look to the late nineteenth and early twentieth century not only because it was a consequential period in race and labor formations in the

United States, one that consolidated normal and abnormal identity, U.S. expansionism, and Western colonialist tropes, but also because conjoined figurations of animality, race, and queerness were not mere sublimated suggestions, but rather were explicitly rendered, drawn, and illustrated.

By revisiting the turn of the twentieth century, I reveal that animality played a visibly mediating conceptual role within the unstable landscape of racialization. Indeed, animalized intimacies were depicted in visual culture that included popular and widely circulated materials such as advertisements and political cartoons. Attending to a small handful of such images, I emphasize the importance of what Claire Jean Kim calls "racial triangulation"[42]—particularly the introduction of Asian race notions into a formerly bipolar racial imaginary of black and white, with an understanding that who was considered "white" was ideologically determined by class and nationality, such that, for instance, Irish immigrants were excluded from its boundaries.[43]

The late nineteenth century in the United States witnessed significant turmoil with regard to shifts in labor, race, and population; when the economy took a downturn, concerns grew among whites about adequate employment, fears that engendered a competitive and scapegoating sense of "Yellow Peril" against the Chinese that emerged in cultural expression as well as in law. This concern was made especially evident, as Lisa Lowe writes, in attitudes and policies around Chinese immigration:

> In a racially differentiated nation such as the United States, capital and state imperatives may be contradictory: capital, with its supposed needs for "abstract labor," is said by Marx to be unconcerned by the "origins" of its labor force, whereas the nation-state, with its need for "abstract citizens" formed by a unified culture to participate in the political sphere, is precisely concerned to maintain a national citizenry bound by race, language, and culture. In late-nineteenth-century America, as the state sought to serve capital, this contradiction between the economic and the political spheres was sublated through the legal exclusion and disenfranchisement of Chinese immigrant laborers.[44]

Lowe notes that increased Asian immigration was facilitated by the interest of the United States in drawing on cheap international sources for labor, while the legal exclusions of Chinese workers were part of a wider strategy to create a racially stratified labor force. As Lowe keenly observes, this had profoundly gendered consequences for later cultural formations and subjectivities. The United States, which had encouraged the use of cheap labor but was simultaneously beholden to its white citizenry, enacted a sequence of laws that limited legal citizenship for Chinese subjects, culminating in the Chinese Exclusion Act of 1882. In this same period, the enfranchisement of black men was legally enacted through the Fifteenth Amendment of 1869, which raised the specter of undesired black citizenship; its enforcement was sporadic and uneven between individual states.

The tensions engendered by these racial exclusions and enfranchisements were registered in a variety of visual media. The cartoon in figure 6 was published in *The San Francisco Illustrated WASP* in 1877. The *WASP* was a magazine that rehearsed anti-Chinese fears in an era of continued Chinese immigration. In the image, we see an animated and physical backlash against Chinese immigration—glossed here as "the Chinese Question"—as a white laborer in California in uniform leading the "Working Men's Procession" punches a Chinese coolie in the mouth while another coolie looks on. The Working Men's Party asserted that the Chinese immigrant laborers were threatening the economic livelihood of whites.

Chinese hair was often referred to in the West as a tail. The British diplomat, Sinologist, and translator Herbert Giles wrote in his book *The Civilization of China*, published in 1911, that "a Chinese coolie will tie his tail round his head when engaged on work."[45] Interestingly, the Chinese man's hands, a common signal of labor and work capacity, are ambiguously absent or concealed by his long flopping sleeves that make his arms dangle "apelike" and passively at his sides, against the obviously active and well-defined fist of the white bearer of the "first blow." With his "knock-knees" and "pigeon-toes" and a head improbably straining to the left, the Chinese man is presented as an ungainly figure who appears to float or flail next to the stout white man whose legs are solidly planted on the ground. His peach fuzz—or facial fur—contrasts with the thicker, virile beard of his attacker. (Interestingly, beards themselves, as masculine secondary sexual characteristics, were subject to monitoring and debate among whites in the nineteenth century, shifting between "barbarous" and "civilized" masculinity.) Ultimately, this Chinese representation has been graphically rendered as animal-like, as simianized.

6. Unattributed illustration. *The San Francisco Illustrated WASP* 2, no. 71 (1877).

7. "Rough on Rats" advertisement, c. 1870–90.
Daniel K. E. Ching Collection, Chinese Historical
Society of America, San Francisco.

A contemporaneous advertisement by E. S. Wells Trade Company for one of its products called "Rough on Rats" (another was "Rough on Corns") essentially promulgates the Chinese *as* rats (or of the same stuff as rats), leaving a tempting empty slot where a banner might otherwise bear their name: the location closest to where the direct object of "it clears out" might be (figure 7).

The rat poison ad, whose explicit purpose is to sell poison, also takes advantage of the wider anti-Chinese discourses that themselves racialized the notion of "hygiene." It relies on a logic of similarity between rats and Chinese people to stir up fears of infection, invoking not only a similarity but a consanguinity (or even a substitution) between the rat and the Chinese man. First, the two bodies merge through his act of eating and by the superposition of a second rat against the man's pants. This merging is augmented by the analogical prompt of the mirroring of the two tails (rat appendage and hair), which makes the rat approaching the man's mouth almost seem like an act of cannibalism. "They Must Go" doubles in meaning, simultaneously referring to the undesired animal pests and literally citing the slogan of the anti-Chinese immigration movement. Another large rat, dead and flat on its back at the top of the ad, indicates the triumph of the poison but also hints at the animal's passivity or submissiveness. We can consider the man's depicted ingestion of the rat a form of bizarre bodily intimacy, one that complements the kinds of human queer sexualities that Nayan Shah meticulously charted in his history of turn-of-the-century San Francisco Chinatown.[46] Shah (who makes glancing reference to rats) details how unruly human intimacies—in the homosociality of bachelor households, the "improper intimacies" of opium dens, and the shared parenting of Chinatown working women—participated together in white domestic discourses of racialized hygiene and public health.

But how and when were the Chinese Americans racialized in animal terms in relation to others? Certainly, animalization was not the exclusive province of the Chinese. Arguably, African slaves first bore the epistemological weight of animalization, when they were rendered as laboring beasts by slave owners and political theorists legitimizing slavery. In 1879, just two years after the "rat tail" cartoon, the political satirist and German émigré Thomas Nast mocked U.S. Senator Blaine's opposition to the modified Burlingame treaty reopening connections with China, giving it favored-nation trade status and allowing greater immigration (figure 8). Here Nast points out that Blaine opposed further Chinese immigration; on this issue, the cartoonist sympathized with Chinese immigrants. Elsewhere, he was known to animalize some "whites" in his illustrations in order to demonstrate white barbarity in relation to Chinese "higher" civilization; these animalized "white people" were Irish. The contested nature of the whiteness of the Irish had a partial basis, notably, in Irish-black proximities in the formation of the American working class.

In this image, the figure to the left, appearing to represent a black man holding a recently legalized voting card (black men's right to vote was legally established in 1865, but was only extended to Southern blacks in 1868), seems to be simianized, as indicated by his hunched posture, diminished size, and relatively small head, complete with a darkened skin tone. The small head also suggests a visual hinting at microcephaly, indicating the close connection between disability, "freakiness," intelligence, race, and animality.[47]

It is tempting here to hypothesize a strange circulation of racialized

VOL. XXIII.—No. 1158.]   NEW YORK, SATURDAY, MARCH 8, 1879.   [WITH A SUPPLEMENT.
PRICE TEN CENTS.

Entered according to Act of Congress, in the Year 1879, by Harper & Brothers, in the Office of the Librarian of Congress, at Washington.

8. Thomas Nast, "The Civilization of Blaine," *Harper's Weekly*, 1879.

figuration: Nast was known to study, and borrow from, British caricature. He further shared (or had adopted) the British disdain for the
Irish, going on to not only simply ape-ify the Irish representations
in his own pictorial repudiations, but arguably participating in what
Anne McClintock refers to as "the iconography of domestic degeneracy." Referring to the "receding foreheads" in the representations of
the Irish in an illustration from *Puck*, McClintock writes that this iconography "was widely used to mediate the manifold contradictions in
imperial hierarchy—not only with respect to the Irish but also to the
other 'white negroes'—Jews, prostitutes, the working-class, domestic
workers, and so on."[48] The representation of the black man here thus
speaks to a possible borrowing by Nast of degeneracy's visual arguments from Irishness and other European others, ironically reapplying
already hybridized iconographies of Africanized whiteness to newly
enfranchised African American men. The travel of such iconographies
reminds us that the travel of bodies, whether coerced or facilitated by
the state, is merely one strand to trace in imperialism's diverse fabric,
which in some ways ignores the "postcolonial" births of nations.

The black man's pose is especially striking in relation to the erect
poses of Blaine and the Chinese man, who stands in front of an array
of imported goods as if he is an ambassador of capitalism. Rather than
standing upright, the black man's body curls over toward the senator;
his right leg is bent up as his foot crooks around his other knee, so
that his balance is unstable, dependent upon the Senator to whom he
clings. John Kuo Wei Tchen analyzes Nast's cartoon:

> Blaine reject[s] the teas, silks, porcelain, and carvings offered by John
> Confucius [what I understand to be Nast's stand-in "good" Chinese
> immigrant], thus trampling on the Burlingame Treaty, while cater-
> ing to the ballot of a gross caricature of a black man who, though
> physically full-grown, is depicted in a childlike posture. Essentially
> Nast was saying that treaties, trade, and superior Chinese culture
> were not important to Blaine as long as he could gain the vote of
> an imbecilic, uncultivated former slave. The drawing was satirically
> captioned "The Civilization of Blaine," with John Confucius asking,
> "Am I not a man and a brother?"—the English abolitionists' slogan.[49]

This depiction can be thought of as animating a *multiracial drama*. The
comparative use of the negative Black example to demonstrate another's secured or accomplished subjecthood is a vast and prevalent

trope that unsurprisingly has come to inform some forms of Asian antiblack racism, in another instance of the success of divide-and-conquer strategies as a way to defuse coalitional antiracist movements. I say multiracial, not multicultural, because such racial triangulations ironize precisely the facile fantasies of multiculturalism's prehistory in the United States.[50]

Thus, I suggest that the simianization of this black man in the cartoon was a convenient trope for Nast. The cartoon recruits the animacy hierarchy to secure the very status of "the human" itself, since those deemed uncivilized or less civilized may simultaneously be thought in terms of primitivism, barbarism, and animality. One simianized figure stands in for the threat to the citizenship of the next human candidate (the Chinese man), who is not in this case simianized.

The simianizing present in "The Civilization of Blaine" neatly aligns with the violence of the desire for the white laborer to expel the Chinese. But things can become also more complex than this simian-other formation, and they may do so queerly. While Tchen remarks on the "childlike posture" of the black man, he does not mention feminization or, to be more precise, the intimate bodily contact between the black man and Senator Blaine, with their hands, wrists, and feet touching. But even more significantly: there is a curious intimacy between Blaine, the anti-immigrant crusader, and the presumably black voting subject nearly in Blaine's arms, holding his vote, with legs in a simpering curtsy and toes touching Blaine's own. Might we begin to think of this as a queer proximity, a queer intimacy? If we do, how does Nast's wish to depict Blaine's catering to black political desire become depicted as queer intimacy? And in what ways does it exceed a typical cartoonist's need to graphically represent strange alliances? What are the implications of the presence of animality in this queer desire? While Tchen has remarked on the animality and barbarity of both Chinese and Irish figures in Nast's images, he seems to allow the black figure's own animality to be spoken for by the genre of "gross caricature," thus attenuating any additional potencies of Nast's visual argument.[51] The queerness also implicates and taints Blaine, as he is chastised here for not listening to the tune of capital as represented by the Chinese merchant and for being drawn into a circuit of bodily intimacy with a black man who presumably stands outside such capital, rendering their relationship at once cross-racial, ambivalently cross-species, and queer.

As these three historical examples illuminate, animal figurations at the turn of the century were by no means simple and were often overlaid with sexual implications. It is commonly understood that animality "sticks" indelibly to specific races. However, thinking these images within the rubric of what I am calling animacy theory, we can see how that animality can shift, attaching itself to different kinds of groups. That the domain of the animal is treated as a zone of deferral means that animality subtends a great deal below the white human man at the top, who in spite of his own superior position, can be dragged down by his own queer association. Paying attention to the relationality among the figures allows us to see the complex queer intimacies involved.

Querying Fu Manchu

The conjunction of animality, Asianness, and queerness persisted beyond the late nineteenth century. I now turn to consider—but hopefully not beat—the "dead horse" of Fu Manchu, the outlandish, turn-of-the-century creation figured by tropes of the Yellow Peril. I do so in part to provide some historical ballast to arguments about queer animal presents, and simultaneously to point to the strength of legacy and historical consequence in the shape and timing of Fu Manchu's appearances in the United States. Fu Manchu is in some ways (one slice of) the bread and butter of Asian American studies; he further occupies the historically dominant focus of Asian American studies on Chinese and East Asian figures. Yet, as a primary site of study, he deserves revisiting with the optic of animacy. "Fu Manchu" is a prewar phenomenon in which cinema charted, embellished, and vitalized a racialized animality beyond its literary mappings.

Fu Manchu appeared in a series of popular novels and mainstream Hollywood films through the first half of the twentieth century. Of course, Fu Manchu has lived well beyond the bounds of his British and North American literary and filmic existence, leaking into fictional representations of evil Asian masculinity, and acting as a key figure of Asian American and scholarly analysis.[52] In the 1960s, he took new form in the Omaha Zoo as an orangutan, "Fu Manchu," who became famous for his skillful escapes: he was so wily, in fact, that he became the subject of many news and scholarly articles that profiled his intelligent, tool-using behavior.[53] Today, he reappears as an early example of the media studies concept of "techno-orientalism."[54] I wish to build on this previous scholarship to reconsider Fu Manchu, not with a mere nod to "feline" attributions by his creator, but with an emphasis on his racialized, cinematic, queer animality. Fu Manchu's animality has not been extensively considered, and I suggest that it provides a particularly useful example for reading covert animalizations in cases where racialized queering is already at stake.

Fu Manchu came to life in a series of novels written by the British author Sax Rohmer (the pseudonym of Arthur Sarsfield Ward) from the 1910s through the 1950s. Apparently, Rohmer had never been out East, only to his local Chinatown. As a writer, he seemed to be titillated by his own observation that broad informal networks of support among immigrant Chinese resembled the queer kinship of British "sworn brotherhoods," complete with ulterior logics and allegiances, if not also swirling, mysterious sexualities.[55] The novels' massive popularity in both Britain and the United States was driven by the sentiment of the Yellow Peril in each region concerning the rise of Chinese immigration and labor in the late nineteenth and early twentieth centuries, as well as shared fears about rising East Asian powers in the mid-twentieth century. Rohmer's series in particular achieved immense popularity in the United States; the novels in turn inspired a series of Fu Manchu films produced in Hollywood, which premiered in the late 1920s (with a special concentration of movies appearing in the 1960s), as well as a short-lived television series.[56]

These wildly popular films constituted a genuine mass-media phenomenon, one so powerful that even today Fu Manchu is a recognizable "type," a shorthand for many Asian stereotypes. The films also provided a consistently extravagant imaginary visual and narrative fount through which to define U.S. citizenship against Asian moral decline. In 1942, the Chinese government protested that the Fu Manchu film then under production would offend a wartime alliance between the United States and China; the film was suspended in response. That a film was taken as an interest of the nation not only reminds us of the centrality of the Hollywood industry to bolstering U.S. nationalisms, but affirms that the exotophobia of the Fu Manchu novels and films was consonant with contemporaneous policies designed to minimize Chinese attempts at citizenship.[57] His appearance on the cultural and national stage was thus accompanied by policies in which Chinese identity was subject to various controlling efforts, including legal efforts at containment, exclusions from citizenship, and public health strategies.[58]

The character of Fu Manchu is described in an oft-cited compendium of terms laid out in an early Rohmer book, *The Insidious Dr. Fu Manchu*: "Imagine a person, tall, lean and feline, high-shouldered, with a brow like Shakespeare and a face like Satan, a close-shaven skull, and long, magnetic eyes of the true cat-green. Invest him with all the cruel cunning of an entire Eastern race, accumulated in one giant intellect, with all the resources of science past and present, with all the resources, if you will, of a wealthy government—which, however, already has denied all knowledge of his existence. Imagine that awful being, and you have a mental picture of Dr. Fu-Manchu, the yellow peril incarnate in one man."[59] Here, Fu Manchu is depicted as an extranational agent with limitless resources. He is a perverse "race man," sinister and intelligent (with a brow like Shakespeare, which interestingly hints at a cultivated intelligence threateningly bordering on "white") and endowed with scientific knowledge, a potent means of mastery over the environment and over social and geographic arenas. To say that Fu Manchu functions as the embodiment of the entirety of China is not to make too great a claim, for as this passage notes, within his person he contains "all the resources . . . of a wealthy government." Tina Chen notes that while "the surface rhetoric of the books condemns Fu Manchu for attempting to build a Chinese empire, the Doctor's techniques of collection and demonstration actually mirror *Western* imperial practice."[60] Moreover, his strength is augmented, it would seem, by an animal spirit: a specifically feline cunning, stature, and ocular appearance.

In addition to this circulation of signs, a number of alternately sympathetic and hostile critics, including Frank Chin, Daniel Y. Kim, and Harry Bernshoff, suggest that Fu Manchu is also homosexual.[61] His queer desire is arguably most dramatized in the Hollywood film *The Mask of Fu Manchu*, produced in 1932, starring the popular "monster actor" Boris Karloff, in which he indicates a certain possessive desire for the character Terrence Granville, even laying his hands on the bare chest of Terrence (figure 9).

The story is set in the Gobi Desert, where a group of British and German explorer-scientists have come to nab the death mask of Genghis Khan before Fu Manchu can acquire it. Here Fu Manchu is, and is not, "catlike." Rather, his presumed felinity is subject to the representa-

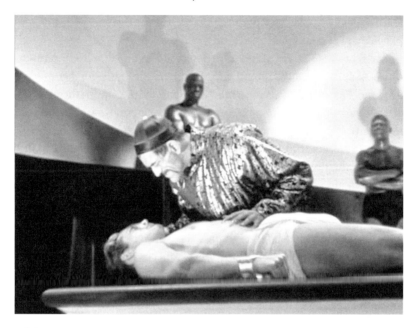

9. Boris Karloff playing Fu Manchu. *The Mask of Fu Manchu* (dir. Charles Brabin, 1932).

tive load of roaming signifiers of catness, resulting in a human–animal blend that includes a distinctly yellow face. Fu Manchu's clawlike nails, for instance, which we find in a select few of the films, bizarrely migrate, appear, and disappear, and take on and lose decoration.

In this film still, Fu Manchu gleefully leans over Terrence, his hands caressing Terrence's bare torso and belly; only a few fingers show the long nails. In the background stand two statuelike black slaves who cast shadows against the walls. The stark lighting of the scene washes out Terrence's face, which appears very pale in contrast to Fu Manchu's prominently darker visage (Karloff performing in yellowface). This touch is irrefutably homoerotic, and Fu Manchu's feminized felinity is itself arguably queer. His long nails, when present, might well have been a citation of Chinese stereotypes based on "actual" royal practices. But considering the roles they played in the films and for viewers as recognizable marks, these feline nails function visually to compete with Fu's intellectual renown, altering the perceptual economy of normative subjectivity by redirecting his sensibility toward the animal. Simultaneously, his femininity hides as felineness, undercutting his otherwise trenchant masculinity by effectively queering it.

At the same time, we might argue that his animality exceeds the feline. Indeed, from what place comes his wealth of facial hair, simultaneously valued as brute, royal, and masculine and as primitive and barbarian? Fu Manchu is often depicted with his pet marmoset, Peko, sitting on his shoulder, near the primary site of subjectivity—the head—suggesting that the monkey "has his ear." The proximity of this simian familiar suggests kinship predicated not on shared blood but on affinity, affection, or some other affective order.

Another image, this from the cover of the DVD collection of the TV series *The Adventures of Fu Manchu*, aired in 1956, shows Fu Manchu with Peko in his lap, grasping its wrists with his hands and presenting the "paws" of the monkey seemingly in place of his own hands (figure 10). The release of this DVD collection points to the ongoing interest in Fu Manchu and exemplifies his persistence in contemporary cultural memory. Here Fu Manchu is seated before a background that includes Chinese lanterns and a large spider hanging on its web, a classic indication of sinister traps. A dark-haired woman in elaborate jewelry and a brocade top exposing her midriff grasps Fu Manchu's face and upper arm, shifting her eyes to the side while he, along with Peko, stares directly at the viewer, leveling an intimidating gaze.

But what interests me most here is the representation of the embrace between the monkey and the human. The hands, viewed as indicators of capacity and creativity (as our most essential tools), class (as in the category of manual labor), and humanness (in their significance to tool-using evolutionary claims of the opposable thumb), are placed in relation to the paws of the monkey. Whose manuality predominates? And what is the force of that dominance? If they refer to a site of subjectivity, is that subjectivity made more sensible, more animate? In Steve Baker's analysis of a variety of contemporary artistic projects involving animals, he discovers a prominence of attention to hands. He suggests this may not be coincidental: while hands seem to centrally and uniquely symbolize human creativity, animals themselves also seem to be "aligned with creativity."[62]

Baker notes that the hand is a central contentious figure in Derrida's assessment of Heidegger's famous claim that the animal is "poor in world": according to Heidegger, an ape's hands are *not* hands because they do not represent the possibility of taking intelligent hold, of grasping something conceptually. What is compelling about Fu Manchu's grasping of Peko's paws is his presentation of the paws over his

10. Cover of *The Adventures of Fu Manchu* (1956). *Alpha Home Entertainment*, Classic TV Series DVD.

own. The paws suggest that all that Fu Manchu grasps is animalistic in nature, or that animality itself drives his will to knowledge and to creativity. Fu Manchu's interior animality is a proposition made explicit and observable in the "pawing" of Fu Manchu's grasping tools: his hands. Fu Manchu is not just animal, not just queer: he is porous along many axes of difference. The clasp of the monkey's hands is also a queered embrace, one that exists in tension with the clearly eroticized woman at his side. In weaving between heterosexual, homosexual, and the asexual (the emasculated sissy that Elaine Kim cites), he mirrors the ambivalently sexualized quality of animals.

Fu Manchu's gestural equivocation between hairy masculinity and clawing felinity literalizes the animalizing appliqués of a colonialist imagination concerned with its others, and is itself (trans-)gendered and transspecies by being rendered as feline. If filmic representations of racialized characters almost have a tradition of chaotic rendering, this "chaos" has a particular tinge. The literally animal signifiers circulating around Fu Manchu occur because he is a racialized figure. This confusion of human-animal and female-male signs may well bespeak the confused other status and the complex materiality of the Asian male body in North American society, to invoke David Eng's important work on this subject.[63]

How intelligible is the (or an) Asian body? "Asian American" sex and gender positions are deeply polarized; the missing Asian male phallus is countered by a female hypersexuality ranging in representation from the submissive geisha to the "dragon lady." Celine Parreñas Shimizu provocatively describes such racialized hypersexuality as "a form of bondage that ties the subjectivity of Asian/American women."[64] Such a sexual-racial polarization seems in the end untenable, and the Asian transgender body becomes both eminently possible as the logical (if socially disallowed) consequence of a significatory overreach, while at the same time, the Asian transgender body survives as an impossible spectacle.[65] Indeed, Fu Manchu's queer gendering poses an embodied threat; the filmic representation of this body, it could be argued, suggests the perceived toxicity of a racially gendered body that simply won't behave. This nonbehaving body echoes the strains of the Yellow Peril, sounding alarms about unwelcome laboring bodies that will not retreat to their country of origin, as well as about the possibility of a rising Asian body of power.

While Fu Manchu is, as a fictional construct steered primarily by non-Asian producers, made "from without," Fu Manchu's "inscrutability" is of a very particular kind. The queer human-animal blend he offers to us—undone and redone in every successive representation— offers no easy roadmap, despite revisitations to this archive by scholars decade after decade. Available and unavailable for reading upon reading, this is a "wily" figure indeed; to the extent that animality variously and multiply subtends the human, I wonder whether he might be thought of as claiming animality, rightfully claiming animality, the animality that we all have and that some of us hide, as a part of his righteous defiance of Western orders of rule and knowledge.

Coda: Visaging Travis

How do past and contemporary sexual publics articulate figures of animality? How do urban and rural containments such as "Chinatowns," "ghettoes," and institutions such as prisons produce and maintain queer animalities? When and where are such tropes *not* affectively charged and animated without relation to colonial impulses? When does disability—glossed cynically as pathology, partiality, old age, and contagious disease, and, alternatively, as machinic cyborg and as natural variation—come into play? When is human "animal sex," whether bestial or queer or rapacious, racially intensified? How are particular "animal" species racialized through specific trajectories of "human" engagement? How do artists work such proximate borders? Some of these questions are returned to in the next chapter. To take the play of meanings seriously means that animality must be considered as a complex thing, material, plastic, and imaginary, at least in coformation with other concepts such as wildness, monstrosity, bestiality, barbarity, and tribality, as well as what it is to be human. This is the stuff of animacy theory.

Finally, how to reconcile animals and their strange temporal presence with the temporality of color? For racialized color, arranged as it is along hierarchies of labor and of primitivity in contrast to modernity, has also been resolutely attached to the past. What body presents? How is that body articulated, even before it speaks? What does it mean for a presenting body, a living body, to shift between white presence and a queer racialized past, between animality and humanity? These human-animal bodies and figures not only fatally but perhaps productively literalize this endless blend. And so this chapter might be thought of as an invitation to consider queer animality not just as a component of technofuturity, but as a site of investment, a commitment to queer, untraceable, animal futurities, morphing time and raciality.

Earlier in this chapter, I declared that I was pointedly focusing on representations of animals rather than their "real" counterparts. Yet I self-consciously end with a discussion of the strange affective politics conjured by the events of and following February 17, 2009, in which a living chimpanzee and former TV animal star named Travis "went berserk" and mauled a woman named Charla Nash (a friend of his owner, Sandra Herold), destroying her nose, hands, lips, and eyelids.

Travis had been reluctant to go in for the night to the home he shared with Herold; Herold called Nash for help. According to Herold, after arriving in her car, Nash approached him with a stuffed toy before her face, and then, by moving it aside, revealed her face, which had been altered by a new hair cut and a makeover. This makeover is codified, of course, as an acceptable disruption of the historical contiguity of individual personhood. We do not know, of course, whether it was her doubled switching of facial presentation that enraged or unsettled him, though Herold herself wondered whether this was so; and it was certainly Nash's face that received heightened damage and was the focus of Travis's attack, along with her hand.

After some efforts to stop his attack, Herold called 911: "Oh, my god! He's eating her! He's eating her face! Shoot him, shoot him!" Herold later explained, "I had to save my friend," meaning Nash. The responding policeman, whose safety seemed threatened by the chimp, who had approached his police vehicle, shot and mortally wounded Travis.

Herold, as Travis's nearly lifelong legal owner and human companion, shared wine with him in the evening, gave him Xanax and other pharmaceuticals, and shared his bed. Indignant comments condemned her ownership of Travis, saying that one should never keep a "dangerous" chimpanzee privately as Herold did, and that there are more appropriate places for them (presumably nature reserves and animal conservation parks). Yet, the "private" realm, while constructed as the inviolable civil right of all under U.S. liberalism, is politically, economically, and racially determined. That the privacy of Herold and Travis's intimate unit (other pictures show them smiling for the camera and kissing on the lips on their home's front steps, with Travis's arm around Herold's shoulder) was deemed condemnable and retroactively fallible — even "sick" — is similar to the declaration of the public right to conduct surveillance of the private sphere when certain improprieties are at stake. This is reminiscent of the enforcement of homosexual sodomy laws in the United States until *Lawrence v. Texas* was decided in 2003. That is to say, this is a story that vexes the controls of public and private space. Travis's tale is a one of a tenuous and failed kinship, one in which he had been a vital participant, finally forsworn. His actions seemed to call for Herold to activate a militarized response ("Shoot him!"), though after being shot by the police officer, Travis tragically retreated into the house he shared with Herold and into his personal cage, where he died.

In view of the relationship of racialized affective surfeit to militarized control, it is not so remote to consider the value of Travis on the public stage as not only a species experiment but as a racialized one that mediates between imprisonment and death. One controversy that followed involved a *New York Post* political cartoon depicting a chimpanzee shot by a police officer, with the caption, "we'll have to find someone else to write the next stimulus bill," arguably forcing the chimp's referent toward President Obama.[66] Like a latent blackness (indeed, black masculinity) that spilled beyond its tenuous threshold of racial equilibrium, it was up to the (police) state to step in, correct, and mediate. The social and individual experiment Travis and his species represent speaks directly to the "visaging," the enfacement, referred to in some divides between humans and nonhuman animals, an enfacement which is implied in the primacy of the sentience-affording visage for vegans who do not eat anything "with a face."

It is interesting to consider what will become politically of the research which has revealed that macaques seem to possess several brain areas (as identified by fMRI, functional magnetic resonance imaging) within which cells are specialized for face recognition, whether human, animal, or cartoon.[67] This result bears some similarity to cognitive-linguistic research that shows that language is but one of a realm of cues that animate conceptual imaging. We also have to remember that humans are not the only possessors of sentience; such a view legitimates (and, according to some thinkers, necessitates) a turn toward various realms of "actuality," whether biological research or animal research or engagements with "actual animals." At the same time, the notion that nonhuman animals have a special interest in faces as faces, whether animal, human, or cartoon, demonstrates an inevitable porosity and interchange between "realities," even if human scientists might not be able to diagnose the epistemic status of each example to a nonhuman animal, that is, the relationship each example has to the "real" for that animal.

If there are inescapable materialities by which we live, it is also true that in many more circumstances than are often acknowledged, what is real is what one thinks is real. Ultimately, my point here is not to naively assert that nonhuman animals must certainly have in quality and quantity direct analogues to "human" capacities. With a nod to the section that opened this chapter on animal language and sentience, I wish to share my doubt about nonhuman animals' simplistic or templatic *exclusion* from such capacities, since even at the level of scientific research there are increasing numbers of ways in which, as these capacities are refigured away from previous, implicitly anthropocentrist constructions, nonhuman animals come to share with humans certain territories of sense, percept, cognition, feeling, and, indeed, language.

In the aftermath of Travis's attack and death, the politics of (dis-)ability also loom large in the form of questions about what counts as a proper or livable life (including Travis's) in the complex biopolitics of human and animal worlds. One respondent to the *New Haven Register*'s coverage of a *Oprah* episode in 2010 which hosted Charla Nash after her release from the hospital, wrote, "Seeing her face and the damage done it really looked like they sewed the chimps [*sic*] tongue on the center of her face . . . I must confess about thoughts inside my head made me ask if she was better off dead , , , but I get this feeling this woman is strong and is loaded with love and is loved deeply by her family and friends, so it is love that will keep her going."[68]

"Better off dead" recalls the equation mentioned in this book's introduction between disabilities marked as "severe bodily perversions" and the cancellation of the life that holds them.[69] Bodies worthy of life: as the disability theorist Paul Longmore has made clear, there are intimate relationships between euthanasia and eugenics discourses, a dependency within the history of euthanasia on the construction of unacceptable disabilities.[70] Furthermore, the passage's repeated invocation of "love" further reminds us of the belief in the corrective and rehabilitative possibilities of affective politics (especially of legitimated kinship and intimacy structures)—affectivities which the exchanges of patriotic fervor and trauma in times of war demonstrate so soundly.

Finally, the commenter's sense that Travis's tongue and the area surrounding the central portion of Nash's face had been *sewn together* intensifies Herold's own pronouncements in the 911 call that Travis was eating Nash, or eating her face, putting both the normal human consumption of other animals' flesh and the common understanding of heightened consanguinity between humans and chimps in stark irony. Both comments, though they are quite different interactions, tell a tale of transposable, cosubstantial matter and of interchangeable kind. But this human–chimp consanguinity, studied, charted, and affectionately hierarchalized within primatology, was a different, proximating consanguinity than that alleged between the Chinese and rats, which rendered them similarly murky, fungible, interchangeable, and comfortably distant (from "us").

The sewing of Travis's tongue to Nash's face threatens a symbolic violence to human integrity that is in spite of its extension of intimacy. On a human face, one finds a chimp tongue that symbolizes not the subjective promise of human language but something "almost the same, but not quite," to cite Bhabha's famous rendering of colonial mimicry, a tongue suitable merely to its "animal functions." The image of Travis's cannibalizing of Nash communicates an apparently horrific intimacy. Like Mary Shelley's monster created by Dr. Frankenstein, the cannibal image is foretold by a haunting of whiteness, a troubling of boundaries that is not only racialized but also sexualized.[71] Ultimately, that "an animal" attacked a human here seems but a sideshow. If the attack first appeared most surprising the tale now seems one of a family gone terribly wrong.

The aftermath to the tale was that Nash was not only on the mend but on a search to acquire a better face and hand via transplant, even as the other protagonists had ceased to live. (Not only was Travis himself fatally shot on the day of the incident, but Sandra Herold soon after died of a ruptured aortic aneurysm; her attorney explained that she had died of repeated heartbreak.) But one hospital has already rejected Nash as a candidate because it could not perform a simultaneous hand and face transplant from the same donor. A representative from the hospital explained that Nash would need sight (which the face transplant would presumably restore) to retrain her new hand, so it was not as if she could easily choose one over the other. Only a near-complete functional replacement, a restoration of both signal sites for Nash's sentient capacities, seemed to make any operation worthwhile. At that moment, somewhere in the world, a heated discussion about whether chimps could successfully donate hearts to humans was under way.

4

Animals, Sex, and Transsubstantiation

I suggested in the first chapter that in animacy's instantiation in Western epistemologies, its coercivity consists of both mundane and exceptional reinforcements. Animacy spans enforcements and governmentalities: not only does it inform state policy, but it is also articulated overtly and implicitly as a "way of life." Austin's "monkey marriage" not only defines the proper field for marriageable subjects, but also defines fields of impropriety, including the claim or right of nonhuman animals to enjoy civil liberties. Speech is not necessary to this conception, and indeed, linguists have relinquished mastery over animacy even as they have attempted as best they could to track its materialization in language.

Animacy hierarchies in Western ontologies are about kind: they assert that *this group* is affiliated with *these properties* (for instance, the assertion that "animals lack language"). In such a hierarchy's conceptual life, kinds are equated with propensities; but in the maintenance of kinds, the hierarchy simultaneously assigns kinds a *generativity*, mapping and marking reproductive and nonreproductive bodies. Reproductivity in its signal bodily and material sites thus plays a key role in contentious debates about the borders between kinds. When carefully managed cross-animate realms change, so must the biopolitical stakes around their realignment. Continuing the previous chapter's concern with queer animality, I turn here to take up questions of materiality, animality, and transness, demarcating the "proper boundaries" around both nonhuman animals and humans so that the drawn biopolitical relations among them can be made more palpable.

I further consider the epistemological and temporal lessons made possible by thinking about animality in terms of sex: in this case, its regulation, its contestation, and its purported desexualization. Indeed, in this chapter's take on "transness," I focus on how animal-human boundaries are articulated in terms of sex and gender by examining perhaps the most consistent missing morphology in cultural representations of animals: the genitalia.[1]

If mattering turns irrevocably on gender—if, as Judith Butler writes, questions of gender are irretrievably interwoven with questions of materiality, and if human substantiation enduringly depends on the expulsion of animals—then it is imperative that we ask questions not only about how animals matter, but how they matter sexually.[2] To examine the transness of animal figures in cultural productions or philosophical discourses (beyond their biology, queerness, or pure animality, for instance) is to also interrogate how humans' analogic mapping to and from animals (within imagined, lived, or taxonomic intimacies) paradoxically survives the cancellation wrought by the operations of abjection, casting a trans light back on the human. By considering the simultaneous relevance of race, gender, sexuality, and geopolitics in animal studies, this chapter builds on recent work that treats animal spaces intersectionally.[3] It makes use of the simultaneous mobility, stasis, and border violation shared among transgender spaces and other forms of trans-being: transnationality, transraciality, translation, transspecies. This is not to conflate these various, importantly distinct terms, but to instead try to think them together in new constellations.

Making the astute observation that "biology has always meant the thing itself and knowledge of what it is, and equally notoriously, these two biologies have not always been identical," Sarah Franklin dubs "transbiology" an intensified making of "new biologicals" via "the redesign of the biological in the context of contemporary bioscience, biomedicine and biotechnology."[4] She identifies what might be thought of as a significant shift in the specific depth of imaginative technologies in crafting matter, a shift in the participants of what Charis Thompson has called "ontological choreography."[5] Here, thinking less in terms of biotechnologies than attending to the role of visual representation and morphology in mattering, I turn directly to the "trans" in "transbiology," redirecting it toward transsubstantiation.

Changes in biology today are tweaking the delineation of kinds. Pharmaceuticals are composed of nonhuman biological material, cloning and stem cell technologies deploy blends of human–nonhuman animal material, and so on; this affects the "sex" of reproduction and fudges lines of lineal descent. Yet it is important to reiterate, for all the significance of today's biotechnological chimeras, that human–animal mixings have already existed in the realm of discourse. In an unstable realm of animacy, relational exchanges between animals and humans can be coded at the level of ontological mediation, or alchemical transformation, one that goes beyond a vitalism that infuses given boundaries with lifeliness. I read these productions as participating in the animacy hierarchy by exercising a kind of substitutional, horizontal logic of species displacement (altering kind), intervening with the slower, largely lineal pace of the sexual reproduction of species (replacing kind with kind). In certain cases, I suggest it is by interactions of substance with human countervalences — *(trans-)substantiation* — that animals may achieve their final form (for humans) or, more significantly, by interacting with animal countervalences that humans achieve their final form. This transsubstantiation has repercussions outside an intellected analogy. It extends beyond intimate coexistence in that it is not only substantive exchange, but exchange of substance, and thus cannot be understood in terms of pure ontological segregation. In some sense, the animate leakage within the strictest hierarchy is what paradoxically enables that hierarchy to become what it is imagined to be; biopolitical governance, conspiring with the "rehoming" assertions of those who traffic wrongly, steps in over and again to contain these leaky bounds.

The terms "animal spaces" and "animal places" are used by Chris Philo and Chris Wilbert in an articulation of critical animal geographies: animal spaces signify the kinds of domains in which nonhuman animals appear and inside which they come into particular being (such as experimental animal labs); animal places signify the "proper location" of animals in a human typology.[6] Myra Hird writes that "nonhuman animals have for some time been overburdened with the task of making sense of human social relations."[7] In my view, race cannot be forgotten as an endlessly variable human social relation for which animals are, also variably, tasked to do constant symbolic work. Given that humans, as indefatigable denizens of the symbolic, inherit such responsibilities and project them onto nonhuman animals, the trick seems to be to objectify this symbolic responsibility given to nonhuman animals, as well as our dependence upon their symbolic labor, and to contextualize it such that our ideas about animality are not automatically reliant affectively or structurally upon this dependence.

In the pages that follow, I begin with biopolitical concerns regarding the regulation of animal sexuality, and the interruptions to animal places wrought by the kinds of animal spaces discussed later. I then turn to the realm of cultural production, bringing into suggestive conversation several late-twentieth-century instances drawn from the realms of film, popular culture, contemporary art, and experimental video, each of which ostensibly juxtaposes nonhuman animals to humans in ways that crucially implicate sex and gender as well as kind. Two of these instances engage—or provoke considerations of—Asian cultural formations, one more transparently or legibly than the other: the film *Max, mon amour* by the Japanese director Nagisa Oshima, involving a human love affair with a chimpanzee, released in 1986; the other, a live installation by the Chinese artist Xu Bing, "Cultural Animal," involving a live pig and a humanoid mannequin, released in 1994. Each instance that I examine—the rhetoric of animal neutering, a film about a love between a chimp and a woman, Michael Jackson's video morphing into a panther, and a performance with a pig that copulates with a human form—plumbs animals' symbolic force within particular imprints of racialization, sexualization, and globalization in an era of geopolitical contestation and coloniality. These cultural productions literalize a human-animal ontological mediation, demonstrating for us its animate currency.

Neutering into Modernity

It has recently become newsworthy in the West that China's "pet ownership"—wherein nonhuman animals live within privatized homes—is on the rise. Pampered, cared for, and loved, Chinese pets are increasingly invoked and experienced as family members. This reemergence of pet ownership (whose closest antecedent is found among early Chinese royalty) has coincided with increased attention by municipalities and communities to the management of populations of nonhuman animal species within cities (rural animal ownership is another matter). Seeking to regulate the uncontrolled spread of these animals, municipalities are increasingly demanding that owners spay or neuter their new kin; and a growing industry of pet-related products are finding an eager market, what has been called the "pet economic sector."[8]

Cindy Patton employs the term *geophagia* to refer to the tendency of nation-states to promulgate and reproduce themselves elsewhere; she diagnoses the U.S. Constitution as itself geophagically imagined, as a template that actively sought to instantiate itself in the context of other nations. Such geophagia can be construed as a temporal parallelization to achieve political synchrony: Patton suggests that Taiwan's repeal in 2002 of a ban on the conscription of gays into the military — a political decision about sex with decidedly national effects — is not only a reach for proper statehood, but an indicator of its reach for inclusion in modernity, alongside (or even ahead of) other powerful nation-states that serve imperially to define or exemplify the very meaning of modernity.[9] One can find markers of geophagia in a *New York Times* article published in 2010, "Once Banned, Dogs Reflect China's Rise," which declares that a pet dog named Xiangzi serves as a "marker of how quickly this nation is hurtling through its transformation from impoverished peasant to first-world citizen."[10]

The transformation Xiangzi indexes is toward China's citizenship and prosperity, two signal markers of "development" discourses. The law professor Chang Jiwen, the Chinese sponsor of a dog-eating ban for submission to the National People's Congress, is quoted as reasoning that the nation's "development" should have consequences for the treatment of animals: "Other developed countries have animal protection laws. . . . With China developing so quickly, and more and more people keeping pets, more people should know how to treat animals properly."[11] While the notion that China is a "developing nation" has become something of a global spectacle, that development may feel slightly more ironic from within China's borders and around its territorial edges; in the midst of "development," the increase in transient feminized labor, migrant work, senior care, and territorial instability is a steady counterpoint to the prospect of a rising middle class.[12]

Michael Wines, the author of the *New York Times* article, suggests that the one-child policy has *created* new needs for dogs in households, either to augment numbers (this seems to subvert the notion that the sizes of families mattered in part because more children meant more contributing economic producers), or to replace children who have grown up and left home. Wines's speculation that one-child families in China experience a kind of social deprivation that they then act to fill with pets only superficially aligns with the "critical pet studies" instigator Heidi Nast's work tracking the rise of "pet-love" feelings and discourses in post-industrial sites, where new configurations of wealth and alienation foster new commodifications and emerging neoliberal affects that shift the status of both animals and human-animal relations.[13] While Wines understands that extant kinship relations texture and condition pet ownership, one wonders whether his speculative association of one-child families in China with loneliness—compared to, say, the cultivation of smaller numbers associated with middle-class families in the United States—has anything to do with implicit assumptions that families in developing countries have an emotional attachment to large broods.

Nast writes that the growth of pet-animal affective bonds emerges from new economic configurations:

> The libidinal economies of pet-animal DAL [dominance-affection-love] have expanded and deepened in certain post-industrial spaces, something I surmise is fueled by a dual process: the hypercommodification of pet-lives and love (especially dogs); and the many alienations attendant to post-industrial lives and places, whether these be related to the dissolution or downsizing of traditional family forms, the increasing footlooseness of individual and community life, or the aging of post-industrial populations. The dual process is in any event tied firmly to neoliberal processes of capital accumulation more generally and the attendant growing gap between rich and poor.[14]

Nast's provocative analysis, coming out of critical geography, might additionally benefit from thinking more about the role of state authority in extant kinship relations and using less a notion of "post-industrial places" tout court, which suggests a teleological progression of capital development toward alienation. She gestures to the economic liberalization of some sites not in the United States, making glancing reference to China, but in my view China's unique biopolitical history challenges us to lend important consideration to things beyond the political-economic strictly understood.

As dog ownership rises in Chinese urban areas, cities have instituted the rule that there can only be one dog per family. New one-dog policies, evidence of a different kind of governmental hand, both suggest that dogs are kin by their obvious patterning on the one-child kinship law (as a kind of biopolitical expansion), and provoke friction at the invocation of kinship on the edges of its propriety. Neutering and spaying thus becomes central to the question of dog domestication in sites such as Beijing, which since 2006 has had a "one dog, one family" policy. "The birth of humans needs to be planned, but anyone can raise a dog?" asked one incredulous blog post in response to reported complaints about the limits on pet numbers. "The resources that you conserve from having less people, you give to dogs? This is a very serious problem. Are you saying that people are worth less than dogs?" wrote one Beijing commenter in a discussion debating the viability of dog ownership.[15]

The questions provoked by this commenter are central to the debates about the animacy hierarchy, in particular its rigors and failures. Where and when nonhuman animals serve as more or less proximate members of human families (or the human family), cultural mappings between nonhuman animals and humans cluster around questions of sex, regulation, substance, and biopolitics. Paradoxically, neutering or spaying animals is a preeminent queering device, since the idealized neutering or spaying halts sexual reproduction, prevents overlittering, and—in the case of pet ownership—redirects desires to the maintenance of pet owner kinship formations within the human household. Observe the following selected arguments from a typical spay and neuter website directed to cat owners:

> Statistically speaking, even if a person finds good homes for a litter of kittens, some of the kittens will grow up and produce litters of kittens.
>
> Even indoor-only house cats often find ways to get outdoors when the sexual urge hits them.
>
> Whether they disappear for good (due to panic, accidents, or enemies) or they return home, kittens are the result.
>
> Unaltered cats have urges that make them irritable and anxious. They yowl or whine frequently, fight with other cats, and/or destroy objects in the house.
>
> Neutering lowers his urge to roam and to fight, and thus lowers chances of disease transmission and woundings.[16]

I bring these points up not to glorify a restorable natural state, but to indicate the ways in which the interaction between animals and humans in the domain of pet ownership discourses is one of biopolitical management, a management of reproduction that has both racialized and sexualized overtones. From another direction, queer, lesbian, and gay folks, with their ostensibly compromised capacity for "biological" reproductive sexuality, might be likened to neutered.

It is not necessary, however, to take recourse to animals to think about neutered queers; in chapter 2, I thought about neutering in relation to suppressed or canceled affect in considering the willful suppression of queerness in anti–Proposition 8 ads authored by neoliberal homonormativities. In addition, as Cathy Cohen has made clear, a queer theoretical analysis must consider the queering by the state of many kinds of bodies as sexually nonnormative, including those located in class and race disprivilege who might otherwise be defined, or self-define, as "heterosexual." "Welfare mothers" are simultaneously constructed as racialized wards of the state, misbehaving, nonproductive creatures who bear their own inordinately large litters and who are destructive to heteronormative family models because they are sexually rampant (and thus stray outside of proper sexual and domestic borders).[17] Indeed, the recent history of the United States has witnessed state-administered sterilization of poor black, Native American, and Puerto Rican women; incarcerated women; and people with cognitive disabilities alike, in the name of eugenically "bettering" the population.[18] Such animacies, I argue, are mapped and ontologically shared among animalized humans and anthropomorphized animals, and are maintained in mutually defining knowledge streams.

This is the stuff of human-animal biopolitics, which is at once linguistic, discursive, state-directed, and sometimes directed toward "health." The literalized figures of such human-animal biopolitics, the "humanimals," vary between the traditionally monstrous blends of human and animal features, posthuman and postmodern cyborg descendants running predictable scripts between organism and machine, and the benign blends of dogs and cats wrapped in human paraphernalia that can be found in rampant numbers on the unapologetically fetishistic website Cute Overload. But it becomes especially interesting to see how the borders between these genres cannot hold up so cleanly.

A recent case makes the "monstrous humanimal" and the terms of its construction ostentatiously clear. Nadya Suleman, the mother of eight children by assisted reproductive technology, otherwise known by the moniker "Octomom," represents a humanimal tentatively racialized as nonwhite (her father is Iraqi) whose contingent dignity turns precisely around her reproductivity. Suleman already had six children before giving birth to octuplets. It is not clear whether the scandalous "Octomom" myth is built around the idea that assisted reproductive technologies were used with the goal of exploiting welfare systems, or whether this "welfare mother's" reproductive act itself was so extravagantly successful that it reached the level of caricature. When Suleman's house was near foreclosure, PETA successfully lobbied her to place its promotional signs in her front yard and offered her a fee of $8,000. The sign said: "Don't let your cat or dog become an 'octomom'—always spay or neuter."

Another marketing competitor, the pornography company Vivid, first unsuccessfully invited her to act in its films (offering her $1 million), and then tried asking her to serve in off-screen work functions for less money. She declined both. Suleman seemed to welcome a technology of media attention that sutured diverse advertising interests to her transmogrified appearance, that is, her own mediated, revised body (with her apparent cosmetic surgery interventions). At the same time, she rejected an alterative technology of vision and mediation whereby her involvement in or proximate to human sexual acts would be explicitly commodified. Both PETA and Vivid were somewhat unimaginative in their marketing decisions: the porn company clearly partook of an unsurprising frenzy of curiosity around her spectacularized body. Suleman-as-Octomom is an overdetermined variation on the racialized, sexually rampant welfare queen who herself nurses improperly on the ghostly public teat, a teat that, inasmuch as it exists, is shrinking and retracting under renewed neoliberal retrenchment in the United States under the sign of fiduciary urgency. Yet she ambivalently occupied the zone between welfare queen and entrepreneur, as she leveraged her own economy of spectacle to make capital decisions.

Transgenitalia

In extending biopolitical thinking to stretch around humans, animals, and human animality, what would it mean to invite a queer *and trans* critique in the instance of animal neutering and castration as they both literally and symbolically appear? The dance between *queer* and *trans* evokes debates that have been taken up in recent scholarship, particularly about what degree one might excavate the *trans* in what has been taken and subsumed under the rubric of *queer*.[19] Ultimately, the opposition of trans and queer suggests a false dichotomy: just as gender and sex are unavoidably linked, so too are trans and queer. They can be considered as independent factors that participate in animal spaces. I use Nikki Sullivan's provocative invocation of "transmogrification" to bring transsexuality into an expansive analytic.[20] Sullivan wishes to undo the segregated assignment of various phenomena involving bodily transformation to specific types of critics and thinkers: for instance, transsexuality to queer theorists, nonnormative body modification practices to countercultural theorists and criminologists, and cosmetic surgery to feminists. The apparent "voluntarism" or "false-consciousness" of one versus another of these practices she deems insufficient justification for their categorical segregation. Haunting these categories is still another, often construed as tendentious when applied to humans, but in my view having profound cultural relevance once we consider the significance of castration or the "cutting" of some kinds of transsexuality: "neutering" and "spaying," which is often considered by municipal policy makers and animal advocates.

Myra Hird invokes the feminist biologist Sharon Kinsman to argue for the idea that human understandings of sex respond not merely to humanity's own intraspecies evidences, but also to those of non-human animals as well, such as fish whose gonads shift from male to female.[21] Concomitantly, Hird importantly does not think of "trans" as an exclusively human construct, and challenges readers to consider the implications of evidence of transness in nonhuman animals. Such analysis perhaps suggests a sense of trans that extends beyond sex alone; as Hird writes, "I want to extend feminist interest in trans as a specifically sexed enterprise (as in transitioning from one sex to another), but also in a broader sense of movement across, through and perhaps beyond traditional classifications."[22]

Hence, *trans-* is not a linear space of mediation between two mono-lithic, autonomous poles, as, for example, "female" and "male" are, not least because the norms by which these poles are often defined too easily conceal, or forget, their interests and contingencies. Rather, it is conceived of as more emergent than determinate, intervening with other categories in a richly elaborated space. Much in the way that the idealized meaning of *queer* signifies an adjectival modification or modulation, rather than a substantive core such as a noun, I wish to highlight a *prefixal trans-* not preliminarily limited to gender. As Susan Stryker, Paisley Currah, and Lisa Jean Moore write, the hyphen "marks the difference between the implied nominalism of 'trans' and the explicit relationality of 'trans-,' which remains open-ended and resists premature foreclosure by attachment to any single suffix [including gender]."[23] Such a prefixal *trans-* is a way to explore that complexity of gender definition that lies between human gender systems and the gendering of animals. By mobilizing a different form of *trans-*, I do not mean to evacuate trans of its gendered possibilities. To the contrary, I reassert the complex, multifactored cultural contingency of transgendered actualizations and affirm that gender is omnipresent, though it is rarely monolithically masculine or feminine.

Of the body parts that might be labeled "organs," the genitals bear tremendous symbolic weight, particularly in the West and Global North; this may be an obvious point, given the significance of Freudian psychoanalysis (which attaches formative significance to the visible difference of sex parts) to Western social tropes. In such schemes, sexual organs simultaneously impute both gender and sexuality and, as so many race and sexuality theorists have demonstrated, race and class. To take but one example, Leo Bersani writes about narratives of sexual development that "heterosexual genitality is the hierarchical stabilization of sexuality's component instincts."[24] Therefore, the "genitals" are directly tied to social orders that are vastly more complex than systems of gender alone. Genitality is both directly and indirectly represented in multiple ways, vanishing here, reappearing there, sometimes prosthetized through other accoutrements (such as so-called penis cars). Genitalia are culturally overdetermined, and, as the seats of reproduction and fecundity, they are sites of biopolitical interest not only for humans but for nonhuman animals.

Animal Spaces: *Max, mon amour*

Shifting into the realm of cultural analysis, I wish to consider the bilingual French and English film *Max, mon amour*, directed by Nagisa Oshima and released in 1986, a film generally treated within cinema studies as a surrealist comedy of manners. When the film begins, Margaret (played by Charlotte Rampling), the wife of a British diplomat named Peter (Anthony Higgins), recounts to her husband that she has fallen in love with a chimpanzee named Max, purchased him, and

11. Max and Margaret on an intriguingly torn mattress. Film still from *Max, mon amour* (dir. Nagisa Oshima, 1986).

taken the animal home. The film is almost wholly set in the bourgeois household, with the exception of a forest where Max is searched for and an asylum where Peter goes to find Margaret. There is a general prevalence of ornament and artifice to match the civil conduct of the human characters (hairy, indecorous Max serves as the blatant exception). The narrative proceeds with the ambivalent games of Peter's coping with Max's entrance into the family, his moving into the family home, and his resistance to Peter's erratic mistreatment. Over the protestations of her husband, Margaret insists upon keeping her relationship with Max. A climactic scene ensues in which a rifle changes hands from Peter to Max and shots are fired, but ultimately the family (including Max) is happily reconstituted. Max and Margaret are depicted in a number of intimate embraces, including spooning tenderly on an unmade bed, its ripped mattress an indication of their love's rupture of the social fabric (figure 11). In this scene, Margaret's silken clothes, impeccably made-up face, and smooth-shaven, properly feminized legs contrast with the simian unruliness of the animal. Max and Margaret lie, gently spotlit, in the middle of the frame; their shadows are cast on the wall behind them within the semi-circular halo that illuminates them. Following some of the recognizable visual motifs of conventional film depictions of star-crossed lovers, Max and Margaret express a purity of devotion that shines in contrast to the squalor around them.

In the structural climax of the film, Peter and Max, the competitive suitors vying for Margaret's attentions, seem to be in literal battle over and around a gun. It is useful to turn here to a consideration of cinematic fetishism, in which onscreen objects displace and entrain desire for both diegetic characters and viewers. For Freud, the fetish object—installed as a displacement of desire for woman, whose castration (in the mother) was an originary unviewable horror—both "remains a token of triumph over the threat of castration and a safeguard against it."[25] Linda Williams's groundbreaking book *Hard Core* examines the role of the fetish in contemporary pornography genres. In a chapter called "Prehistory: The Frenzy of the Visible," she attends to the establishment of the ensemble of social, psychic, and technological apparati in the prehistory of cinema, in which Eadweard Muybridge's "animal studies" of horses and other animals in motion, and later of men and women, take critical part.[26] Within Muybridge's images of women, Williams argues, one can detect a fairly resolute fetishization of women by the surfeit of seemingly necessary companion objects and by the lack of self-driven action, whereas the men in images have been inherently active and unadorned and seem to inscribe the proper gestural domain of possible action. From this perspective, the peculiar technological artifice within which precinematic animals were produced by Muybridge's locomotion studies—unadorned, mobile, and focal, yet firmly woven into the scientific discourses of visuality—gives them an uncertain position in relation to the fetish. In the climax of Oshima's film, Max has seized a rifle from Peter, who meant to use it either to keep order or to kill him; when Max runs from spot to spot in the house, firing randomly, it is not clear whether he intends to use the gun, or how, or against whom. If the moving, onscreen animal haunts modern cinema, if the gun is irretrievably phallic, and if the ape is an uncertain fetish, then what is the substitutional value of a penisless ape shooting a gun, and for whom?

In this comedy of manners, the rifle potentially competes with Max as the cinematic object representing perhaps the most blatant violation of proper and "civilized" action. Yet colonialism has enjoyed just this coincidence of the two objects, Max and the rifle: to preserve a peaceful, civil interior, barbarity and wildness on its outer edges must be extinguished and the barbarians brought under (militarized) control. Max is, and is not, an "animal" in the nonhuman sense, just as a colonized subject is, and is not, a "human" in theories about colonialism. Max's fully characterized animalness and animality neatly, though perversely, fall within the lines of Homi Bhabha's notion of colonial mimicry, in which colonial discourse produces an other that is "almost the same, but not quite"; the only thing that is perverse, here, is what the visuality of the film offers us: the prioritization of humanized *animal* figuration (and Max's animal role) over animalized humanness. Within the logic of Oshima's filmic representation, Max thus symbolizes both Peter's lack of sexual control over his wife and his fecklessness as a diplomat in waning colonial times, wherein the insecurity of the colonialist is revealed by his anxiety over control. When, at film's end, the gun is put away and Max is folded into the happy family at the dinner table, the resolution is precisely a colonial one: the sexuality that Peter promises, but that only Max can fulfill, is resolved as Max is absorbed into the family, but precisely as a castrated animal without the possibility of progeny and which might as well be the family pet (Bhabha's "not quite").

During the climactic scene, in the realm of filmic satisfaction, we might say that a penisless yet phallic Max supplants the penis of Williams's famous "money shot" (which she uses to describe the suturing of filmic narrative as climax, fetish object, and phallicity).[27] Instead of the "money shot," however, in Oshima's film we get a "monkey shot": an ape shoots a gun seemingly at random, and what should feel climactic (indeed, the moment is structurally climactic) feels like a misfire, a failure, a bad shot. This is similar to some critics' overall assessment of Oshima's film, which was that *Max, mon amour* was just not very good; it was something of a commercial flop outside of Japan and has been called an "anomaly" and a "misfire."[28] According to Maureen Turim, who asserts that the film represented Oshima's attempt to appeal to Western tastes, "*Max, mon amour* would not prove to be successful enough with critics or at the box office to elicit much demand for Oshima as a virtual expatriate."[29] But at the level of the film, Oshima's commercial goals need not be identified with his creative ones. In particular, one might alternatively read his interspecies project as an *achievement* of failure, an indicative misfire, a signal of the emasculated collapse of the colonial upper classes who can only end up living not dangerously, but ridiculously. It is difficult to miss, after all, the underside of the "comedy of manners" that Oshima willingly produced using Max. As Bhabha writes, "The effect of mimicry on the authority of colonial discourse is profound and disturbing. For in 'normalizing' the colonial state or subject, the dream of post-Enlightenment civility alienates its own language of liberty and produces another knowledge of its norms."[30]

In a critically positive psychoanalytic reading of *Max, mon amour*, Barbara Creed frames the film as one example of the new "zoo-centric" cinema that reflects its interest in resolving questions that remain today of a Darwin-influenced blurring of the boundary between human and nonhuman animal. Creed notes that Margaret's desire for Max foregrounds an even-more mysterious female jouissance that lies threateningly outside of the male symbolic order (and thus beyond the husband diplomat's ken).[31] But we might say too, thinking more closely about the consequential nature of Margaret's lover, that Max's sexing and gendering is itself unstable. First, the role of language in Max's animation, I suggest, is minor. While Max's *linguistic* gender is male throughout, the embodied creature is not terribly convincing as a chimpanzee. The nonintegrity of the creature is made evident by the fact that the eyes shift around inside the sockets of the chimpanzee hood as Max moves, recalling the role of the imperfect ape costume in the directorial efforts in *Planet of the Apes* (directed by Franklin Schaffner, released 1968) in effecting no more than a hybrid human-apeness. (Interestingly, the English word *creature* is derived from Middle English; its earliest evidenced referents include objects of creation, both human and animal.)

To a camp-loving (and perhaps forgiving) queer skeptic, the middling chimp costume's lack of any visible genitalia begs further questions, poor 1980s special effects notwithstanding. To my knowledge, the visual culture of animal genitalia has not been significantly addressed outside of the domain of scientific illustration. The appearance of animal genitalia in visual cultures surely serves, in any case, as a reflection of invested human interest in animals. In *Making Sex: Body and Gender from the Greeks to Freud*, Thomas Laqueur's historical account of gender/sex ideology reminds us of the historical recency of the conception that male and female sexes are somehow opposing. Pausing to reflect on the visual representation of the sex organs of nonhuman animals, Laqueur comments that our species cares little that, say, the genitals of a female elephant are rendered to look like a penis in an 1881 scientific illustration, "because the sex of elephants generally matters little to us."[32] Yet animals considered to have analogous properties to humans (such as the great apes, or those which have been the subject of agricultural research), presumably bear more weight of interest in their sexual particularity.

While in *Max, mon amour* such an absence of obvious genital features, all else being equal, might possibly (but not necessarily, given the visibility of certain female displays!) provoke a tentative reading of the figure as female, it is also true that the default movie sex for costumed monkeys and apes can remain unspecified, genderless, in a literalization of the generic unsexed animal type. (This is true, of course, of the vast majority of representations of fictional humans, animals, and monsters alike, from Ken dolls to Donald Duck to cartoon abominable snowmen, in which the male genitalia are rendered as curved bumps. Female counterpoints like Barbie also lack genitalia but have fully developed, even exaggerated, secondary sex characteristics.) In addition, individual animal specificities such as sex cannot survive in a costume unless it is intended as "anatomically accurate," bucking costume traditions of neutering. In the somewhat ostentatious case of Max, such undeterminability of visual sex is an indication of the ambivalence with which cultural spaces confront animals as sexed creatures.

Conveniently perhaps for the design of the film *Max, mon amour*, no linguistic contradictions need be enacted: the French grammatical gender for chimpanzee (*le chimpanzee, lui, il*) is the same as the purported gender and sex of the chimpanzee Max, who is supposed to be a masculine, male chimp. Yet for all the profusion of linguistic gender, in *Max, mon amour*, the incursion of species difference also introduces the presumably threatening possibility of a *genderless* relation, produced by the genericity of the type but literalized in the costume itself. Margaret and the chimp's affections thus yield something that is *trans* in the sense of the undecidability, elusiveness, or reluctance toward the fixity of the chimp's sex, which in spite of its linguistic reinforcements surpasses its otherwise presumptive maleness; that is, to what extent can one trust that a male chimp is sexed *or* gendered "like" a human male?

What cannot be ignored in *Max, mon amour* is the virtual stampede of Africanized racial invocations; these are overdetermined by the diplomatic status of Margaret's British husband and the Parisian locus of the film as both a colonial metropolis and an ambivalent host to racialized colonial subjects. Such racialized staging is further evident from moment to moment in the chimp's expressive limitations; marked "impoliteness" and unfamiliarity with "civilized" surroundings; and surfeit of embodiment, aggression, and emotional lability in the face of white upper-class cultural sophistication, formal "goodwill," and expressive minimalism. All of these factors are conditioned by seasoned colonial narrative and visual tropes.[33]

The unstable national provenance of the film arguably enriches the film's racial possibility: On the one hand, it can be identified as part of Oshima's trajectory outward from Japanese cinema (which he often stated he despised) and toward, in part, Western cinema, including European avant-garde and animal tropes. On the other hand, against popular external understandings of the Japanese as racially "homogeneous," Japan's own history with race—including its interest in black history in the United States—extends far earlier than *Max, mon amour*.[34] The recognizable fakeness of the costume's face invites comparisons to blackface minstrelsy (which remained popular in Europe long after it faded in performance cultures in the United States), in which there lingers the possibility that a mask conceals a differently racialized human. This lingering possibility undermines the film's pointedly surrealist overtones with a historical legacy of European evolutionary racism tied to colonialism. While blackface practices have a relatively recent history within Japanese hip-hop subcultures and aesthetics, we can also consider the possibilities of citation and intertextuality with regard to animal tropes, racialization, and faciality within European, U.S., and Japanese film histories.[35]

Akira Lippit writes that "the complex matrix that adheres to the name 'Oshima' . . . is in fact . . . an intertextual corpus that both does and does not belong to Oshima himself."[36] *Max, mon amour* is an unreliable barometer of Oshima's own unfixed authorship within a fluid transnational frame, one in which the complexities of Japanese race relations with regard to blackness are both suggested and deferred. Within film studies, where the film is often treated as a mere footnote in Oshima's canon, there remains confusion over precisely what the film's stylistic exceptionality indicates and a concomitant level of doubt about the degree of this movie's "Japaneseness" (not only because of its all-Western cast and its French setting).[37]

Cultural Animal

The intertextuality characteristic of Oshima's *Max, mon amour* continues at a more obvious level in the Chinese conceptual artist Xu Bing's installation and performance work "Cultural Animal" (first shown in 1994), in which a live male pig, with "nonsense" words made up of letters from the Roman alphabet painted all over its body, was introduced to a static male mannequin posed on all fours with "nonsense" Chinese characters inscribed on its body (figures 12.1–12.4). In front of a curious audience at the Han Mo Art Center in Beijing, the pig eventually mounted the mannequin, in a sexually aggressive way, according to descriptions of the pig's approach. In personal accounts of this piece, Xu Bing explained that he had applied the scent of a female pig onto the mannequin, presumably to encourage this sexualized behavior.[38]

Highly regarded in the globalized art world and the recipient of a MacArthur grant in 1999, the artist, who moved to the United States from China in 1990, is consistently interested in questions of translation, language, and communication beyond or outside human understanding, as this work demonstrates.[39] He is best known for his invented script of nonsensical calligraphy, or "false characters," that frustrates any process of reading (for the viewers who know Chinese) or translation (for the viewer not literate in Chinese). In "Cultural Animal," he literally em-bodies his false characters by placing them onto the surface of both an animal (the pig) and an animalized man (that is, a mannequin whose pose—open to be penetrated from behind—also potentially queers him). What are we to make of this spectacle of animal genitality and its connection to transnationalism and sexuality?

"Cultural Animal" was developed from a previous performance by Xu Bing called "A Case Study of Transference" (which, despite its title, he disavowed as a psychoanalytic project). This work involved two pigs, one a male boar who had been inscribed with nonsense Roman script, and one a female sow who had invented Chinese-looking characters printed on. This earlier iteration, which was also presented in front of a live audience at the Han Mo Arts Center in 1994, had a more explicitly reproductive subtext, one that conjured notions of East-West racial mixing or miscegenation: the stated intention of the piece was that the pigs should mate. As the video documentation of

12.1–4. One live pig, one paper-mache mannequin, ink, discarded books, cage, forty-square-meter enclosure. Xu Bing, "Cultural Animal," 1993–94.

the event shows, it was strangely difficult to get the pigs interested in each other.[40] Nevertheless, in this performance, the two illegible character systems, along with the two porcine bodies, moved alongside and against each other, and thereby interanimated.

With the substitution of a static human body for a pig in "Cultural Animal," Xu Bing thus solved a major logistical problem: he only had to get one pig to do his bidding rather than two. He also introduced an interspecies aspect to the piece, though he inverted industrialized society's normative animate control relations of (human) subject over (animal) object by rendering the human static and passive and the pig active and alive. Stills from the video documentation of the performance show the pig mounting the human figure from behind, as well as nuzzling the mannequin on the face and pressing its neck against the sculpture's front arm. The possibility of a sexual act involving a human with a nonhuman animal raises the human-perspective specter of bestiality. In this transspecies encounter, still other possibilities are raised because of the animal's uncertain gendering and because its

145

sexual status, while undetermined, bears a peculiar intensity: pornography, queerness, and cultural and race mixing. In the work's video and photodocumentation, the animal's penetrative capacities are central, while the mannequin's own genitals are not rendered easily visible.

What significance should be applied to the apparent reversal of active human and passive animal? In this representation and performance, "the animal" cannot be so easily filled in by the "dead," "fake" figure, despite that figure's quadripedal stance: it is templatically "human." If the traditions of human-animal encounter in representation and performance privilege or enhance the liveness or subjectivity of the human against the counterexample of the animal, then "Cultural Animal" scrambles given codes of reading and reception. In this work, the pig's Roman-alphabet nonsense characters brushed up against and eventually mounted the prone body of the mannequin, itself inscribed with false Chinese characters, thereby setting up a potential power dynamic of submissive and receptive Asianness as defined against beastly Western dominance. The entire scene, which was staged on a floor littered with open books, could be read as one of linguistic and sexual aggression of the "West" toward the "East," but let us not forget that the pig also had its tender approaches. What is more, both the sign systems used here were unstable, illegible, and hence conjured only a phantasmatic version of both "East" and "West" as read against and through each other.

"Reading" is an equal participant in the spectatorship of this performance. Xu Bing's nonsense words are commonly interpreted as scrambling received semiotic relations between East and West. While such a lexically dependent strategy might in itself seem a rather obvious rendering of the impossibility of cultural translation, when juxtaposed with the actors of the performance and their emergent actions, this scrambling simultaneously generates a possible critique of the ready recourse of human-animal renderings into symbolic certainties (or the ready assignation of passive mannequin to the "East" and penetrating pig to the "West"). What the pointed and productive restaging of otherwise common priorities makes possible here is a Deleuzian "becoming-animal": without the fixity of animal-human difference in place, the audience is provoked into the multiplicity of possible encounters of self and other, perhaps even of the dissolution of borders between animal and human and self and other.

Does the imprinting of nonsensical text and the intervention of animality really complicate the dyad of East and West in "Cultural Animal," where each faces the other? Xu Bing's work seems to partake of some critique of transnational exchange, particularly of Western hegemonic modes of representation. At the same time, he has espoused somewhat controversially conservative viewpoints that seem to attenuate a fully deconstructive and dialectical reading of "East" versus "West," a reading favored by Xiaoping Lin's positive review;[41] he has shown no interest in launching a more-pointed critique of either U.S. or Chinese politics. As he said in an interview in 2008, "The old concept about art and government being at odds has changed. Now artists and the government are basically the same. All the artists and the government are running with development."[42] In other words, both art and government for Xu Bing are aligned with the space of commerce and the market—or "development," to circle back to the rhetoric of pet neutering—which potentially smoothes over political frictions. At the same time, "Cultural Animal" raises questions about the connection between various forms of trans- encounters, including transnational, transgender, and transspecies.

Ultimately, the introduction of species difference in Xu Bing's work yields a yawning gap around the unresolved question of gender and sexuality, precisely around questions of the generic and gender. If Oshima's Max, for instance, is a blend between actual (if materialized through costume only) and figural chimpanzee, should there not be another layer of gender confusion between human/animal and actual/figure? Carla Freccero suggests there is; she takes up Derrida's engagement with his cat in his essay "L'animal que donc je suis." Freccero notes a degree of creative play between the biological sex and grammatical gender of Derrida's female cat (a noun that is grammatically gendered masculine), as well as shifts in Derrida's vulnerability and gendered relating to her.[43] In a critical scene during which his cat observes him naked, Derrida's anxious concerns about gender, masculinity, and sexuality emerge. Freccero notes that Derrida meanders in address between the masculine, generic *le chat* and the feminine, specific *la chatte*. Derrida thus genders the cat in multiple, potentially contradictory ways and invites the presumption that the cat's and his own gender are forcedly affected by the relationality between them.

I return here to the last chapter's invocation of Austin's "marriage with a monkey." To this I add the notion that the genericity of "a monkey" has certain consequences: a creature without a gender threatens the smooth running of heteronormative society that relies on a robust organization of gender; and its sexed uncertainty threatens to bring a queer sexuality into the institution of marriage. I suggest that though Austin insisted in some sense that the performative verbs themselves (like *wed* in "I thee wed") were fixed in purpose and meaning and thus robust, his attribution of "mockery" to an animality linked to discourses of colonial and species threat reveals, perhaps, a fear that the institution of marriage (or conventions of language, or rigidities of gender and sex, or divisions of race and nation) might be maligned and indeed transformed by a performative's misuse. The insecurity I attribute to Austin here is equivalent to a recognition of the importance of iterative renewal for the performative itself to retain its normativity.[44]

Thus, while considering Max's "bad" costume may seem an indulgence or just a "nonserious" joke, Austin's monkey example suggests that any decision about including or excluding genitals on a figured nonhuman animal cannot help but be loaded: species difference itself is fraught with anxieties about race and reproduction. Thus, transanimality can refer to gender and species with sexuality, geopolitics, and race in full scope. Otherwise put, an analysis of transanimality is enriched by identifying the quiet imputations of race that are so often shuttled along with the animal.

Transmogrification

While much has been written of histories in which nonwhite racialized men are often, due to racism, subject to symbolic castration and representation as nonhuman animals, less has been suggested of the possibility that the castrated animal is not only a substitute for but coextensive and forming meanings equally with castrated racialized men.[45] Frantz Fanon's *Black Skin, White Masks*, in analyzing the postcolonial psychic state of a racialized subject, theorizes relations among animality, castration, and black (sexual) threat, and in so doing offers a condensed image of the social possibility of simultaneous *castration* and phallic *presence*, even hypermasculinity.[46] Given the sacrosanct importance of the penis or phallus, we might extend the concurrence of castration and phallic presence to the possibility that nongenitality could *impute* genitality or the threat of genitality's eventual presence. But if the absence or presence can sometimes be intensified as a threat that *consolidates* maleness, the pairing can also be attenuated in such a way that transsexuality emerges as curiously legible.

Writing about Michael Jackson—more the phenomenon than the person—Cynthia Fuchs analyzes the ways that race, gender identity, and sexuality all intervene to produce a sporadically present phallus in Jackson. Fuchs comments, "the problem of his penis remains . . . continually cited by his own choreographed crotch-grabbing. A sign of autoerotic sexuality (read: perverse, unreproductive, and homosexual), his unseen penis resists visibility, that prevailing emblem of Western cultural Truth."[47] In describing Jackson, Fuchs deliberately and perhaps provocatively uses the term *transsexual*. She does so not as a thesis about his lived experience, but rather as a diagnosis for the emergent sexed interstitiality of Jackson, an interstitiality that evokes phallic presence as often as it absences it, and that is surrounded by other kinds of body modification and illusion, including appearances by Jackson that uncannily approximate the stylings of Diana Ross.

Similarly suspending judgment about Jackson's transsexuality, I would like to leaven Fuchs's account with a consideration of the animal-animality that sat next to Jackson for most of his life and ask what place this animal-animality might have in his (sexualized) realization. While it might be a simple matter to attribute his affection and concern for certain specific nonhuman animals to an innocent, "childlike nature," as allies did in the hope that it would be effective both as a defensive explanation amid the discursive intensity that surrounded allegations of pedophilia both in and outside the juridical sphere, it is productive to consider his animal interests on their own terms.

Among the most recognized of Jackson's animal signs was the morphing black panther in his video "Black or White," released in 1991 (his frequently photographed companion chimp, Bubbles, was another). In the video, a black panther walks out of a room, then transmogrifies into Jackson, who in the original version of the video goes on to dance with no musical accompaniment and to enact physical violence on inanimate objects, breaking windows, smashing a car windshield, setting a building on fire. Was the animal form of the black panther a reference to the Black Panther Party? The Black Panthers and the larger Black Power movements of the 1960s and 1970s have continued to echo within national "multicultural" and "postracial" presents in the United States as the most iconic images of black nationalism and militancy, and so are a potent end to a video whose lyrics "it don't matter if you're black or white" optimistically declare that race does not "matter." In an archived interview with MTV filmed in 1999, part of a special event celebrating its "100 Greatest Videos," Jackson explained:

> I wanted to do a dance number [and] I told my sister Janet, I said, "You remind me of a black panther." I said, "Why don't you do something where you transform into a black panther and you transform into yourself again?" She said, "I like it," but she didn't go with it. . . . The two of us, we always think alike. So I did it. And in the dance, I said, "I want to do a dance number where I can let out my frustration about injustice and prejudice and racism and bigotry," and within the dance I became upset and let go. I think at the time people were concerned with the violent content of the piece, but it's, like, easy to look at. It's simple.[48]

Jackson seems to explain away as serendipitous (rather than premeditated) the nature of his arrival upon the black panther; and indeed, his choice of the animal may well have been so. But in performing *as* a black panther, Jackson admits that he "let go" and acted out his feelings of racism and injustice. "Letting go" means relaxing into a tendency, a placement, an embodiment, and detaching from some alienable thing. "Being" a black panther (or a Black Panther) permitted (a moment of) the impermissible, both for Jackson as a political figure impassioned by justice and for Jackson as a man whose masculinity was undeniably queer. But Jackson's "letting go" itself conflates two becomings. The first is a human delivery of frustrated, reactive violence. The second is a turning into an animal that itself symbolizes or sublimates that frustration. Thus the panther—in its chromatic blackness and hence humanoid racialization, its species competence for smart pursuit and capture, and its capacity for violence upon other animals—embodied, stood in for, rather than took on, Jackson's violent affective stances.[49] This is a signal moment, I suggest, of transmogrification as transsubstantiation—for the critical shift is not merely of form, but of affect itself.

Trans-Connections

Returning to Fuchs's assessment of the meandering symbolics of Michael Jackson and his missing phallus, we can widen the argument to include both the invocation of animality and animals via a shared

affectivity and Jackson's gender-defying "transsexuality." Transsubstantiation succeeds, in my view, unless it is modeled on voluntaristic
transfungibilities that are *already* considered proper to certain other,
racialized nonwhite bodies. In the case of Xu Bing's work, sexuality
as a form of racialized, and nationalized, communication by humans
and animals alike is revealed as a fiction, and there remains an obdu-
rate impasse between these transspecial crossings. And indeed, fungibility is not always fantastical or whimsical, but can take on punitive
and disciplinary effects; fungibility is precisely what frames Saidiya
Hartman's critique of the racialization of black bodies in the antebel-
lum and postbellum South.[50]

In the case of Max, the fictive chimpanzee in an animal suit in a
fictional film, his transspecies identity is incontestable. Narratively,
Max is a chimpanzee with unruly passions who is deeply attached to
Margaret; visually, "Max" is a chimpanzee costume with no known
sex and a somewhat disembodied voice, barely concealing the actor
inside, who is of unknown sex, gender, and age. The standards of
opacity applied to this actor are much lower than those applied to
Rampling in character as Margaret. The consequences of reading the
not-so-chimp chimp are manifold. Another layer is opened up; the
chimp figure, which is already itself a complex blend of species, race,
gender, and sexuality, animates a body without organs, releasing our
determinative hold on the events in the film as the sincere construction of truth, and allowing surrealist ironies to unfold. What is transanimality here is not that we sometimes see the chimp as alternatively
chimp and unskilled human actor, so much as the fact that the presence of this "flimsy chimp" can serve as a key that enables us to move
outside and away from the overdetermined racialized and other spaces
Max occupies, and to critically read the confluences by which he has
been constructed.

In two successive coauthored works, *Anti-Oedipus: Capitalism and
Schizophrenia* and *A Thousand Plateaus*, Gilles Deleuze and Félix Guattari describe what they call a "body without organs."[51] The body without organs is that body that actively refuses its own subjectivity by
engaging the dis-ordering of its "organs." In the body without organs,
no given organ has merely one functionality, and the organism itself
cannot be represented as an ordered system. Instead, the body without organs makes impossible *any* coercive systematicity by affirming
an infinite functionality and interrelation of the "parts" within, "parts"

that can only be individuated by one of an infinite number of permutations of a body into "parts."[52]

Deleuze and Guattari's body without organs essentially describes a *condition* of animate transsubstantiation. We can return to Austin's restrictive colorable "capacity" as a condition of the successful performative: materialization for Austin succeeds only when a function is not only present but presumed operative. Austin's early view of the performative, while illuminating for a skeletal understanding of the most discernible instances of materialization, is haunted and ultimately undone by its own animate monkey, which *has* a color, and which has, dare we say, infinite capacities to pair, to marry, to cosubstantiate.

Quite unlike Deleuze's "body without organs," the "animal without genitals" would seem to be a body-with-organs-without-genitals, that is, a body with organs from which the genitals have been extracted or pointedly neglected. Nevertheless, the "animal without genitals" has an affective valence that warrants closer attention. Just as biological research on organism systematicity is headed toward a recognition of more multiplicity, the animal-without-genitals marks or symbolizes a kind of affective impulse toward a human hope. At the same time, there is a repulsion away from a boundaryless being, for it reiterates the porosity of the very human-animal border. Thus, the animal-without-genitals *affirms* the body without organs, while carrying dramatically variant affective registers. The ghostly logic of the racialized castrated human male–present phallus explored by Fanon and Fuchs is perhaps why, alternatively, the racialized figurative animal that is deployed for purposes of human signification is a body *with* organs *without* genitals, since the (reproductive) body with organs *needs* genitals. Furthermore, affectivities, while they may help leverage narratives to a satisfying conclusion, also yield a result that is ambivalent about the abjection of animality in the face of the weakly solidified human, because the analogies are so vibrant and indeed vital.

To move even further to a generative account of transanimality, what of the transsubstantiation that *other* animals make possible? Can we look to the kinds of interspecies redefinitions of biology wrought in contemporary "dolly mixtures," to cite Sarah Franklin?[53] What sharedness of transsexuality is possible, and what transitions? The trans critic Eva Hayward's article "More Lessons from a Starfish: Prefixial Flesh and Transspeciated Selves" takes an innovative approach to its own textual materialities in considering the potentials of starfish flesh (as evoked by a song by Antony and the Johnsons, "Cripple and the Starfish," released in 2000) to interrupt normative narratives of castration, amputation, and regrowth. Thinking of "cut" and its rhetorical and onomatopoetic effects and the ontologizing prefixes of *re-* and *trans-*, Hayward's essay is written as a "critical enmeshment," less a personal account than an "entangling within the stitches of ongoing processes."[54] Hayward looks to starfish as a kind of species partner in the sense of sharing a "sensate ontology." In this conception, limbs, as not merely absented or "lost" parts but rather as partners in a trans-speciation, become otherwise. It seems to me that both Hayward and the song itself might suggest that rather than a penis being fetishized as the primary appendage, its significance dissolves in its removal into that of just one limb among many. In this account, the voluntary removal of sex organs leads to a *possible* kind of rejuvenation in a sense of completed or completing selfhood: in Hayward's very moving words, it is an articulate refusal of the forbidding materiality implicated in the discourse of the "absenting" of "native parts" that is often leveled against transsexuals: "transsexing is an act of healing."[55]

Still, Hayward's essay might benefit from a more engaged consideration of disability politics, particularly given the use of the word *cripple* in the Antony and the Johnsons song. Claiming transsexing as healing would be more effective were it more closely tied to disability theory, especially given the pathologization against the shared motivations for the negativity leveled against the believed "monstrosity" of both amputees and transwomen. Like Robert McRuer, Hayward successfully invokes disability theory's complication of the negativity of dis- as loss, absence, and failure.[56] Given this relationship, to celebrate the agential transformation of trans cutting comes into tension with disability study's accounts of amputation, most of which are understood to be nonvoluntary; hence, Hayward could more fully consider the affective provocations of the song's deployment of the word *cripple*. This juxtaposition gets right to the heart of current debates around transness, because transsexuals, much like gays and lesbians, often are compelled to own a story that tells that they were "born" this way, in a body that needs to be "fixed" to reach true selfhood (such stories may be required, for instance, to be eligible for sexual reassignment surgery). But if we take seriously Franklin's assessment that there are ways in which biology is *made, not born*, then we should be cautious

about naively romanticizing what Hayward calls the "generative en-
actment of . . . healing." Perhaps instead, the language of transsubstantiation might provide an alternative way to understand how bodies of
all sorts undergo regimes of regulation, and also how they resist those
regimes.

I end this chapter by invoking a short film, "Range," screened at the
San Francisco International LGBT Film Festival in 2006 as part of a
curated selection of short films titled "Transfrancisco," which juxtaposed rural masculinities (and potentially even transmasculinity) to
the castration of animals. Made by the transgender filmmaker Bill
Basquin, "Range" poetically pairs visual representations of white rural
masculinities in agricultural countryside.[57] The film is composed of
muted colors and sweeping landscapes in which human bodies are un-
exceptional and seemingly minor participants. An extensive voiceover
about stewardship refers to the speaker's interest in "leaving the land
better than when you first came to it," leaving open the question of
the status of livestock on that land.

The film is marked by an extended scene showing the repetitive
"cuttings" of young lambs at the end of a conveyor belt: the ewes are
getting "tail docked," and the male sheep are being castrated. Basquin has written that his films present a kind of ambivalence or resistance to queer readings; he understands his works as being "from
a queer point of view without being explicitly queer in subject matter."[58] At the same time, the castration he depicts in "Range" potentially ironizes a "portrait of quiet reckoning about family relationships
and farming" as well as the trans filmmaker's relation to reproduction
and to masculinities.[59] "Range" stages its scene of "neutering" in rural
North America and is an invocation of thwarted environmental responsibility and care, of the fragile, sometimes broken ties between
entities who inhabit a shared landscape both inanimate to animate and
animal to human. This film is marked by its studied *differential* biopolitics regarding the (sexed) animate nature of the co-construction of
animals and humans.

In the conceptions offered in this chapter, several senses of "trans-"
have been mobilized and put into conversation: transgender (living
outside normative gender definition or undergoing a shift in gender identity), transmogrification (the changing of shape or form to
something fantastical), translation (across languages), and transspecies
(across species). Each of these terms suggests a movement or dyna-

mism, from one site to another, as in the sense of "across." I made the case for a trans- theorizing that recognizes the distinctness of queer, but at the same time embraces the collaborative possibilities of thinking trans- alongside and across queerness. In analyzing a number of cultural productions and their (often hostile) articulations or imputations of transness, with the exception of Eva Hayward's essay, this chapter worked at some distance from *actively claimed* (whether human or not) transgender and transsexual lives and identities. It did not seek to impose an uncritical or obligatory relation to the reproductive politics of neutering and spaying, which at so many levels have very little to do with human trans lives; indeed, such a pat analogy could be quite offensive if taken at face value. Yet this chapter sought to analyze and diagnose the cross-discursive connections already available and drawn between animals and humans, racial castration and biopolitical neutering and spaying, under a rubric of transmogrification sensitive to the complex politics of sex, gender, and sexuality. The coercive conceptual workings of these cultural productions and their way of crafting forms of cultural exile are premised on already marginal loci in gender, race, species, and sexuality matrices. Simultaneously, there are zones of possibility that work around and against such coercions, such as the analogic survival of transness that can always be purported back to the human.

Deleuze and Guattari's "body without organs" is both honored and merely suggested in the examples elaborated in this chapter. This concept's simultaneous limitation and promise is precisely that the genitals (or nongenitals) matter, but are not necessarily constrained by normative gender and sexuality. Even the "animals with/out genitals" possess a transmateriality that is characterized by a radical uncertainty, a destabilization of animacy categorizations that mean to keep "kinds" together, and a generative affectivity; but as Hayward reminds us, we should not be limited to thinking with and through the simplest analogies. And so this chapter might be thought of as an invitation to consider queer-trans animality within a more porous understanding of animacy, even in its politically most closed of circumstances, and not as a tired and fatal venue for human self-making but as a site of unpredictable investment for untraceable animate futurities.

PART III ∗ METALS

.

5

Lead's Racial Matters

Here I pluck an object from the lowest end of the animacy hierarchy: lead metal, a chemical element, an exemplar of inanimate matter. In the two previous chapters, I detailed how animality is coarticulated with humanity in ways that are soundly implicated in regimes of race, nation, and gender, disrupting clear divisions and categories that have profound implications ramifying from the linguistic to the bio-political. In this final part, I bring animacy theory to bear on metals; first by looking at recent racialized discourses around lead, and in the next chapter by focusing on mercury toxicity to discuss the vulnerability of human subjects in the face of ostensibly inanimate particles. These particles are critically mobile and their status as toxins derives from their potential threat to valued human integrities. They further threaten to overrun what an animacy hierarchy would wish to lock in place.

Toys off Track

This chapter considers the case of "lead panic" in the United States in 2007 regarding potentially toxic toys associated with Chinese manufacture. I label this recent lead case a "panic" to suggest a disproportionate relationship between its purportedly unique threat to children's health and the relative paucity of evidence at its onset that the contaminated toys themselves had already caused severe health consequences.[1] I measure this panic against other domestic public health lead concerns, including spectacles of contagion, to investigate lead's role in the complex play of domestic security and sovereign fantasy (defined here as the national or imperial project of absolute rule and authority). I suggest that an inanimate but migrant entity such as industrial lead can become racialized, even as it can only lie in a notionally peripheral relationship to biological life. Rather than focus exclusively on the concrete dangers to living bodies of environmental lead, which are significant and well documented, I consider lead as a cultural phenomenon over and above its material and physio-medical character.

In the summer of 2007 in the United States, a spate of specific recalls and generalized warnings about preschool toys, pet food, seafood, lunchboxes, and other items began to appear in national and local papers and television and radio news.[2] In this geopolitical and cultural moment, the most urgent warnings were issued regarding toys. Lead's identity as a neurotoxic "heavy metal" was attributed to a set of toys whose decomposable surfaces when touched yielded up the lead for transit into the bloodstreams of young children, giving it a means for its circulatory march toward the vulnerable, developing brain. Nancy A. Nord, acting chair of the Consumer Product Safety Commission, issued a statement that declared, "These recalled toys have accessible lead in the paint, and parents should not hesitate in taking them away from children."[3]

Descriptions of the items recalled tended to have three common characteristics. First, they pointed to the dangers of lead intoxication as opposed to other toxins. Second, they emphasized the vulnerability of American children to this toxin. Third, they had a common point of origination: China, for decades a major supplier of consumer products to the United States and responsible for various stages in the production stream: "As More Toys Are Recalled, Trail Ends in China," reported the *New York Times* in June 2007.[4] These alerts arose out of direct testing of the toys rather than from medical reports of children's intoxication by lead content in the indicated toys; as one *Consumer Reports* article said, "our latest tests find the toxic metal in more products."[5] In other words, no children had yet to fall demonstrably ill from playing with these specific toys. One image for a lead testing kit, the Abotex Lead Inspector, shown on the company's website, shows a smiling white baby seated next to a plush toy (figure 13). The baby's right sleeve appears to have been pushed farther up its arm, so that its

13. Abotex Lead Inspector Lead Test Kit.
From the promotional website, 2007.

prominent skin contact with the toy can visibly indicate the intimate bodily contact between toys and children in the course of everyday play.

The toy's obviously facial front naturalizes the toy's status as a primary interlocutor for the infant. Its anthropomorphization reifies parents' fantasy that the toy must be a familiar and safe substitute for a "person." If the toy flower presents a friendly face to the socializing infant, the testing kit suggests that this idealized scene of interactivity has a threatening undercurrent. The logo features a silhouette of a man's face and a magnifying glass, a deliberate anachronism that makes it seem as if this kit will turn a parent into Sherlock Holmes, able to hunt down clues, searching for visible traces of lead as if looking for fingerprints in a board game murder mystery.

The Abotex Lead Inspector can investigate for a consumer which toys and other personal effects have toxic levels of lead. Its color-

Resultant Color Produced	Faint Yellowish Tint	1-3 ppm
Approx. Lead Release in parts per million (ppm) of the sample. PATENT #1,256,782	Light Brown	5 ppm
	Medium Brown	10 ppm
	Dark Brown	25 ppm
	Black	over 50 ppm

14. Abotex lead color chart. From the promotional website, 2007.

coded test strips can be bought in quantities of eight to one hundred. Once one uses the testing strip, they can refer to a reference color guide (figure 14), for which the diagnostic colors range from a "faint yellowish tint" (the least toxic range) to "medium brown" to "black" (most toxic). Critical race scholars have usefully parsed the distinctions between "colorism" and "racism," investigating how regionally and culturally specific discourses (including legal ones) regarding tones, shades, and colors may or may not synch up with relevant discussions on race.[6] Yet the graded valuation of color—the higher valuation of light shades and lower valuation of darker shades—remains a popular habit of mainstream colorism in the United States, and the Abotex reference chart complies with this chromatic logic.

At the height of the lead toy scare, media outlets paraded images of plastic and painted children's toys as possibly lead-tainted and hence possible hosts of an invisible threat; guest doctors repeated caveats about the dangers of "brain damage," "lowered IQs," and "developmental delay," directing their comments to concerned parents of vulnerable children. Toy testing centers were set up across the country, and sales of inexpensive lead test kits like the Abotex Lead Inspector rose as concerned parents were urged to test their toys in time for the holiday season in 2007, in effect privatizing and individualizing responsibility for toxicity in the face of the faltering dysfunction of the FDA and EPA, whose apparent failure to regulate these objects was thrown into sharp relief.

One of the more prominent visual symbols of this recall debacle was that of toy trains, generally smiling, in different colors and identities. In this illustrative photograph accompanying an article on the toy recall in 2007 in the *New York Times*, an anthropomorphized engine is graphically headed off the tracks (figure 15). The photograph affiliates the toy panic with one particular toy, Thomas the Tank Engine, the eponymous head of the Thomas & Friends series. Originally

15. Thomas the Tank Engine headed off the tracks. Lars Klove, *New York Times*, June 19, 2007, from "RC2's Train Wreck," by David Barboza and Louise Story.

a creation of the British author Wilbert Awdry in a book published in 1946, Thomas the Tank Engine has spawned an entertainment industry that today spans the globe; its central significance to the toy panic is discussed later in this chapter. In this photograph, Thomas's open mouth and raised eyebrows suggest surprise at his derailing as the wooden tracks under his wheels gently curve away. The "maker" of Thomas & Friends toys, the U.S. company RC2 (whose manufacturing is outsourced to China), also produces Bob the Builder and John Deere toys, model kits, and the Lamaze Infant Development System; the prevalence of toys related to construction and industrial transportation reflects a slant toward fostering young masculinities.[7]

Other media images specific to lead-tainted toys abounded: stuffed animals, plastic charms, necklaces and bracelets, teething aids, and toy medical accessories such as fake blood pressure cuffs (these medicalized playthings were particularly ironic, since this toxic toy transposed expected subjects and objects: children were turned from future doctors and nurses back into the patients of public health). Pictures of the decontextualized toys alternated with images that included overwhelmingly white and generally middle-class children playing with the suspect toys.

While notions of lead circulated prolifically, lead itself was missing from these renderings. Neither the molecular structure of lead, nor its naturally occurring colors, nor its appearance in raw form or industrial bulk were illustrated. Rather, images of the suspect toys and the children playing with them predominated in visual representations of the toxic threat. Even the feared image of a sick American child that underlay the lead panic was not visually shown, only discussed in the text as a threatening possibility. Together, the associative panoply of images—the nursery-school primary color toys associated with domestic, childlike innocence and security—served as a contrastive indictment. The lead toxicity of painted and plastic toys became the newest addition to the mainstream U.S. parental (in)security map.

The ensemble of images seemed to accelerate the explosive construction of a "master toxicity narrative" about Chinese products in general, one that had been quietly simmering since the recalls in 2005 of soft Chinese-made lunchboxes tainted with dangerous levels of lead. Journalists, government offices, and parents drew alarming connections between Chinese-made products and environmental toxins apace. Their lists now included heparin in Chinese-made medicines, industrial melamine in pet food, even Chinese smog, which had become unleashed from its geographic borders and was migrating to other territories. The visual representations of Chinese toxicities not related to lead that flourished in 2007 included rare-earth magnets haphazardly arrayed in the intestines of a child's X-rayed body; medicine vials; toothpaste tubes; cans of dog food; lipstick tubes; dogs lying on veterinary tables; and Chinese female workers in factory rows, in what Laura Hyun Yi Kang has called "one of the emblematic images of the global assembly line."[8] If RC2 shared legal responsibility for the lead found in Thomas the train, this fact seemed lost on the news media; it was the Chinese site of assembly (and the U.S. child as the site of contact or ingestion) that received the lion's share of attention.[9]

A generalized narrative about the inherent health risk of Chinese products to U.S. denizens thus crystallized. But this narrative is a highly selective one dependent on a resiliently exceptionalist victimization of the United States. Chinese residents are continually affected by the factories called their "own," through the pollution of water, air, food, and soil. A growing awareness of the regular failure of local and national governments to strengthen protections for residents and workers from industrial toxins has led to a dramatic rise in community protests, lawsuits, and organized activist movements.[10] These industries are deeply bound up with transnational industrialization, in which China has been a major participant for decades, as well as the vulnerabilities it generates. According to David Harvey, the governments of industrializing nations are tempted to "race to the bottom" in their striving for participation in systems of transnational capital. In the process, they are more than willing to overlook unjust labor remunerations or benefits and the lack of protection from adverse labor conditions. As a result, local populations and industry workers, because they are deeply tied to the very environments in which these industries are animated, must forcibly consume (literally) the byproducts of those industries.[11]

Within the United States in 2007, mass media stories pitched Chinese environmental threats neither as harmful to actual Chinese people or landscapes, nor as products of a global industrialization that the United States itself eagerly promotes, but as invasive dangers to the U.S. territory from other national territories. These environmental toxins were supposed to be "there" but were found "here." Other countries, including Mexico, were named in relation to manufacturing hazards; yet, perhaps in proportion to its predominance in world markets, China remained the focus of concern for the vulnerability of the United States to consumer product toxicities. It seems no coincidence that just before this year, in 2006, China overtook the United States in global exports, a fact documented by the World Trade Organization and widely reported throughout 2006 and 2007.[12] This rise in manufacturing led to fears about the trade deficit, fears hardly contained—and in fact in some sense paradoxically fueled—by Commerce Secretary Carlos Gutierrez's proclamation that the swelling Chinese output was "not a threat."[13]

Alarm about the safety of Chinese products entered all form of discourse, from casual conversations to talk shows to news reports. In what might be called a new, shrewd form of unofficial protectionism, Stateside citizens were urged to avoid buying Chinese products in general, even though such products are essentially ubiquitous given the longtime entrenchment of trade relations between the United States and China. That an estimated 80 percent of all toys bought in the United States are made in China is the sign of such entrenchment. An investigative reporter recounted that attempting to avoid anything "made in China" for one week was all but futile. He wrote, "Poisoned pet food. Seafood laced with potentially dangerous antibiotics. Toothpaste tainted with an ingredient in antifreeze. Tires missing a key safety component. U.S. shoppers may be forgiven if they are becoming leery of Chinese-made goods and are trying to fill their shopping carts with products free of ingredients from that country. The trouble is, that may be almost impossible."[14] One lesson of this panic was that inanimate pollutants could now "invade" all kinds of consumer products, and other pollutants could always climb on board.

The Chinese toy panic in 2007 was a twist on an earlier theme in recent U.S. history regarding the toxicity of lead. Since 1978, the year that the U.S. Consumer Product Safety Commission banned residential paint containing lead, there have been public-awareness campaigns and legislation regarding exposure from house paint. Lead-based paint is present in many buildings constructed before 1978, though public-awareness campaigns and municipal abatement programs have been quite successful in reducing the threat of residential lead to the middle and upper classes. More recently, however, environmental justice activists from polluted neighborhoods and public health advocates have insisted that lead toxicity remains a problem for children in impoverished neighborhoods. Lead poisoning among black children was thus figured as an epidemiological crisis linked to the pollution of neighborhoods populated largely by people of color, including older buildings whose once-widespread lead paint had not been remediated, and where lead-polluting industrial centers were located. But in 2007, news media coverage this kind of lead toxicity began to float and fade, overtaken by the heightened transnational significance of lead. Toys from China quickly became the primary source of threat, displacing this previous concern.[15]

I thus argue that a new material-semiotic form of lead emerged in 2007. This new lead was, despite its physiological identity to the old lead, taking on a new meaning and political character and becoming animated in novel ways. Why were painted trains and beaming middle-class white children chosen to represent the lead toxicity this time? If the spread of transnational commodities reached into all classes and privileges, how did middle-class white children morph into the primary victims of *this* environmental lead, when poor black children had previously been represented as subject to the dangers of domestic lead? Why could only China, or occasionally a few other industrial sites not in the United States such as Mexico and India, be imagined as lead's source? Ultimately, what, or who, had this new lead become?

Animate Contaminants

At first glance, lead is not integral to the biological or social body. In the biomythography of the United States, lead is "dead." Rather than being imagined as integral to life, and despite its occurrence in both inorganic and organic forms, lead notionally lies in marginal, exterior and instrumental, and impactful relation to biological life units, such as organic bodies of value. The concept of animacy suggests there can be gradations of lifeliness. If viruses, also nonliving, nevertheless seem "closer" to life because they require living cells for their own continued existence, lead seems more uncontroversially "dead" and is imagined as more molecular than cellular. The meta-rubric of "animacy theory" proves useful here, as lead appears to undo the purported mapping of lifeliness-deadliness scales onto an animate hierarchy. Not only can dead lead appear and feel alive; it can fix itself atop the hierarchy, sitting cozily amid healthy white subjects.

Furthermore, lead deterritorializes, emphasizing its mobility through and against imperialistic spatializations of "here" and "there." The lead that constitutes today's health and security panic in the United States is figured as all around us, in our toys, our dog food, and the air we breathe, streaming in as if uncontrollably from elsewhere. Lead is not supposed to, in other words, belong "here." Even popu lar reports of the export of electronics waste to developing countries for resource mining still locate the toxicity of lead, mercury, and cadmium away from "here"; their disassembled state is where the health hazard is located, and disassembly happens elsewhere.[16] Now, however, the new lead is "here," having perversely returned in the form of toxic toys. Lead's seeming return to the middle and upper classes exemplifies the "boomerang effect" of what the sociologist Ulrich Beck calls a "risk society": "Risks of modernization sooner or later also strike those who profit from them. . . . Even the rich and the powerful are not safe from them."[17] The new lead thus represents a kind of "involuntary environmental justice," if we read justice as not the extension of remedy but a kind of revenge.[18]

While the new lead fears indicate an apparent progressive development of the interrelations of threat, biology, race, geographic specificity, and sovereign symbolization, lead's present-day embodiment may not be such an unusual admixture. It is instructive to trace lead's imbrication in the rhetorics of political sovereignty and globalized capital, remaining attentive to what is present and what is absent. If lead is at the present moment imagined to come from places *outside* the geographic West—in spite of the longtime complexity of transnational relations—and to threaten definitive U.S. citizenry, then how might we assess its status against a history of race rendered as biological threat, and a present that intensifies the possibilities of biological terrorism? How might we contextualize the panic around lead as a hyper-stimulated war machine in which the U.S. government perceives and surveils increasing numbers and types of "terrorist" bodies? And how does a context of an increasingly fragile U.S. global economic power texture and condition this panic, one that sits adjacent to discussions of contamination and contagion?

While lead has long worn an identity as a pollutant, associated with industry and targeted in environmentalist efforts, today's lead might first suggest a new development in the domain of contagion discourse. Contagion can be invoked precisely because the touching and ingestion of lead represents, for children, a primary route of exposure, just as with "live" biological agents. Yet there may be still further structural forces at play. Priscilla Wald, writing about complex narratives of biological contagion, has shown how epidemiology itself can be informed by circulating "myths," understood as stories that are authoritative and serve to buttress communitarian identity.[19] One could argue that the black children who disappeared from the lead representations did so precisely because the new lead was tied to ideas of vulnerable sovereignty and xenophobia, ideas that demanded an elsewhere (or at least not interior North America) as their ground. However, as I will argue later, black children did not quite disappear. In the United States, the genuine challenge of representing the microcosmic toxicity of lead and a human group's vulnerability to it defers to a logic of panics, falling back on simplified, racially coded narratives. Such narratives, by offering ready objects, doubly conceal the deeper transnational, generational, and economic complexity of the life of lead.

The behavior of lead as a contaminating, but not technically contagious, toxin (but, again, not necessarily as a pollutant in wall paint or as an airborne dust) contains many of the elements of Wald's "outbreak narrative," a contemporary trope of disease emergence involving multiple discourses (including popular and scientific) that has been present since the late 1980s. Wald asserts that the specific form of the outbreak narrative represented a shift in epidemiological panics because it invoked tales that reflected the global and transnational character of the emerging infection and involved the use of popular epidemiological discourses to track the success of actions against the disease. Lead, however, is not a microbe, not an infectious agent; it does not involve human carriers like those profiled in Wald's examples of outbreak narratives. The lead panic depends not on human communicability but the toxicity of inanimate objects, so it is technically not the stuff of contagion. What it does clearly and by necessity involve, however, is transnational narratives of the movement of contaminants in the epidemiology of human sickness. In migration (the Pacific Rim) and source (China), the lead story significantly resembles the SARS epidemiological and journalistic trajectories of 2002, when the "outbreak" occurred. Finally, lead's major route of contamination is by ingestion, and it is epidemiologically mappable; when lead is attached to human producers, even if transnationally located far away, a kind of disease vectoring still can happen, even if its condition is not (even transitively) communicable.

Yellow Terrors

There is in fact very little that is new about the "lead panic" in 2007 in the United States. At least, we can say that it is not sufficient to turn to popular and scientific epidemiology's overapplied cry that contemporary ailments bear the mark of this globalizing world's heightened interconnectivities (a cry that says, for instance, that lead travels more than it used to, which would require us to accept, somehow, that lead came only from China). In fact, anxieties about intoxications, mixings, and Chinese agents have steadily accompanied U.S. cultural productions and echo the Yellow Peril fears articulated earlier in the twentieth century. That lead was subject to an outbreak narrative works synergistically with these anxieties, and these narratives may indeed have been partially incited or facilitated by them. One wonders in particular about the haunted vulnerability of "Western" sites that Elizabeth Povinelli incisively describes as ghoul health:

> Ghoul health refers to the global organization of the biomedical
> establishment, and its imaginary, around the idea that the big scary

bug, the new plague, is the real threat that haunts the contemporary global division, distribution, and circulation of health, that it will decisively render the distribution of *jus vitae ac necris*, and that this big scary bug will track empire back to its source in an end-game of geophysical bad faith. Ghoul health plays on the real fear that the material distribution of life and death arising from the structural impoverishment of postcolonial and settler colonial worlds may have accidentally or purposefully brewed an unstoppable biovirulence from the bad faith of liberal capital and its multiple geophysical tactics and partners.[20]

Povinelli traces a kind of looming materialization, in the form of threatened health, of the latent affects of imperialist "just deserts."

The recent lead panic echoes, yet is a variation of, the turn-of-the-century Orientalized threat to white domesticity, as detailed by Nayan Shah in relation to San Francisco Chinatown in the late nineteenth century and early twentieth.[21] Shah describes local investments in white domesticity in this period and its connection to nationalism and citizenship. Two perceived threats to white domesticity came in the form of activities believed to reside exclusively in Chinatown: prostitution and opium dens. Significant among concerned white residents' and policy makers' fears at the time was the contractibility of syphilis and leprosy, which was imagined to happen in direct contact with the Chinese, whether this contact was sexual or sensual in nature. Notably, they also worried that the passing of opium pipes "from lip to lip" was a major route of disease transmission; this image resonates with the licking scene of contamination of the lead-covered toys, a scene to which I return later.[22] This indirect mode of imagined transmission resonates with the nature of the lead panic, for the relation of contamination in the case of both the opium pipes (disease contagion) and the new lead (pollution, poisoning) is one of transitivity. While the imagined disease transmission mediated by an opium pipe was more or less immediate and depended on proximity, if not direct contact, between human bodies, the new lead is imagined to be associated with national or human culprits somewhere far away.

Since the current reference to lead produces an urgent appeal to reject Chinese-made products, and since mentions of China arouse fantasies of toxins such as lead, heparin, and so on, then in effect, lead has in this moment become just slightly Chinese (without being personified as such). That is to say, on top of the racialization of those involved, including whites and Chinese, lead itself takes on the tinge of racialization. This is particularly so because lead's racialization, I suggest, is intensified by the *non*-proximity of the Chinese who are "responsible" for putting the lead in the toys: that is, lead's presence in the absence of the Chinese, in a contested space of U.S. self-preservation, effectively forces lead to bear its own toxic racialization. As toys become threatening health risks, they are rhetorically constructed as racialized threats. This racialization of lead and other substances both replicates a fear of racialized immigration into the vulnerable national body at a time when its economic sovereignty is in question and inherits a racialization of disease assisted by a history of public health discourse.

The corrupted Chinatown arguably still lives, albeit now understood as an entire nature covered in irresponsible factories that spread their poisons far and wide. In the twenty-first-century lead panic, exogenous (that is, "unassimilated") mainland Chinese still stand to face the old accusations of ill hygiene and moral defect. Thus, today's images of toy-painting laborers too readily attract narratives of moral contagion: they demonstrate irresponsibility toward "our" consumers and blithe ignorance of the consequences of their work, properties that effectively reinforce their unfitness for American citizenship. This is a moral standard that has already been increasingly imposed on the working class by legal and social expressions of U.S. neoliberalism.

Chinese lead panics are sticky; they are generated by, and further borrow from, many already interlaced narratives. The spread of war discourse within the West and of the imaginary fount of bioterrorist plotting, dramatized by the U.S. government in its second Gulf war, was a convenient additive to narrations about toxins.[23] Bioterrorism involves the intentional use of toxic agents that are biologically active, even if not "live" themselves, against populations. They often cannot be perceived by the naked eye. While bioterrorist intentionality cannot be attached to the lead narrative (the China case might more aptly be called "bioterrorist negligence"), it is nevertheless fairly easy to read the discourses on lead as a *biosecurity threat*, conflating the safety of individual bodies with the safety of national concerns.[24] Other biosecurity threats have also been recruited as "Asian," in the case of contagious diseases such as SARS and bird flu. Consultants and safety advocates deemed red and yellow colors—precisely those colors used to indicate heightened levels of "security threat" in U.S. airports—to have particularly dangerous levels of lead and suggested color as an effective criterion ("profile") by which toys should be identified and returned.[25]

Thus, lead was an invisible threat whose material loci and physical provenance, much like a terrorist "sleeper cell," needed to be presumed in advance and mapped—not only geographically but sensorily, sometimes through visual coding schemes like color itself (recall the Abotex lead test color chart which codes faint yellow the least toxic, black the most).[26] Popular responses both in the United States and in other countries affected by the China toy recall bore this out; one blog entry's title, for instance, was the indignant "Why Is China Poisoning Our Babies?"[27] News about heparin contamination in pharmaceuticals originating from China became particularly explosive when it was thought to be deliberate, highlighting the sense of insidious invasion in the same way that bioterrorism does.[28] Given the apparent, blithe disregard or dysfunction of both the Chinese and U.S. governmental safety controls along the way, the sign of biosecurity and protection falls on the head of a young child who wishes to play with a toy, and by implication, that child's parents. Indeed, the body of the young white child using a toy train is not signified innocently of its larger symbolic value at the level of the nation; its specific popularity suggests this metonymic connection.

The last few decades have seen a strengthening of affects around terrorism, associating it with radical extranationality as well as nonstate agentivity. Jasbir Puar has incisively examined the escalating agitation around purported "terrorism," particularly its potential to consolidate national interests (including white and neoliberal homonationalisms) in the face of such a perceived threat.[29] Indeed, nonstatehood, while always potentially unstable, has come into a mature relationship with the imagined *possibility* of terrorism. This is evidenced, for example, by the fact that in 2010, Senator Joe Lieberman proposed that Congress enact the revocation of citizenship from those who demonstrate financial support or other forms of allegiance to organizations deemed "terrorist" by the United States. Under these conditions, the invisible threat of cognitive and social degradation in the case of lead meant that the abiding, relatively more methodical, and diversified work of environmental justice activists on lead toxicity was here transformed into something that looked less "environmental" and increasingly like another figure in the war on terror, a war that marked the diffuseness, unpredictability, and sleeper-cell provenance of enemy material and its biological vectors.[30]

This "war on terror" was doubly pitched as a neomissionary insistence on the dissemination of the "American way," including its habits of free choice and its access to a free market at its core defined by the proliferation of consumer products. Thus, the very title of a *New York Times* article by Leslie Wayne published in 2009 about corrosive drywall for new homebuilding sourced from China, "The Enemy at Home," betrays toxic drywall's coding as a biological threat metaphorized as war (itself not at great notional distance from "biological warfare").[31] The idea of this "enemy at home" makes lead into a symptomatic signifier of a war of capital flows, particularly the struggle over trade protectionism and the Chinese resistance to allow the Chinese yuan to float against the dollar, a resistance that has only recently seen a measured lessening as of this date of writing (2011). Lead is animated to become simultaneously an instrument of heightened domestic panic, drawing from and recycling languages of "terror," and a rhetorical weapon in the rehearsal of the economic sovereignty of the United States. A story by the financial-interest magazine *Forbes* at the height of the toy recall made these slippages baldly evident: "Chinese Toy Terror."[32]

What are blended in this collapse of narratives, and what are of particular interest here for animacy, are precisely the subjects and objects, recipients and perpetrators, terrorists and innocents, of lead toxicity. In other words, the fused stories about lead *displace* the normal agents of the contagion narratives and scramble the normal pairings between protector and protected and self and other. As such, they cannot rhetorically function as effectively as they might strive to function. This easily recognizable failure of boundaries may be the sole rehabilitative counterthrust of the new lead panic.

Lead's Labors

The image of the vulnerable white child is relentlessly promoted over and against an enduring and blatant background (that is, unacknowledged) condition of labor and of racism: the ongoing exposure of immigrants and people of color to risk that sets them up for conditions of bodily work and residence that dramatize the body burdens that projects of white nationalism can hardly refuse to perceive. Blithely overlooked—or steadfastly ignored—are the toxic conditions of labor and of manufacture, such as inattention to harmful transnational labor and industrial practices that poison, in many cases, badly protected or unprotected workers.[33] Other persistent conditions include the invisibility within the United States of the working, destitute, or agrarian poor in favor of idealized consumers who are white and middle or upper middle class; electronic wastes as extravagant and unattended exports of the United States to countries willing to take the cash to mine it; the dumping of toxic wastes and high-polluting industries into poorer neighborhoods within municipalities; and common practices in the United States of exporting products of greater toxicity than is permitted within its own borders.[34] Here, the cynical calculus of risk, race, and international trade continually reproduces a specific configuration of toxic expulsion to othered lands or peoples. As Cheri Lucas Jennings and Bruce H. Jennings report the international economic director of the World Bank suggested that third-world countries might be better off trading for the toxic waste of first-world countries, since "poverty or imminent starvation" were a greater threat to life expectancy than the toxicity of the waste they would receive.[35] Within the United States, these authors point to the greater access to less persistent toxins (such as pesticides) by those with economic privilege, leading to a bifurcated distribution of greater and lesser toxic infusion along lines of both class and race.

The contemporary fears in the United States about lead contamination and mental degradation are complexly interwoven with race, class, and cognitive ability, both as they externally manifest (that is, the racialization of imports from China) and as they dovetail with internal registers of classism and regional stereotyping. Take, for example, one toy, Hillbilly Teeth, made in China and distributed by the company Funtastic (of Houston, Texas), which was recalled due to concerns about lead in 2008 (figure 16). The recall notice of this product issued by the U.S. Consumer Product Safety Commission singled out the gray paint on the teeth as the source of lead.[36] Though it was coded as threatening or harmful due to its potentially tainted plastic (which would by design be placed in the child's mouth), one could equally find alarm in its perpetration of classed, ableist, and ruralized violence in its identity as a toy.

The package's cardboard backing depicts a smiling, presumably "nonhillbilly" white male child wearing the denture insert, and the

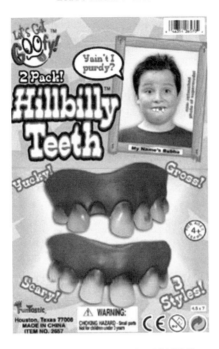

16. Funtastic's "Let's Get Goofy" Hillbilly
Teeth, made in China, recalled in 2008.
Source unknown.

discolored, out of proportion, and otherwise imperfect teeth are designated "yucky," "gross," and "scary." An inset fake frame, labeled "My
Name's Bubba," has a cartoon speech bubble ("Yain't I purdy?") that
uses a distorted caricature of rural or Southern accents. The prefatory
and framing "Let's Get Goofy!" resembles the youthful refrain "Let's
Get Retarded!" and signifies a willful and temporary loss of rationality
and cognitive measure. The extant class coding of the "bad teeth" further builds on the myth of rural and working-class degradation by
hinting at the acute dental issues that often accompany addiction to
methamphetamines (aka "meth mouth"). Methamphetamines are the
most recognized drug problem in "hillbilly country," that is, the rural
South and Midwest. The juxtaposition of *Hillbilly* and *Teeth* reminds
us that both the urban gentrified center and the pastoral myths of
the United States have their own white undersides.[37] Against such a
consolidated scenario, the leaden gray-tinted tooth paint seems even
more intent on the protection of a limited few, the urban kids who

have the voluntary luxury, every year on Halloween, of assuming the mask of fallen class and intellectual ability, only to snap it off later.

A different toy, however, sat at the center of the lead panic in 2007: the expensive toy series Thomas the Tank Engine, seen earlier. Thomas and his "friends" are immensely popular objects and are accompanied by a range of lucrative tie-ins, including a television show, games, activity books, candy, and other merchandise bearing Thomas's characteristic blue "body" and round gray and black face. These are not only meant for children. The series is marketed to middle-class parents who insist on high-status "quality" products, which in this case are tuned toward boys and quite explicitly direct their proper masculine development. An article from the *New York Times* in 2007 explicitly associated the toys' high prices with their presumed quality and safety. The article bears one visual image, a photograph of the "James Engine" from the Thomas series, and a description of one member of the vulnerable population (identified as children), a white four-year-old boy whose mother points to the expectation of "quality" for these toys and whose class membership appears to be middle to upper middle class: "The affected Thomas toys were manufactured in China. . . . 'These are not cheap, plastic McDonald's toys,' said Marian Goldstein of Maplewood, N.J., who spent more than $1,000 on her son's Thomas collection, for toys that can cost $10 to $70 apiece. 'But these are what is supposed to be a high-quality children's toy.'"[38] Presumably, the "cheap," working-class McDonald's toys are the toxic ground on which the nontoxic quality toys are to be built and compared.

Goldstein may have a point about the train's symbolic privilege, at least. Trains occupy an iconic place in the mythology and economic actuality of the creation of the American West. Symbolically and materially, trains are intrinsically connected to commerce and the circulation of economic goods as well as, in the United States, to a hidden history of Chinese labor. Both the extension of railroad systems to the American West and the development of the Sacramento River Delta in California heavily depended on imported Chinese labor that was rendered invisible in certain interested histories of labor.[39] Narratives about lead toxicity in toys from China largely obscure the conditions of Chinese labor in the production of these toy trains.[40] Nevertheless, these narratives deploy the fact of labor obliquely, in an explication of the pathway of toxicity (lead must be painted on). How to explain this incipient visibility?

An accusatory narrative in which Chinese are the criminal painters of the toy Thomas trains sets things up differently from the story of the Chinese laborers who extended the railroads to the American West: while the latter were made invisible in the interest of the white ownership of land, property, and history, for the toy painters the conditions of labor needed to be made just visible enough to facilitate the territorial, state, and racial assignation of blame, but not enough to generally extend the ring of sympathetic concern around the workers themselves.[41] Indeed, I found very few instances among concerned parents or journalists in the United States in which lead was also understood to be a source of toxicity for the immigrant or transnational laboring subjects who take part in the manufacture of the product.

So, the story of lead, a story of toxicity, security, and nationality, is also necessarily about labor: when it is registered, and when it is hidden, and who pays what kind of attention to whose labor. The regular erasure, or continued invisibility, in the lead narratives of the textile sweatshops, device assemblers, and toy painters, who are largely young women who have migrated into the Chinese cities from rural satellites, renders quite ironic the care work that is so poignantly provided by the toys—and transitively by the women who make them. The transitive criminalization of Chinese toy assemblers is all the more ironic when we consider the routinization of childcare inside the United States by African Americans and immigrants from Central and South America, the Philippines, South Asia, the Caribbean, and elsewhere, for middle-class parents of all ethnicities.[42] In some respects, the economy itself and changing kinship structures have increasingly meant that parents hire help while they work away from home, a creep of the care crisis into higher echelons of society, as feminist labor scholar Evelyn Nakano Glenn notes.[43] From the 1980s, middle-class mothers increasingly joined the labor force as neoliberalism took hold in the racialized sphere of the care of children: as they increasingly left the house and their children, "mothers had to accomplish more intimate care in less time," suggesting that care work be taken up by others in their place.[44] The racial mapping of the desirable subjects in the United States thus occurs in the context of the erasure of its disposable ones; I refer here to Grace Chang's notion of (immigrant female) "disposable domestics."[45]

Just as lead particles travel, so too does Thomas the train. It is a mobile vehicle, not only symbolically but also materially, one that has journeyed from England to the United States to China and back again. And indeed, a trip I took to China in 2010 revealed many knock-offs of Thomas, who is just as popular there as he is in the United States. These packaged toys, puzzle books, and candies were immediately recognizable but had slightly incorrect English spellings of his name, such as "Tromas," or "Tomas" (figure 17), as if to match the impossibility of perfect translation. These "illegal" copies show that, like the lead he allegedly carries with him on his back, Thomas is not containable within a given trajectory of movement and desire. The global spread of this commodity complicates the one-way vector of contamination from China to the United States, indicating a multidirectional flow. And yet, little is still known within the United States about how these toys may or may not harm Chinese children or the Chinese workers who produce them.

I referred earlier to a mode of transmission—from contaminated toy to child—as one of transitivity. For the late-capitalist, high-consumption, and highly networked sectors of the world, transitivity has arguably become a default mode not only of representation but of world-relating. The asymmetry of this world-relation is no barrier to the toxic effectivity of simmering racial panics. The sphere of the world that is well rehearsed in the flow of transnational commodities, services, and communications has become the perfect "host" for such transitivity, or at least the collapsing of transitive relations into conceptualizations of immediate contact. Patricia Clough, in her theorization of the complex, even nonhuman, agencies and affects participating in television and computer-consuming information societies, aptly writes that "even as the transnational or the global become visible, proposing themselves as far-flung extensions of social structure, they are ungrounded by that upon which they depend: the speed of the exchange of information, capital, bodies, and abstract knowledge and the vulnerability of exposure to media event-ness."[46]

An advertisement on the airport trolleys in Shanghai Pudong Airport (figure 18) in June 2010 demonstrates this relentlessly productive metonymic and economic transitivity. The text reads, "Your Eyes in the Factory! Book and Manage your Quality Control on www .AsiaInspection.com," in stark white letters on a red background; below the website name is an icon of inspection, the magnifying glass. In an inset picture, a male worker—possibly an inspector, possibly an assembler—handles a product. The transitivity here is not between the Chinese workers and the toys they have assembled, but rather

17. Super Tomas Series toy train set, outdoor market, Guilin, China, 2010. At lower right, the first three Chinese characters are *to-ma-sz*, a phonetic spelling of Thomas. Photograph by the author.

18. Airport trolley ad for AsiaInspection.
Photograph by the author, June 26, 2010.

of participants in production monitoring. It exists between the eyes of international corporate managers, the advertisement's English-reading addressees, and another set of eyes that is ambiguously either that of local Chinese inspectors or that of remote cameras that focus on Chinese workers. The ad further represents the interest in surveillance, glossed here as more benign "quality control," that arose after the toxicity of Chinese products illuminated Chinese production as a troubled site.[47]

Blackened Lead

Some years ago, as I indicated earlier, before the domestic narrative largely disappeared in favor of the Chinese one, the greater public was invited to consider the vulnerability of black children to lead intoxication. What happened to this association? Did it simply disappear, as I first hinted? Or did it meaningfully recede? I turn here to take a closer look at the medicalization of lead. Lead toxicity is medically characterized as at least partly neural; that is, it involves the nerve system, most notably comprising the brain and nerve pathways throughout the body. Medical accounts of lead toxicity, including those invoked in the toy lead panic of 2007, invoke its ability to lower the intelligence quotient (IQ) of a child. The IQ measure bears a distinctly eugenicist history and remains the subject of controversy regarding whether it has adequately shed its originary racial and socioeconomic biases.[48] Indeed, to what extent might we imagine that lead-induced IQ loss not only threatens the promise of success in an information economy, but also involves subtle racial movement away from whiteness, where the greatest horror is not death but disablement, that is, mental alteration and the loss of rational control?

Julian B. Carter's study of neurasthenia, or "nervous exhaustion," and its characterization in the 1880s by the neurologist George Beard as a specific property of genteel, sensitive, intelligent, well-bred whiteness (rather than, it was assumed, as a property of the working or peasant classes) gives us a more specific backdrop against which to consider neurotoxicity and its connection to the new lead's poster boy, the white middle-class child. Carter argues that the very vulnerability expressed by neurasthenia as a property cultivated primarily in privileged whites, both men and women, is what legitimated their claim to power in modernity, even as industrialization was blamed as a cause of the condition.[49]

Within the United States, "blackness" has its own specific history with regard to rhetorics of contamination, not least the "one drop of blood" policies against racial mixing and miscegenation. Later policies of racial segregation in the Jim Crow South were also linked to white fears of contamination. Referring to the debates in *Plessy v. Ferguson*, Saidiya Hartman writes of white concerns about the "integrity of bodily boundaries and racial self-certainty." She notes, "As *Plessy* evinced, sitting next to a black person on a train, sleeping in a hotel bed formerly used by a black patron, or dining with a black party seated at a nearby table not only diminished white enjoyment but also incited fears of engulfment and contamination."[50]

Lead contamination in the United States continues to be scrutinized for its racial bias, albeit unevenly. One recent contested conjunction of African American populations and lead was a study led by the Kennedy Krieger Institute. This study, conducted between 1993 and 1995, tracked lead levels in the children of Baltimore public housing occupants (primarily African Americans) who were exposed to various degrees of lead toxicity in residential paint, without adequate warning of the dangers of that lead. A storm of debate erupted around this study, in which healthy families were recruited to live in lead-contaminated houses. (This experiment harked back to the notorious Tuskegee Institute study, conducted between 1932 and 1972, which monitored poor black men who had syphilis but neither treated nor informed them in any way about the disease.)[51]

I have claimed that the year 2007 represented a year of transition, as a new and imaginatively more dominant, exogenous Chinese lead was entering the public domain. In this very same year, National Public Radio symptomatically both remembered and forgot received knowledge about domestic lead toxicity. First, a National Public Radio (NPR) show called "Living on Earth" updated its coverage of a longitudinal study on the urban poor and lead toxicity. That same year, another NPR show noted the higher levels of lead toxicity among African American children and pronounced these statistics "puzzling," leaving it at that.[52] "Puzzling": this illogic or failure of deduction occurred despite all kinds of widely available evidence pointing to increased urban regional pollution, lower access to information, and lower financial capacity to remediate or conceal lead paint. This easy disregard explains how black children in representations of toxic lead largely disappear and are replaced by white children: the national security project of the United States is less interested in profiling African American children as victims of lead poisoning, especially when the "new" lead is now situated as an externally derived attack.

Even the "remembering" of urban toxicity in the NPR "Living on Earth" show in 2007 is of a certain kind. This show updated its audience on an acclaimed longitudinal study on lead's effects on children that was begun in the 1970s, led by Kim Dietrich of the University of Cincinnati, and revisited over the years by NPR. Dietrich reported that early exposure to lead toxicity can be linked to later criminal behavior. By design, the study was focused on "inner-city" children, according to Dietrich, "who are largely minority."[53] In the NPR update in 2007, which functions as a symptomatic piling-up of racial constructs, Dietrich actively legitimated the interviewer's prompts, gathering a stunning assemblage: poverty, proximity of weapons, violence, lead, and poor nutrition together as collective determining factors for inner-city criminality:

GELLERMAN (interviewer): So if you look at inner cities, if you look at the poor, if you look at their exposure to weapons, you look at their exposure to violence, you look at their exposure to lead, and

their poor nutrition. Is this sort of the perfect combination of factors for crime?

DIETRICH: Yes, it's in a sense, the perfect storm. Uh, the environment
provides a lot of incentives for crime. The child is in a community
where he or she sees violence—the availability of guns, the availability of illicit drugs. So I would say that the inner-city environment provides the weapon, lead pulls the trigger.

"Lead pulls the trigger." This metaphor of weaponry is used to characterize a latent violent criminality domestic to the United States, naturalized to an urban underclass of color, using a co-construction of
guns, "ghettoes," and racialized pathology. In some sense, it is an old
story: to pump someone full of lead is to kill them. But the form
and objects of death have become molecular, and intentionality has
shifted to neglect, and a fragile self-identification rather than potency
reshapes the threat into the other person, conflated with the lead that
afflicts them.

Contrast this metaphor of weaponry to the title of the *New York
Times* article on toxic Chinese drywall, "The Enemy at Home," which
partakes of a war metaphor not because of some naturalizing co-
construction of guns, "ghetto," and racialized pathology, but in relation to a *transnational* (that is, extra-domestic) exchange that simultaneously seems to threaten representative individual bodies and
criminalize Chinese trade participation. This enemy, that is, should
not be at "home," with this word understood both as a generalized
national body and as the domicile of family units (who are in a position to afford the construction of new homes).

One wonders to what degree any newfound alarmism about the
vulnerability of black children to environmental lead can succeed,
given the abiding construction of *affinities* between racist constructions of blackness and those of lead, long integral to the American
racial and gendered corporeal imaginary.[54] A racial construction of
blacks as already unruly, violent, contaminated, and mentally deficient lies inherent in the current neoliberal economy, which not only
positions people of color in a labor hierarchy that matches them with
literally disabling forms of manual labor, but is also conditioned and
supported by a growing and incredibly powerful prison industrial
complex structured according to race, class, and gender.[55] If lead exposure itself is associated with cognitive delay, enhanced aggressivity,
impulsivity, convulsions, and mental lethargy, then we might read

such characterizations of blackness as attributions, or intimations, of disability, as much as we already understand them as damaging racial profiles. Eric Lott's study of blackface minstrelsy relates the suturing of impulsivity or sudden bodily displacement to fears about black masculinity in this performance culture in the United States. Lott reads Charles Dickens's account of the dancing in a New York blackface performance as stunned by its spasticity: "the whole passage reads as if Dickens did not really know what to do with such energy, where to put it."[56] Would lead toxicity, hence overdetermined with legacies of the negative characteristics of blackness, succeed quite so successfully as an imagined property of other racialized bodies, such as the Mexican braceros of the Second World War and modern-day maquiladora workers, both of whom have suffered from lead toxicity?[57] If disability can be read into constructs of blackness, disability itself is also a critically important axis of difference. Scholars such as Nirmala Erevelles and Andrea Minear point out the dangers of being both black *and* disabled; the authors suggest that within critical race feminism, while disability is sometimes recognized, it can often analytically function for scholars as a "nuance" of intensity rather than its own structural difference, leading to a loss of complexity in the reading: "the omission of disability as a critical category in discussions of intersectionality has disastrous and sometimes deadly consequences for disabled people of color caught at the interstices of multiple differences." These are just some ways in which criminality, race, and disability can be mutually produced and reproduced.

Thus, it is not necessarily correct to judge that African American youth are now no longer viewed as vulnerable to lead. Rather, it is easier to imagine that in this pointedly transnational struggle between major economic powers, black children are now the less-urgent population under threat. It is, instead, as if black children are constructed as more proximate to lead itself, as naturalized *to* lead; they serve as new ground to the newest figure.

In the case of the Thomas trains, lead toxicity is racialized, not only because the threatened future has the color of a white boy, but also because that boy must not change color. The boy can change color in two ways: First, lead lurks as a dirty toxin, as a pollutant, and it is persistently racialized as anything but white. Second, black children are assumed to be toxic; and lead's threat to white children is not only that they risk becoming dull and cognitively defective, but precisely that they lose their class-elaborated white racial cerebrality, and that they become suited racially to living in the ghettoes.[58]

Queer Licking

Let me return to the visual symbolic of media coverage of lead tox-icity. The florid palette of toy-panic images yielded two prominent and repeating icons. The media representations favored a pairing of images: on the one hand, the vulnerable child, more frequently a young, white, middle-class boy; and on the other hand, the danger-ous party: Thomas the Tank Engine. The iconic white boy's lead tox-icity must be avoided: he should not be mentally deficient, delayed, or lethargic. His intellectual capabilities must be assured to consoli-date a futurity of heteronormative (white) masculinity; that is to say, he must not be queer. This is not only because one of lead's toxici-ties reported by the Centers for Disease Control and Prevention is reproductive disability and infertility; I suggest here that one aspect of the threat of lead toxicity is its origin in a forbidden sexuality, for the frightening originary scene of intoxication is one of a *queer lick-ing*. Here again is the example of the white boy, who in the threaten-ing and frightening scene is precisely licking the painted train, a train whose name is Thomas, a train that is also one of the West's preemi-nent Freudian phallic icons.[59] This image of a boy licking the train, though clearly the feared scene of contamination, never appears lit-erally, or least I have not found it appearing literally; rather, if a boy and a train are present, the boy and the train are depicted proximately, and that is enough to represent the threat (the licking boy would be too much, would too directly represent the forbidden). But sugges-tions are sometimes loaded onto the proximities. In one representa-tive image from a website alerting its readers to RC2's recall of Thomas the Tank Engine trains, we see the head and chest of a blond boy lying alongside a train that is in the foreground. The boy's moist lips are parted and smiling, his eyes intent and alert; he grasps a dark-hued train car with his right hand, gazing slightly upward at it. The other cars, receding toward the camera, fall out of focus. The scene is—at the very least—physically and emotionally intimate, pleasurable, and desirous.[60]

On its website, the Centers for Disease Control and Prevention issued a fact sheet about lead, including the following statement under the heading "how your child may be exposed": "Lead is invisible to the naked eye and has no smell. Children may be exposed to it from consumer products through normal hand-to-mouth activity, which is part of their normal development. They often place toys, fingers, and other objects in their mouth, exposing themselves to lead paint or dust."[61] The language here, which means to reassure anxious parents, twice uses the word *normal* in describing children's orality: their hand-to-mouth activity is "normal . . . part of their normal development." This redundancy betrays a nervousness about children, with its language of proper development and its delineation of what is or is not permissible in normal play.

Returning to that fantasy that images could only approximate: what precisely is wrong with the boy licking the train? Two things are wrong: one, the boy licking Thomas the Tank Engine is playing improperly with the phallic toy, not thrusting it forward along the floor, but putting it into his mouth. Such late-exhibited orality bears the sheen of that "retarded" stage of development known as homosexuality. I am invoking the impossible juncture between the queernesses "naturally" afforded to children and the fear of a truly queer child.[62] I recently had a conversation with a British man in his seventies about the lead panic within the United States. With a twinkle in his eye, he said, "We had that lead in toys when I was young! Perhaps we just didn't suck them?" To me, his comment highlights the kind of temporal limitations on some kinds of national memory, the invested forgetting that is necessary for such a lead panic to become so enlivened.

Given that lead's very threat is that it produces cognitive disabilities, the scene of the child licking his toxic train slides further into queerness, as queer and disabled bodies alike trouble the capitalist marriage of domesticity, heterosexuality, and ability. The queer disability theorist Robert McRuer writes of the development of domesticity within capitalism that the "ideological reconsolidation of the home as a site of intimacy and heterosexuality was also the reconsolidation of the home as a site for the development of able-bodied identities, practices, and relations."[63] Exhibiting telltale signs of homosexuality and lead toxicity alike is simultaneously to alert a protected, domestic sphere to the threat of disability. One could say that lead itself is queered here as a microcosmic pollutant that, almost of its own accord, invades the body through plenitudes of microcosmic holes (a child's skin), sites the state cannot afford to acknowledge, for the queer vulnerabilities they portend.

Animacy theory embraces the ramified sites and traces of shifting being. It claims first that the tropes by which lead threatens to contaminate "healthy" privileged subjects relies fundamentally on animacy hierarchies. Lead can drag vulnerable people *down*, through variously "lesser" positions of animateness, into the realms of the "vegetable" or the nonsentient. At the same time, it has already weighed on some bodies more than others. The strength of anxieties about lead toxicity microcosmically, and very compactly, demonstrates that race, class, sexuality, and ability are unstable. These are not assured categories or properties that could operate intersectionally in a binary analysis, but are rather variably "mattering participants" in dominant ontologies that cannot therefore securely or finally attach to any body. Animacy theory objectifies animate hierarchies, assessing their diverse truth effects against the mobilities and slippages that too easily occur within them, and asks what paths the slippages trace. The next chapter focuses on the peculiar affective mediations wrought by toxicity, expanding beyond the paranoid images of altered bodies and minds produced by the fearful ensembles of U.S. biosecurity that are recounted in this chapter.

Notwithstanding my claims about lead's racialization in relation to a Chinese context, lead is of course not always specific to China. Rather, like any toxin, perhaps especially because it is not alive, it can be detached and reattached to diverse cultural and biological forms. This means that it is readily racialized, but with a set of preferences provided by the discursive structures it inhabits. Lead as a toxin, more generally, has already become in this global context racialized in excess as nonwhite; for instance, Mexican lead-tinged candy also received much media attention in 2007.[64] Yet lead's attachment preferences are perhaps not so flighty as one might first think; the "yellow hue" of today's lead seems to swirl in with the "brown" and "black" layers of lead's naturalized image.

I have suggested here that the mediation of lead in and around categories of "life" in turn undoes lead's deadness by reanimating it. In other words, lead has the capacity to poison definitively animate beings, and as such achieves its own animacy as an agent of harm. By examining the signifying economies of health, imperialism, and degradation that paint race onto different bodies, and by directing attention to the multiplicity of "contact zones" of those engaging lead—from working on the assembly line, to using the new products that contain them, to the downstream use of the products, to the recycling and mining of them—we witness the inherent brokenness of "races," "geographics," and "bodies" as systems of segregation, even as they remain numbingly effective in informing discourses of combat, health, and privilege. An environmental history of toxic objects must minimally register the gendered, laboring, and chronically toxically exposed bodies of globalized capital, which systematically bear less frequent mention in narratives of toxicity than the cautionary warnings from the seat of U.S. empire. With this registration, lead's spectacle remains connected to the possible forging of justice.

6

Following Mercurial Affect

Toxins are everywhere. The story goes they weren't here before. They lurk in personal products, our industry-spewn air, our soil, our food, below houses, and in waste receptacles where they will not degrade for years. They reside inside our bodies. They are blamed for disabilities and death, including autism, asthma, chronic illness, cancer. In the attention to worldwide pollution, human bodies and ecosystems alike have entered its broad arc of toxic destruction. Though Lawrence Buell in 1998 identified the early period of contemporary "toxic discourse" in the United States with the emergence of Rachel Carson's *Silent Spring* in 1962, notions and discursive sites of toxicity seem to have blossomed and transmogrified somewhat beyond Buell's astute literary mapping of the rhetorical underpinnings of toxic discourse: rude awakenings, nostalgic yearnings for pastoral purity.[1] Recent years have witnessed a tremendous growth of knowledge productions relating to the toxic ecology of the human body, which is linked to an industry of toxin-testing private and nonprofit agencies that hope to manage safety dangers regarding threats to home and body. These are accompanied by stories about the toxic load that people in various geographies at various life stages carry.[2] Coverage of toxic catastrophes compulsively refers to other such events.

The previous chapter on lead attended to medicalized representations of lead toxicity and their collusion with discourses about race and human development. While the discussion of lead introduced the figure of lead toxicity as a measure of public fear, this chapter focuses squarely on toxicity itself, in both its cultural structures and its affects, this time with attention to mercury and the "mercurial."

Here I move from exploring toxicity's contemporary pervasiveness as a notion, to exploring its purported and experienced mechanisms in the human body. This shift concerns the role of metaphor in biopolitics, since the seemingly metaphorical productions of cultural expressions of toxicity are not necessarily more concrete than the literal ones, which are themselves composed of complex cultures of immunity thinking. Reflecting on the ambiguous subject-object relations of toxicity, I use animacy theory to ask how the flexible subjectness or objectness of an actant raises important questions about the contingencies of humanness and animateness. These contingencies are eminently contestable within critical queer and race and disability approaches that, for instance, disaggregate verbal patients from the bottom of the hierarchy. Since, as I argued in chapter 1, animacy hierarchies are simultaneously ontologies of affect, then such ontologies might benefit from a reconceptualization of "the order of things," particularly along unconventional lines of race, sexuality, and ability.[3]

Toxicity's Reach

Toxins have moved well beyond their specific range of biological attribution, leaking out of nominal and literal bounds. A politician will decry the "toxic" political atmosphere;[4] Britney Spears will sing "Don't you know that you're toxic / And I love what you do";[5] an advice columnist will caution us to keep a healthy distance from "toxic" acquaintances.[6] One book is written for workers "suffering the ravages of a toxic personality," describing what they do as "poison, corrupt, pollute, and contaminate. . . . We define the toxic personality as anyone who demonstrates a pattern of counterproductive work behaviors that debilitate individuals, teams, and even organizations over the long term."[7] Thus, toxic people, not just chemicals, are appearing in popular social discourse, suggesting a shift in national sentiment that registers an increasing interest in individual bodily, emotional, and psychic security. For the rhetoric of security inevitably has ramifications not simply related to health: as the previous chapter delineated, recent concerns about the toxicity of lead were especially charged in terms of race, sexuality, ability, and nation.

Let us probe the affective dynamics of one example in detail, the paradoxical conceit of the now-popular phrase "toxic assets," associated with policies of financial deregulation in the United States that entered a new phase in the early 1990s. Notably, the toxic assets of significance that originated at that time and that are held responsible for global economic fallout are the financial products composed of grouped mortgages tied to a hypervalued and unstable residential real estate market. We might say that this complex financial product, this "toxic asset," is a "good" precisely because it entails capital value; yet it has unfortunately become — considering the discourse in which "toxic asset" has meaning — not only "toxic" but also perhaps "untouchable" (as an affective stance), "unengageable" (as tokens of exchange with limited commensurability), and perhaps even "disabling" (that is, it renders the corporation that buys it up also invalid). The term *toxic assets* thus reflects an effort to externalize — but also to indict for their threatening closeness (to home) — corrupt layers of financial organization.

These examples illustrate that there seems to be a basic semantic schema for toxicity: in this schema, two bodies are proximate; the first body, living or abstract, is under threat by the second; the second has the effect of poisoning, and altering, the first, causing a degree of damage, disability, or even death. In English, this adjectival meaning of *toxic* — of or related to poison, which means that a body or its blood could be harmed by an external agent — has endured since the 1600s, according to the OED, and it was concretized into the noun *toxin* in 1890; it is debatable when the metaphorical use emerged. If we are willing to assign "literal" to toxicity's application to the human body and "metaphoric" to all others, then these metaphorical mappings are not always very sound. Linnda Durre, author of *Surviving the Toxic Workplace*, identifies certain personalities as toxic; among them is one she dubs "The Delicate Flower": "If someone is sitting there constantly saying: 'You're wearing perfume. I'm going to have an allergy attack,' or: 'You're eating meat. That's so disgusting,' it's like grinding, grinding, whining, whining every day of your life."[8] Durre would rather expunge the workplace of such complaints; she fails to consider that the design of a workplace might well place certain people, including those susceptible to allergy attacks, at a radical disadvantage. If the definition of *toxin* has always been the outcome of political negotiation and a threshold value on a set of selected tests, its conditionality is no more true in medical discourse than in social discourse, in which one's definition of a toxic irritant coincides with habitual scapegoats of ableist, sexist, and racist systems. Toxicity's "first" (under threat) and "second" (threatening) bodies are thus in the eye of the beholder.

Faced with toxicity's broad and hungry reach, the contemporary culture of the United States is witnessing both the notional release and proliferation of the metaphor of toxicity, while also marking its biopolitical entrainment as an instrument of difference. While the first seems important for allowing a kind of associative theorizing, it is simultaneously important to retain a fine sensitivity to the vastly different sites in which toxicity involves itself in very different lived experiences (or deaths), for instance, a broker's relation to "toxic bonds" versus a farm worker's relation to pesticides. Furthermore, the deployment of the first can leave untouched—or even depend on—the naturalized logic of the second. Disability scholars have discussed the deployment of disability as a trope that ultimately reconsolidates ability; David Mitchell and Sharon Snyder have elucidated the idea of "narrative prosthesis," a kind of narrative deployment of disability that entrenches a kind of *ableist* idealization of privileged subject positions.[9] Indeed, we might argue that the workplace psychologist Linnda Durre is doing just that in her formulation of "The Delicate Flower." As Michael Davidson reminds us, we cannot consider the prosthesis only at the level of narrative trope, given the widespread problems around access to such essential medical devices; he writes, "sometimes a prosthesis is *still* a prosthesis."[10] Think about how often culture recruits languages of disability: "the corporation was crippled"; "don't use me as a crutch." The "toxic" people debated in self-help guides and pop songs should not be detached from an understanding of how toxins function in, and impair, actual bodies and systems. Furthermore, such "impairment," as some scholars and activists assert, should be understood as a societal production, and not (only or even) as a problem proper to an individual that must be cured or corrected.

Immunitary Fabric

All cultural productions of toxicity must be rethought as an integral part of the affective fabric of immunity nationalism. When immunity nationalism is individuated through biopower, in a culture of responsibility, self-care, anxious monitoring, and the like, toxicity becomes a predictable figure. The apprehension of a toxin relies minimally on two discourses: "science" and "the body." Science studies and feminist studies have worked to study and materially reground these two figures which often stand as both ontologically basal and hence unindictable. In *Bodies That Matter*, Judith Butler engages the biological insofar as she asks us to reconsider the discursive pinning of "sex" to biology and of "gender" to the realm of social and cultural life; but as she warns us, assigning originary status to "sex" or biology obfuscates gender's contribution to (and ontologizing of) sex; that is, both gender and sex "matter."[11] Rather than displacing the extant materiality of the body, she focuses on its partially ontologizing figurations. It is often hard to get a grip on what, precisely, "the body" is supposed to mean and what we ask it to do, and on how we demand of it so much symbolically, materially, and theoretically.

Questions of "the body" become particularly complex when taking into account the various mixings, hybridizations, and impurities that accompany contemporary bodily forms, from genetically modified food to the cyborg triumphed by Donna Haraway.[12] What, indeed, becomes of life now that Haraway's vision has in some regard prevailed? Though her "Manifesto for Cyborgs" is over twenty-five years old, it has proved eerily prescient in its view of the ever-seamless integration of machines, humans, animals, and structures of capital. Human bodies, those preeminent containers of life, are themselves pervaded by xenobiotic substances and nanotechnologies. Toxicity becomes significant now for reasons beyond the pressing environmental hazards that encroach into zones of privilege, beyond late-transnational capitalism doing violence to national integrities. Because of debates around abortion (such as those about when life is technically said to begin) and around the lifeliness or deathliness of those in "persistent vegetative states," not only can we not tell what is alive or dead, but the diagnostic *promise* of the categories of life and death is itself in crisis, not least when thinking through the "necropolitics" that Achille Mbembe proposes for postcolonial modes of analysis.[13] For when biopolitics builds itself upon "life" or "death" or even Agamben's "bare life"[14]—much like kinship notions that build only upon humans and hence fail to recognize integral presences of nonhuman animals—it risks missing its cosubstantiating contingencies in which not only the dead have died for life, but the inanimate and animate are both subject to the biopolitical hand.

Nan Enstad notes that toxicity forces us "to bridge the analytical polarization of global and local by placing the body in the picture" and to consider commodities in new ways in the context of global capitalism, for instance, "capitalism's remarkable success at infusing lives and bodies around the world with its products and by-products."[15] Yet, considering the reach of toxicity thinking described earlier, I would like to expand her fairly concrete take on "the body" (for all the discursive complication she admits) by suggesting that many bodies are subject to the toxic—even toxins themselves—and that it is worth examining the toxicities that seem to trouble more than human bodies. Indeed, it is one way for us to challenge the conceptual integrity of our notions of "the body." For biopolitical governance to remain effective, there must be porous or even co-constituting bonds between human individual bodies and the body of a nation, a state, and even a racial locus like "whiteness." This is especially salient within the complex political, legal, and medical developments of immunity.

For toxicity's coextant figure is immunity: to be more precise, *threatened immunity*. Immune systems are themselves constituted by the intertwinings of scientific, public, and political cultures together.[16] Even further, we know that the medicalized notion of immunity was derived from political brokerages. It is no surprise that discourses on sickness bleed from medical immunity discourse into nationalist rhetoric. Ed Cohen's *A Body Worth Defending* details the history of immunity as a legal concept, tracking its eventual adoption into medicine, a step that eventually enabled people to speak of immune systems with a singular possessive, as in "my immune system."[17] Cohen's historicization of immunity gives insight into the breadth of contemporary expressions of immunity and toxicity, and their many affects in relation to threat. Analyzing the period after this discursive migration, Emily Martin's anthropological study of twentieth-century immune systems, *Flexible Bodies*, details a twentieth-century shift in contemporary thinking about immunity to something private or personal—"maintained by internal processes"—away from a previous focus on public hygiene, in which immunity was seen as "related to unconnected factors from the outside."[18] This internalization, even privatization, of immunity helps to explain the particular indignation that toxicity evokes, since it is understood as an *unnaturally* external force that violates (rather than informs) an integral and bounded self. This is what Cohen calls the "apotheosis of the modern body," the abandonment of humans' integral relation to their environments and the insistence on a radical segregation of self and world fueled by a bellicose antagonism.

We can further consider the Italian political philosopher Ricardo Esposito's elucidation of the ways in which immunity seems to work as a kind of destructive "negative protection of life."[19] In Esposito's "immunizing paradigm," immunity is contracted on a "poisoned" affect of gratitude (on the basis of membership in a community) that undercuts the final possibility of individual immunity. Esposito identifies the shaky prescription of the introjection of the negative agent as a way to defend against its exterior identity. Intriguingly, through "poisoned" affect, or an affect of gratitude that is somehow fatally compromised, toxicity thus sneaks into Esposito's elaboration of immunity in the realm of affect rather than as a formal object; it is thus never fully addressed beyond the given questions of negativity in relation to immunity. This may not be surprising, as the history of immunity does not confirm that toxicity was there from the start. But if it was not there, then what was?

It could be productive, I think, to use this theorization of immunity to ask questions of the absence or presence of toxicity (both are here) as a means of approaching immunity, and particularly to take the consideration of "poisoned" affect and its compromise to individual immunity further. I suggest that toxicity incontrovertibly meddles with the relations of subject and object required for even the kind of contractual immunitary ordering that Esposito suggests. Thus, while the *threat* of toxicity is held to a clear subject-object relation, *intoxication* (of an object by a toxin) is never held to an advantageous "homeopathic" quantity (in light of the biopolitical interjection of negativity): indeed, this is the function of poisoned affect seen fully through. Not only is political immunity challenged, the very nature of this alteration cannot be fully known. Who is, after all, the subject here? What if the object, which is itself a subject, has been substantively and subjectively altered by the toxin? Could we tell a history of intoxication in relation to political immunity that sits next to Esposito's? There are clearly many more questions than answers here about the history of the political affect of immunity.

Toxic Worlding

Recall that matters of life and death have arguably underlain queer theory from the early 1990s, when radical queer activism in relation to AIDS blended saliently with academic theorizing on politics of gender and sexuality. More recently, Lee Edelman takes up a psychoanalytic analysis of queerness's figural deathly assignment in relation to a relentless "reproductive futurism."[20] Jasbir Puar points to life and death economies that place some queer subjects in the privileged realm of a biopolitically "optimized life," while other perverse subjects are consigned to the realm of death, as a "result of the successes of queer incorporation into the domains of consumer markets and social recognition in the post–civil rights, late twentieth century."[21] Similar affective pulses of surging lifeliness or morbid resignation might reflect the legacy of the deathly impact of AIDS in queer scholarship. Suggesting a "horizonal" imagining whose terms are pointedly not foretold by a pragmatic limitation on the present, José Esteban Muñoz in *Cruising Utopia* offers a way around the false promise of a neoliberal, homonormative utopia whose major concerns are limited to gay marriage and gay service in the military: lifely for a few, deathly for others.[22]

To enact a method that prioritizes a queer reach for toxicity's "worlding," I want to interleave considerations of toxicity and intoxication with a "toxic sensorium": a sense memory of objects and affects that was my felt orientation to the world when I was recently categorized as "ill." It seems never a simple matter to discuss toxicity, to objectify it. It is yet another matter to experience something that seems by one measure or another to be categorized as a toxin, to undergo intoxication, intoxification. This difference raises questions about toxic methodology, which in some way inherits anthropology's question about what can be done to respond to crises of objectivity. While no simple solution exists, it is my interest to attenuate the exceptionalisms that attain all too easily in, for instance, the previous chapter's assessment of lead toxicity's discursive range: it is possible for a reader to comfortably reside in a certain sense of integral, nontoxic security in that analysis.

To intensify toxicity's intuitive reach, I engage toxicity as a *condition*, one that is too complex to imagine as a property of one or another individual or group or something that could itself be so easily bounded. I would like to deemphasize the borders of the immune system and its concomitant attachments to "life" and "death," such that the immune system's aim is to realize and protect life. How can we think more broadly about synthesis and symbiosis, including toxic vapors, interspersals, intrinsic mixings, and alterations, favoring inter-absorption over corporeal exceptionalism? I will not address these questions from a point of view of mythic health. Rather, I will tell a tale from the perspective of the existence that I have recently claimed, one that has been quite accurately considered "toxic."

In other words, I move now from a theoretical discussion of meta-phors about threat into what feels, for me personally, like riskier terrain, the terrain of the autobiographical. As academics are often trained to avoid writing in anything resembling a confessional mode, such a turn is fraught with ambivalence. I theorize toxicity as it has profoundly impacted my own health, my own queerness, and my own ability to forge bonds, and in so doing, I offer a means to reapproach questions of animacy with a different lens. This theorization through the "personal" is not intended as a perfect subjectivity that opposes an idealized objectivity. Rather, it is meant as a complementary kind of knowledge production, one that in this context invites both the sympathetic ingestion (or intoxication) of what remains a marked ex-perience, and the empathetic memory of past association. It centers on a set of states and experiences that have been diagnosed as "mul-tiple chemical sensitivity" and "heavy metal poisoning," and can be used to think more deeply about this condition and what it offers to thinking about bodies and affect. As such, my repository of thoughts, experiences, and theorizations while ill—ones that queerly and pro-foundly changed my relationship to intimacy—could be considered a kind of "archive of feelings," to use Ann Cvetkovich's important ter-minology.[23] These are feelings that are neither exclusively traumatic, nor exclusively private, nor a social archive proper to certain groups: they are feelings whose publics and intimacies are not clearly bounded or determinable. Such feelings—and their intimacies—offer a way to come at normative affect's margins. Where Lauren Berlant notes, of less institutionalized interactions, that "intimacy names the enigma of this range of attachments . . . and it poses a question of scale that links the instability of individual lives to the trajectories of the collective," I mean to destabilize where the toxic and its affects can be located.[24]

I have for the last few years suffered from the effects of mercury toxicity, perhaps related to receiving for a decade in my childhood weekly allergy shots which were preserved with mercury, and having a mouth full of "metal" fillings which were composed of mercury amalgam. That said, I am not invested in tracing or even asserting a certain cause and effect of my intoxication, not least because such an endeavor would require its own science studies of Western medicine's ambivalent materialization of heavy metal intoxication as an identifiable health concern. Rather, I wish to chart such intoxications with and against sexuality, as both of these are treated as biologized and cultural forms with specific ethical politics. In early-twenty-first-century U.S. culture, queer subjects are in many ways treated as toxic assets, participating in the flow of capital as a new niche market, yet also threatening to dismantle marriage or infiltrate the military, and thus potentially damaging the very economic and moral stability of the nation. But what happens when queers become intoxicated? Recall the earlier secondary *Oxford English Dictionary* meanings of *queer* as both "unwell" and "drunk," the latter of which is now proclaimed to be obsolete; such meanings shadow queerness with the cast of both illness and inebriation. While Muñoz meditates on the possibilities of ecstasy—the drug—as a metaphor for pleasurable queer temporalities,[25] I explore an intoxication that is not voluntary, is potentially permanent, is ambivalent toward its own affective uptake, and produces an altered affect that may not register its own pleasure or negativity in recognizable terms.

Let me get specific and narrate what my "toxic" cognitive and bodily state means, how it limits, delimits, frames, and undoes. Today I am having a day of relative well-being and am eager to explore my neighborhood on foot; I have forgotten for the moment that I just don't go places "on foot," because the results can be catastrophic. Having moved to a new place, with the fresh and heady defamiliarization that comes with uprooting and replanting, my body has forgotten some of its belabored environmental repertoire, its micronarratives of movement and response, of engagement and return, of provocation and injury. It is for a moment free—in its scriptless version of its future—to return to former ways of inhabiting space when I was in better health. Some passenger cars whiz by; instinctively my body retracts and my corporeal-sensory vocabulary starts to kick back in. A few pedestrians cross my path, and before they near, I quickly assess whether they are likely (or might be the "kind of people") to wear perfumes or colognes or to be wearing sunscreen. I scan their heads for smoke puffs or pursed lips pre-release; I scan their hands for a long white object, even a stub. In an instant, quicker than I thought anything could reach my organs, my liver refuses to process these inhalations and screams hate, a hate whose intensity each time shocks me.

I am accustomed to this; the glancing scans kick in from habit whenever I am witnessing proximate human movement, and I have learned to prepare to be disappointed. This preparation for disappointment is something like the preparation for the feeling I would get as a young person when I looked, however glancingly, into the eyes of a racist passerby who expressed apparent disgust at my Asian off-gendered form. I imagined myself as the queer child who was simultaneously a walking piece of dirt from Chinatown. For the sake of survival, I now have a strategy of temporally displaced imaginations; if my future includes places and people, I pattern-match them to past experiences with chemically similar places and chemically similar people. I run through the script to see if it would result in continuity or discontinuity. This system of simultaneous conditionals and the time-space planning that results runs counter to my other practice for survival, an investment in a refusal of conditions for my existence, a rejection of a history of racial tuning and internalized vigilance.

To my relief, the pedestrians pass, uneventfully for my body. I realize then that I should have taken my chemical respirator with me. When I used to walk maskless with unsuspecting acquaintances, they had no idea that I was privately enacting my own bodily concert of breath-holding, speech, and movement; that while concentrating on the topic of conversation, I was also highly alert to our environment and still affecting full involvement by limiting movements of my head while I scanned. Sometimes I had no breath stored and had to scoot ahead to a clearer zone while explaining hastily "I can't do the smoke." Indeed, the grammatical responsibility is clear here: the apologetic emphasis is always on I-statements because there is more shame and implicature (the implicit demand for my interlocutor to do something about it) in "the smoke makes me sick," so I avoid it. Yet the individuated property-assignation of "I am highly sensitive" furthers the fiction of my dependence as against others' independence. The question then becomes which bodies can bear the fiction of independence and of uninterruptability.

I am, in fact, still seeking ways to effect a smile behind my mask: lightening my tone, cracking jokes, making small talk about the weather, or simply surging forward with whatever energy I have to connect with a person on loving terms. I did this recently when I had to go with a mask into Michael's crafts shop, full as it is of scents and glues and fiberboard. The register clerk was very sweet, very friendly, and to my relief did not consider the site of our intersubjectivity to be the two prominent chemical filter discs on either side of my mask. "Wearing the mask with love" is the same way I learned to deal with a rare racial appearance in my white-dominated hometown in the Midwest, or with what is read as a transnationally gendered ambiguity. It seems the result I receive in return is either love or hostility, and it is unpredictable. Suited up in both racial skin and chemical mask, I am perceived as a walking symbol of a contagious disease like SARS, and am often met with some form of repulsion; indeed, "SARS!" is what has been used to interpellate me in the streets.

As many thinkers have noted, the insinuation or revelation of a disability, particularly invisible disability, dovetails interestingly with issues of coming-out discourses of sexuality and passing. Both Ellen Samuels and Robert McRuer have discussed the ways in which "coming out" as disabled provocatively overlaps with, and also differs from, "coming out" as queer.[26] How does a mask help interrupt the notion of "passing"? How does it render as "damaged" (or, at least, vulnerable) a body that might otherwise seem healthy? Not wearing a chemical mask counts as a guise of passing, of the appearance of non-disability: I look "well" when I am maskless in public, at least until I crumple.

The use of the literal mask as an essential prosthesis for environmentally ill subjects is notable in light of Tobin Siebers's deployment of "masquerade" as an *exaggeration* of disability symbols to manage or intervene in social schemas about ability and disability.[27] This dialogic friction between *actual* mask as facial appurtenance—the mask's literal locus on the face—and mask or masquerade as a racial, non-disabled, or sexuality *metaphor* points to the central significance of face as intersubjective locus, and it exemplifies the expropriability of a facial notion of embattlement to the rest of the (human) body or to social spheres of interaction;[28] but it also points to the complexities that emerge when the actual facial signification of disability rubs up against the facial mask metaphor. Arguably, a chemical mask can serve as its own masquerade, but it also slips and slides into orthogonal significations. Its reading as *exaggeration*, in particular, competes with its reading as racializing and masculinizing toxic *threat*, where the skin of the mask ambivalently locates the threat on either side of it. The same ambivalence may be attributed to the "skins" of some toxic bodies, whereas the synecdochal attribution of toxicity applies either to the (rest of the) toxic body itself (the mask standing for the human SARS vector) or to an exterior, vulnerable body that renders it so (Fanon's "skin," which the "mask" covers, standing in for the colonial racialized visualities that render his blackness toxic to a white collective).[29] Is, then, the toxic body the disabled body? Or is the toxic body that collective body that biopolitically inoculates itself against a stronger toxin by affording itself homeopathic amounts of a "negative" toxin (disabled bodies) while remaining in a terrible tension with these negated entities?

Given my condition, I must constantly renegotiate, and recalibrate, my embodied experiences of intimacy, altered affect, and the porousness of the body. The nature of metal poisoning, accumulated over decades, is that any and every organ, including my brain, can bear damage. Because symptoms can reflect the toxicity of any organ, they form a laundry list that includes cognition, proprioception, emotion, agitation, muscle strength, tunnel perception, joint pain, and nocturnality. Metal-borne damage to the liver's detoxification pathways means that I cannot sustain many everyday toxins: once they enter, they recirculate rather than leave. I can sometimes become "autism-spectrum" in the sense that I cannot take too much stimulation, including touch, sound, or direct human engagement, including being unable to meet someone's gaze, needing repetitive, spastic movements to feel that my body is just barely in a tolerable state; and I can radically lose compassionate intuition, saying things that I feel are innocuous but are incredibly hurtful. The word *mercurial* means what it means—unstable and wildly unpredictable—because the mercury toxin has altered a self, has directly transformed an affective matrix: affect goes faster, affect goes hostile, goes toxic. Traditional psychology here, I suspect, can only be an overlay, a reading of what has already transformed the body; it cannot fully rely on its narratives.

Largely two quarters of the animated agents of the metropolis— that is, motor vehicles and pedestrians, but not the nonhuman animals or the insects—can be toxic to me because they are proximate instigators. The smokestacks, though they set the ambient tone of the environment, are of less immediate concern when I am surviving moment to moment. Efficiency is far from my aim; that would mean traversing the main streets. Because I must follow the moment-to-moment changes in quality of air to inhale something that won't hurt me, turning toward a thing or away from it correspondingly, humans are to a radical degree no longer the primary cursors of my physical inhabitation of space. Inanimate things take on a greater, holistic importance. It also means that I am perpetually itinerant, even when I have a goal; it means I will never walk in a straight line. There are also lessons here, reminders of interdependency, of softness, of fluidity, of receptivity, of immunity's fictivity and attachment's impermanence; life sustains even—or especially—in this kind of silence, this kind of pause, this dis-ability. The heart pumps blood; the mind, even when it says, "I can't think," has reflected where and how it *is*. Communion is possible in spite of, or even because of, this fact.

To conclude this narration of a day navigating my own particular hazards: I've made it back home and lie on the couch, and I won't be able to rise. My lover comes home and greets me; I grunt a facsimile of greeting in return, looking only in her general direction but not into her eyes. She comes near to offer comfort, putting her hand on my arm, and I flinch away; I can't look at her and hardly speak to her; I can't recall words when I do. She tolerates this because she understands very deeply how I am toxic. What is this relating? Distance in the home becomes the condition of these humans living together in this moment, humans who are geared not toward continuity or productivity or reproductivity but to stasis, to waiting, until it passes.

In such a toxic period, anyone or anything that I manage to feel any kind of connection with, whether it's my cat or a chair or a friend or a plant or a stranger or my partner, I think they are, and remember they are, all the same ontological thing. What happens to notions of animacy given this lack of distinction between "living" and "lifely" things? I am shocked when my lover doesn't remember what I told "her" about my phone earlier that day, when it was actually a customer service representative on a chat page, which once again brings an animating transitivity into play. And I am shocked when her body does not reflect that I have snuggled against it earlier, when the snuggling and comforting happened in the arms and back of my couch. What body am I now in the arms of? Have I performed the inexcusable: Have I treated my girlfriend like my couch? Or have I treated my couch like her, which fares only slightly better in the moral equations?

Or have I done neither such thing? After I recover, the conflation seems unbelievable. But it is only in the recovering of my human-directed sociality that the couch really becomes an unacceptable partner. This episode, which occurs again and again, forces me to rethink animacy, since I have encountered an intimacy that does not differentiate, is not dependent on a heartbeat. The couch and I are interabsorbent, inter-porous, and not only because the couch is made of mammalian skin. These are intimacies that are often ephemeral, and they are lively; and I wonder whether or how much they are really made of habit.

Animate Objects, Inanimate Subjects

By its very definition, the toxin, as much as it may have been catego-rized as inanimate, is more than mere matter, for it has a potency that can directly implicate the vulnerability of a living body. Prototypi-cally, a toxin requires an object against which its threat operates. This threatened object is an object whose defenses will be put to the test, in detection, in "fighting off," and finally in submission and absorption. But some confusion occurs when we note that the object of toxicity, its target, is an animate one—and hence potentially also a kind of sub-ject—and that the toxin, the subject of toxicity, is inanimate. Think-ing back to the linguistics of animacy hierarchies detailed in chapter 1, we note that in this case, various categories of assessment, particularly of worthiness to serve as agents or patients of verbs, tell opposing stories. In a schema of toxicity, likely subjects are equally likely ob-jects, despite their location in very different parts of the animacy hier-archy. In a scene of human intoxication, for toxins and their human hosts, the animacy criteria of lifeliness, subjectivity, and humanness (where the human wins) come up short against mobility and sentience (where the toxin wins). And this is before even considering what oc-curs in that moment and the ensuing "life" of intoxication; toxicity becomes us, we become the toxin. The mercurial, erethic, emotion-ally labile human moves toward quicksilver, becomes it. There is, in-deed, something "unworlding" that might be said to take place in the cultural production of toxic notions. A "normal" world's order is lost when, for instance, things that can harm you permanently are not even visible to the naked eye. Temporal orders become Moebius strips of identity: How could it do this to me? And yet in that instant, the "me" that speaks is not the "me" before I was affected by it.

Recent attention to inanimate objects, from Jennifer Terry's work on the love of inanimate objects such as the Eiffel Tower and the Berlin Wall to news coverage of men having serious emotional relationships with their dakimakura pillows, represents certain kinds of reversals of expectation regarding a kind of vitality that objects are afforded within human worlds.[30] Thinking beyond the rubric of fetishism, it is useful to build upon this work to ask questions of the subjects *facing* these objects and to consider how to mark their subjectivity as such or *why* we do so. Consider, for instance, the example of my couch, with which my relationality is made possible only to the degree that I am *not* in possession of human sociality. We might indeed let go of an attachment to the idea that social states or capacities are possessed by one animate entity and think rather in terms of transobjectivity.[31] Transobjectivity releases objectivity from at least some of its epistemological strictures and allows us to think in terms of multiple objects interspersed and in exchange. Stacy Alaimo's term *transcorporeality* suggests we think beyond the terms of the bodily unit and affirm the agencies of the matter that we live among.[32] The sentience of the couch, in our meeting and communing, then becomes my own sentience as well.

Nikolas Rose, in *The Politics of Life Itself*, has observed the impact of recent dramatic changes in the field of biology, particularly in the life-making capacities of genetics and the role of pharmaceuticals in vital self-management.[33] To Rose, these shifts constitute an epistemological and technical event, and he pronounced that contemporary biopolitics must now be considered *molecular* in character. This focus on molecularity is important when thinking about neurotoxicities, which I consider less a part of the spread of pharmaceutical self-management than a sign of the mediations we must now make about toxins between environmental "givens" (that toxins surround us) and self (that toxins are us).

In particular, what are the "affectations" or socialities attributed to toxicity, and what is the "affect" attaining between a toxin and its host? I consider two different senses of molecularity, one of which takes the notion of a particle at face value, the other of which leaves behind a strict biological or physical schema and considers a particle's affective involvement on radically different scales. I also want to make more explicit a relationship between xenophobia and xenobiotics; xenobiotics are substances understood to be not proper to the human body, that is, inherently alien to the body, whether or not they are recognized as such by it.

Both lead and mercury are chemically classified as metals. They are often further described as "heavy metals," a category whose chemical definition remains contested since "heavy" variously refers to atomic weight and molecular density. Heavy metal toxins have sites of entry, pathways of action, and multiple genres of biochemical-level and organ-specific reaction in the body. Lead and mercury are both classified as neurotoxic, which means that they can damage neurons in the brain. Sensory impairment correlated to mercury's neuronal damage, for instance, can include loss of proprioception, nystagmus (involuntary eye movement), and heightened sensitivity to touch or sounds. But their effectivity is potentially comprehensive: "Like most other toxic metals, lead and mercury exist as cations, and as such, can react with most ligands present in living cells. These include such common ligands as SH, phosphate, amino, and carboxyl. Thus they have the potential to inhibit enzymes, disrupt cell membranes, damage structural proteins, and affect the genetic code in nucleic acids. The very ubiquity of potential targets presents a great challenge to investigations on mechanisms of action."[34]

The ubiquity of potential targets further informs us that the transformation by a toxin and its companions can be so comprehensive that it renders their host somewhat unrecognizable. Furthermore, to state perhaps the obvious, research on contemporary toxicities—or indeed, to broaden our field of inquiry, on historical intoxication—confirms for us our experiences: that under certain conditions, some of them enduring or seemingly permanent, social beings can also become radically altered in their sociality, whether due to brain-specific damage or not. They are overcome, overwhelmed, overtaken by other substances. Although the body's interior could be described as becoming "damaged" by toxins, if we were willing to perform the radical act of releasing the definition of "organism" from its biological pinnings, we might from a more holistic perspective approach toxicity with a lens of mutualism.

The biologist Anton de Bary, who developed a theory of symbiosis in 1879, defined three types: commensalism, mutualism, and parasitism. Thinking of toxins as symbiotes—rather than, for instance, as parasites which seem only to feed off a generally integral being without fundamentally altering it (which would perhaps be our first guess)—not only captures some toxic affectivity but enables me to shift modes of approach. Ultimately, amounts—that is, scales—are inconsequential here; it is affectivity that matters, and the distinction between parasite and symbiosis is irrelevant. It is worth noting here that my thinking bears some resemblance to Deleuzian interspersal and symbiosis. Deleuze and Guattari write substantively about "molecularity" in relation to becoming-animal, referring to "particles" as belonging or not belonging to a molecule in relation to their proximity to one another; but such molecules are defined not by material qualities but rather more so as entities whose materiality is purposefully suspended.[35] Thus, they compare "verbal particles" to "food alimentary" particles that in a schizophrenic's actions enter into proximity with one another.

Deleuze and Guattari's thinking is useful in the sense that I attempt not only to accentuate proximal relations among categorically differentiated entities (across lines of animacy), but equally to emphasize the insistent segregations of "material" into intensified condensations (affective intensities) of race, geography, and capital. In this light, the toxicities tied to heavy metals function as a kind of "assemblage" of biology, affect, nationality, race, and chemistry. And yet, their analysis leaves little room for distinctions between "actual" and "abstract," particularly in their creative distinction between molecularity and molarity. Thus, I find it useful to hold on to a certain concrete materiality here, insofar as it offers a potentially critical purchase for thinking through queer relating and racialized transnational feeling, and further because mere metaphors, as we have seen, can sometimes overlook their own effectivity in literal fields.[36]

Queering Intimacy

There is a potency and intensity to two animate or inanimate bodies passing one another, bodies that have an exchange—a potentially queer exchange—that effectively risks the implantation of injury. The quality of the exchange may be at the molecular level, airborne molecules entering the breathing apparatus, molecules that may or may not have violent bodily effects; or the exchange may be visual, the meeting of eyes unleashing a series of pleasurable or unpleasurable bodily reactions, chill, pulse rush, adrenaline, heat, fear, tingling skin. The necessary condition for toxicity to be enlivened—proximity, or intimacy—means that queer theories are especially rich for thinking about the affects of toxicity. At the same time, queer theories can further benefit from the lessons of disability theory, particularly by rethinking its own others.

Thinking and feeling with toxicity invites us to revise, once again, the sociality that queer theory has in many ways made possible. As a relational notion, toxicity speaks productively to queer-utopian imagining and helps us revisit the question of how and where subject-object dispositions should be attributed to the relational queer figure. But even further, queer theory is an apt home for the consideration of toxicity, for I believe the two—queerness and toxicity—have an affinity. They truck with negativity, marginality, and subject-object confusions; they have, arguably, an affective intensity; they challenge heteronormative understandings of intimacy. Both have gotten under the skin. Yet queer theory's attachment to certain human bodies and other human objects elides from its view the queer socialities that certain other, nonhuman intimacies portend. What are the exceptionalisms that can haunt such theorizing?

Let us revisit the scene from the previous chapter of the child who inappropriately licks his lead-toxic painted train, the scene that is constantly conjured as one that must be avoided at all costs. The mobility of ingestible air and the nonemptiness of that air demonstrate that the act of lead licking is a fantasy of exception. It is not only a fantasy that not-licking is a viable way to contain heterosexuality in its bounds, but it is also a fantasy that not-licking is a viable way to contain the interconstitution of people and other people, or people and other objects. Look closely at your child's beloved, bright-red train: you may choose to expel it from your house, for the toxins that the sight of it only hints at; but you will pay the cost of his proper entrainment. What fingers have touched it to make it so? How will you choose to recover your formerly benign feelings about this train? Love has somehow to rise above the predetermined grammar of such encounters, for the grammar itself predicts only negative toxicity.

So how is it that so much of this toxic world, in the form of perfumes, cleaning products, body products, plastics, all laden with chemicals that damage us so sincerely, is encountered by so many of us as benign or only pleasurable? How is it, even more, that we are doing this, doing all this, to ourselves? And yet, even as the toxins themselves spread far and wide, such a "we" is a false unity. There is a relationship between productivity's queers (not reproductivity's queers, that is) and hidden, normative intoxications.

Those who find themselves on the underside of industrial "development" bear a disproportionate risk, as environmentalists and political economy scholars alike have shown.[37] In her article "Akwesasne: Mohawk Mother's Milk and PCBs," environmental justice activist Winona LaDuke describes a multipronged activist project led by the Mohawk midwife and environmentalist Katsi Cook.[38] Cook developed the "Mother's Milk" PCB-monitoring breast milk project, begun in 1984 and ongoing today, in response to the demonstrated toxic levels of PCBs on the Akwesasne reservation, which straddles the border between the United States and Canada and is located very close to a primary emitter of PCBs, a General Motors site established in 1957 which is now a Superfund site. This proximity—and GM's improper disposal practices—meant that both the St. Lawrence River and the Akwesasne wells, the sources of water on which the Mohawks relied, had toxic concentrations of PCBs. Indeed, Akwesasne is one of the most highly polluted Native American reservations.

Cook emphasizes strengthening women's health so that their critical role as the "first environment" of babies be taken seriously for existing and future bodily toxicity. These molecular intimacies—particles passed on via breast milk to babies—are implicated in regimes of gendered labor and care. Cook's activism connects the poisoning of the turtles to the fate of the Mohawks in a cosmology that reiterates the shared potency of live turtles and earthly support. Turtles are critically important in the Mohawk cosmology, which connects them to the earth itself; LaDuke mentions that North America is called "Turtle Island," which comes from a common Native American origin story. Such a cosmology does not depend, for instance, on the narrow ecology of edibles that informs mainstream U.S. food safety advocacy (wherein bigger animals eat smaller animals, a logic that articulates the threat of ocean fish to humans). It serves as a reminder that to the degree that mainstream animacy frameworks have become dominant law, such law could potentially be recodified if the animate orders on which it depends were interrupted. The interruptions demand recognizing the contradictions within matter itself—whether through accepting that worldviews (and their cosmologies) are legitimately contestable, especially in a time of problematization and retrenchment diagnosed as "posthuman," or through revitalized understandings of matter's own complexity that can cross the discursive boundaries of science.

Cosmologies, of course, are as much written into Western philosophies as they are in Akwesasne cultures, and the life and death hidden within their objects has a binding effect on their theoretical impulse. In her important book *Queer Phenomenology*, Sara Ahmed gives extensive, unabashed attention to tables, at one point writing extensively about her "orientation" (in a larger discussion of sexuality and orientations) toward a table of hers and that table's orientation toward her. She writes, "we perceive the object as an object, as something that 'has' integrity, and is 'in' space, only by haunting that very space; that is, by co-inhabiting space such that the boundary between the co-inhabitants of space does not hold. The skin connects as well as contains. . . . Orientations are tactile and they involve more than one skin surface; we, in approaching this or that table, are also approached by the table, which touches us when we touch it."[39] Ahmed works here with an important and profound assertion by Maurice Merleau-Ponty that sensory engagement binds sensing and sensed objects to one another; in this way, my skin is simultaneously the skin of the world. Yet, if we were to stretch this intercorporeality further, it appears that Ahmed still presumes the proper integrity of her body and of the table, an exclusion of molecular travel that permits her to position one thing against another. Ahmed is talking mainly about the *perception* of integrity; but I wonder what happens when percepts are to some degree bypassed, for instance, by the air itself. When physically copresent with others, I ingest them. There is nothing fanciful about this. I am ingesting their exhaled air, their sloughed skin, and the skin of the tables, chairs, and carpet of our shared room.

Ahmed's reading thus takes the deadness and inanimacy of that table as a reference point for the orientation of a life, one in which the table is moved according to the purposes and conveniences of its owner. And while it would be unfair to ask of her analysis something not proper to its devices, I do wonder how this analysis might change once the object distinctions between animate and inanimate collapse, when we move beyond the exclusionary zone made up of the perceptual operands of phenomenology. The affective relations I have with a couch are not made out of a predicted script and are received as no different from those with animate beings, which, depending on the perspective, is both their failing and their merit.

My question then becomes: What is lost when we hold tightly to that exceptionalism which says that couches are dead and we are live? For would not my nonproductivity, my nonhuman sociality, render me some *other* human's "dead," as certainly it has, in case after case of the denial of disabled existence, emotional life, sexuality, or subjectivity? And what is lost when we say that couches must be cathected differently from humans? Or when we say that only *certain* couches as they are used would deserve the attribution of a sexual fetish? These are only questions to which I have no ready answers, except to declare that those forms of exceptionalism no longer seem very reasonable. Indeed, the literary scholar John Plotz's careful review essay on new trends in materiality theories, "Can the Sofa Speak? A Look at Thing Theory," itself never arrives at confronting the possibility of the sofa's speech, seeming to presume that the question of sofas remains at the level of humorous titular play, no explanation needed.[40]

It seems that animacy and its affects are mediated not by whether you *are* a couch, a piece of metal, a human child, or an animal, but by how holistically you are interpreted and how dynamic you are perceived to be. Stones themselves move, change, degrade over time, but in ways that exceed human scales. Human "patients" get defined, via their companion technologies, as inanimate, even as they zip right by you in a manual wheelchair. And above and beyond these factors related to the power of interpretation and stereotype, there is the strict physicality of the elements that travel in, on, and through us, and sometimes stay. If we ingest each other's skin cells, as well as each other's skin creams, then animacy comes to appear as a category itself held in false containment, insofar as it portends exteriorized control relationships rather than mutual imbrications, even at the most material levels. Nancy Tuana, reading New Orleans after Hurricane Katrina in terms of interactionist ontology, writes, "There is a viscous porosity of flesh—my flesh and the flesh of the world. This porosity is a hinge through which we are of and in the world. I refer to it as viscous, for there are membranes that affect the interactions."[41] Furthermore, the toxicity of the queer to the heterosexual collective or individual body, the toxicity of the dirty subjects to the hygienic State, the toxicity of heavy metals to an individual body: none of these segregations perfectly succeeds even while it is believed with all effort and investment to be effective.

In perhaps its best versions, toxicity does not repel but propels queer loves, especially once we release it from exclusively human hosts, disproportionately inviting dis/ability, industrial labor, biological targets, and military vaccine recipients—inviting loss and its "losers" and trespassing containers of animacy. We need not assign the train-licking boy of the previous chapter so *surely* to the nihilistic underside of futurity or to his own termination, figurative or otherwise. I would be foolish to imagine that toxicity stands in for "utopia" given the explosion of resentful, despairing, painful, screamingly negative affects that surround toxicity. Nevertheless, I am reluctant to deny the queer productivity of toxins and toxicity, a productivity that extends beyond an enumerable set of addictive or pleasure-inducing substances, or to neglect (or, indeed, ask after) the pleasures, the loves, the rehabilitations, the affections, the assets that toxic conditions induce. Unlike viruses, toxins are not so very containable or quarantinable; they are better thought of as conditions with effects, bringing their own *affects* and animacies to bear on lives *and* nonlives. If we move beyond the painful "antisocial" effects to consider the sociality that is present there, we find in that sociality a reflection on extant socialities among us, the queer-inanimate social lives that exist beyond the fetish, beyond the animate, beyond the pure clash of human body sex.

Affective Futures

A chapter on mercurial affect would not be complete without some accounting for autism. While autism's etiology remains controversial, a significant number of accounts tie childhood autism to the neurotoxicity of environmental mercury, with much attention to vaccines.[42] (This is surely not true of all accounts. Some people, including Amanda M. Baggs, who appears later, explicitly disavow it.) Environmental mercury occurs in two forms, inorganic and organic (methyl) mercury. Much of the debate has occurred over whether the inorganic form of mercury is toxic to human bodies. Much of the noncontroversial, undebated alarm about mercury toxicity has focused on fish, which are not damaged by methyl mercury, even as they accumulate it; once ingested, methyl mercury is toxic to human beings. However, many have claimed that the inorganic form of mercury can be converted partially by the human body into the organic form. The classic developmental understanding of autism does not conform to the popular understanding of "mercuriality," most commonly associated with Minamata or "mad hatter's syndrome." Mercuriality focuses on adult responses to mercury intoxication, which by definition are not about child development. My invocation of autism in relation to "mercurial affect" here is not a closed one and is most certainly not a theory. It is a purposeful inclusion in a history that has yet to be told, and is hence, as I write today, to a certain degree experimental. The inclusion is part of my attempt to plumb the connections between toxic elements and toxic bodies; that is, bodies which are deemed "sick" are either seen as affected by toxic elements to the point of entering disability categories or are themselves considered a polluting scourge upon human normative securities.

To begin, I revisit a question I posed at the end of chapter 2: what are the possibilities of rejoinder, of response, for those considered nonsubjects or errant subjects? For it has not escaped me that there is an ironic, yet all too true, possibility of reading medicalization into the descriptive linguistics terminology for the components of actions. Verbal actions are described as being executed by *agents* and performed on *patients*. As a linguist, I can use this jargon with pleasure and the excitement of precision. Yet its use also sometimes hurts, because in conventional use, the noun *patient* refers to an object of Western medical treatment. The linguist Suzanne Fleischman writes that Western biomedical discourse on disease "tends to cast the sufferer in the role of a passive substrate, or medium, on which the more interesting player in the game, the disease, operates."[43] Hence, disabled and ill people, particularly given their medicalized locations in U.S. society, occupy a rather strict container and a subhuman locus on animacy hierarchies; that is, *other* humans "operate on" these ones. Here I examine not only the possibilities for simple rejoinder—being a subject of one's own expression—but for a challenge to the very animacy hierarchy, which is simultaneously an ontology of affect.

I turn first to perhaps the best-known spokesperson for autism, Temple Grandin, whose self-representation speaks to the animacy hierarchy in a very interesting way, for it is both rendered in first-person experience and explained using discourses of science. Grandin gained fame precisely through her accomplishments in animal welfare, including descriptions of how nonhuman animals think and feel, and her autobiographical accounts of living with autism. In an extraordinarily communicative book, and in interviews and other writings, Grandin expresses precisely the ambivalence reported by many people with autism and Asperger's regarding their "human" expressibility: that while she may communicate very well, this is a skill she has had to learn through unusual means, and that the most natural and consonant communication for her occurs with nonhuman animals (which, perhaps contrary to expectation, she calls simply *animals*).[44] Though she does not herself claim this, Grandin's work makes possible the insight that a turn toward nonhuman animals need not be considered itself an antisocial turn, and that people with autism need not be thought of as antisocial. Rather, Grandin traces a set of positive relations among autistic people and nonhuman animals.

Nor are all autistic people's claims merely about communalisms, kinship, or affection with nonhuman animals. A plethora of scholarship, expressive arts, and reported experience speak to a greater significance of inanimate objects than is normatively expected. The activist and writer Amanda M. Baggs has, as part of her work articulating a neurodiversity framework, made and circulated several videos in which she "translates" her experience of the world for a nonautistic viewership. In 2007, Baggs created a video titled "In My Language." The You-Tube video is accompanied with an explanation that the video's purpose is not to do a "look-at-the-autie peep gawking freakshow"—a constant risk for disabled people's self-expression—but a "statement about what gets considered thought, intelligence, personhood, language, and communication, and what does not."[45] The first part, Baggs annotates, is "in my language" and consists only of her vocal, touch, and hearing sense interactions with objects in the context of her apartment: metal chains, staplers, plastic Slinkies, door handles, dresser knobs, paper, books. The second part is a "translation, or at least an explanation," for English readers: overlaid on Baggs's interactions with more objects, lines of text appear on the screen that are simultaneously automated as computerized text-to-speech. (A dog often appears in the background.) Significantly for this chapter, the video represents to me an important juncture between expressibility commensurable with normative human language and expressed distance from that normativity. Baggs points out two critical ironies within mainstream beliefs that hinge attributions of personhood and proper sociality on material practices, specifically interactions with things:

Far from being purposeless / the way that I move / is an ongoing response to what is around me. / Ironically, the way that I move /

when responding to everything around me / is described as "being in a world of my own" / whereas if I interact with a much more limited set of responses / and only react to a much more limited part of my surroundings / people claim that I am / "opening up to true interaction with the world." . . . However the thinking of people like me / is only taken seriously / if we learn your language, / no matter how we previously thought or interacted. . . . It is not enough to look and listen / and taste and smell and feel, / I have to do those to the right things / such as look at books / and fail to do them to the wrong things / or else people doubt I am a thinking being / and since their definition of thought / defines their definition of personhood / so ridiculously much / they doubt that I am a real person as well.

Baggs thus very effectively reverses the given economies of language and affect. The transobjective tack is subtly suggested by the notion that her relationality with objects could be interrupted by an exclusive focus on human sociality, indeed that such relations might be somehow *enabled* by the absence of attention to human sociality. The lesson I take from this passage is that we would be well advised not simply to denounce Baggs's transobjectivity as problematic from some normative perspective, but rather to ask what it might mean of objects, what it might say of humanness and the ways it must push on the carefully guarded subjectivities proper to the human. Furthermore, to pathologize such object relationships out of hand would also be to pathologize a great many kinds of long-standing, but politically suppressed, cosmologies. These include the Potawatomi world-relating mentioned in chapter 1 and other cosmologies dubbed *indigenous* that are less characterized by a categorical, stringent attachment to human exclusivity.

Examining relationships between people with illness, or autism, and inanimate objects is not without its risks, for it can easily resemble—or be taken up as—a repathologization or a validation of pathologization. That is to say, while these relationships are important to recognize, they should not be unreflectively used to naturalize such people and objects to lower positions on hierarchalized animacy scales, while normative positions themselves are renaturalized to the top. For example, Licia Carlson observes that human intellectual disability is commonly brought up in arguments about speciesism and in general populates philosophical arguments about animals; thus, the intellectually disabled are unthinkingly used to populate "the face of the beast" in more than glancing terms.[46] My own belonging in this human-object field of recognition (as someone, for instance, whose illness brought me into renewed and vitalized intimacies with inanimate objects) does not shed me of responsibility for asking what it is I am doing, what is the status of my example, and how to move toward, not away from, justice in my use of an archive.

But I also draw—perhaps surprisingly—from the affective politics of Ann Cvetkovich's important work on lesbian cultures of trauma. Writing about therapeutic work on incest and its tendency to carefully disavow any possible relationship between incest and lesbianism, she asks, "But why can't saying that 'sexual abuse causes homosexuality' just as easily be based on the assumption that there's something right, rather than something wrong, with being lesbian or gay?"[47] I do not mean to conflate incest, queerness, or disability so much as to use this moment to think about the affective politics—within and without scholarship—of desiring the canonically undesired: desiring disability, desiring queerness, desiring objects. As Robert McRuer and Abby Wilkerson write, there is a special resistant sense of "desiring disability," unlike fetishizations of disability, that embraces "practices that would work to realize a world of multiple (desiring and desirable) corporealities interacting in nonexploitative ways."[48] Ultimately, Baggs makes desiring disability possible not only by articulating such relatedness through a visual modality that disidentifies with the gestural tropes of "severe disability," but by simultaneously releasing the hold of an ableist language fully dependent on strict animacy hierarchies that are assimilated and are reasonably legitimate only for a very specific set of people.[49] It is a crip-theoretical text.[50]

Tito Rajarshi Mukhopadhyay, a South Indian immigrant to the United States who has published poetry and narrative articulations of his autism experience from an early age, participates in this debate in a direct way. Among the objects taking importance in his learning world is a long mirror, with which he remains in dialogue. Later, he writes, "The curtains that moved in the wind, the big and small leaves that moved a little more with the air because of their suspended positions, the little bits of paper, or the pages of an open book under a fan were classified as autistic. They were affected with autism because they flapped, because they would not respond to any blocks, because they did not talk, and I was sure that they would not be able to imitate the clinical psychologist."[51]

Mukhopadhyay applies a status mobility to objects that might not otherwise be their province for a neurotypical thinker. It is not, Mukhopadhyay asserts, irrelevant to think that a curtain might be autistic too. The normative "violation" Mukhopadhyay commits is to refuse the animate locatability of autism toward those objects and to remember that it is only a *possibility*, not a given. Mukhopadhyay's writing simply disregards the sure pathologization of the transobjective worlds that some autisms engage. To loosen the pathologizing ties that bind normalcy to normalcy, or nonnormalcy to nonnormalcy, in human object worlds is to reassert the status mobilities of "humans," "animals," and "objects" in the many worlds they populate.

Let me say more about a particular object—a stone—as it has been encoded and applied to human sexualities. Within butch or femme lesbian culture, being "stone" or "stone butch" is a particular erotic and sexual formation. It does not suggest an outright lack of agency or power—as an animate hierarchy might predict—but a particular sexual economy of affect in which the butch's sexual pleasure can emerge from the touch instigated by her, whereas she prefers not to be touched by her lover. The stoneness of butch can also refer to the masculinities of expressive life for butches: feelings held in, the appearance of unfeeling. "Being stone" is thus not merely a queer affect; it also tugs at and traverses the animacy hierarchy's affective economy with regard to both feeling and touch.[52] "Stones in My Pockets, Stones in My Heart," Eli Clare's early discussion of trans and butch locations, sexual abuse, and the importance of telling troubled histories for movement politics, can be read as shadowed by the affective print of stone butch, offering us a relation between the feeling and being of butch into the material forms of stones: stones in the pocket warmed by Clare's hands, stones in the heart, stones lying together in an array.[53]

Clare wrote in this essay as a female-bodied person searching for places between butch and trans: "I turn my pockets and heart inside out, set the stones—quartz, obsidian, shale, agate, scoria, granite—along the scoured top of the wall I once lived behind, the wall I still use for refuge. They shine in the sun, some translucent to the light, others dense, solid, opaque. I lean my body into the big unbreakable expanse, tracing which stones need to melt, which will crack wide, geode to crystal, and which are content just as they are."[54] The stones are of Clare's heart (integral) and in Clare's pocket (exterior); Clare is and is not stone; Clare is and is of stone. Rather than considering the stones as simple structuring metaphor, we can read this piece as one about an intimate co-relation, one defined by both integrality and proximity, in which the stones—themselves multiple and variant, diversely opaque or translucent—also feel, need, shift, transform. Their draw to Clare, and Clare's engagement with them, complete a kind of environmental assemblage, of names, expression, subcultures, affects, prosthesis, material existence, and being.

It is simply wrong to say that, for instance, people with autism and stone butches—both of whom are popularly depicted as lacking emotion—are "affectless." Neither the untouchability that some people with autism possess (for instance, many people with autism describe it as an overwhelming surfeit of sensory information), nor the sexual untouchability of certain butch-identified women need be thought of as a construction of self in response to a historical trauma. Yet touching by others in spite of an orientation of not being touched can be experienced as traumatic. J. Jack Halberstam aptly points out that stone butchness is often wrongly popularly portrayed as a pathological state of femaleness, while men, for instance, who do not wish to be penetrated are simply viewed as normal.[55] Extending this point further, we might imagine that to the extent that sexual or abled identities rely on particular histories, those histories should not be so stably sutured to definitions of physical or sexual harm's own historicity. A definition of harm that is reliant on the possibility of present or imminent injury, rather than reliant on a vision of reiterations of past trauma that defines a person's pathology or disability, locates hurt, like Clare's stones, ambivalently: both inside and outside of the body, both inside and outside of the self, both in sociopolitical structure and in the individual instance.

But what is a toxic body, after all? How can we reconceptualize a harmful body when our bodies are themselves deemed harmful to others? It is useful here to turn to queer theory's uptake of the toxic, where it retained a certain resonance and a certain citational pull. Eve Sedgwick's use of *toxic* to describe an *expellable* interiority (one that shameful elements are not, since they are proper terms of one's identity) is taken up in Muñoz's *Disidentifications* to refer to discursively toxic elements, the "toxic force" of illicit desire, and images and stereotypes toxic to identity, all uses that seem to repeat Sedgwick's ultimately exterior, or alienated, quality of toxicity.[56] For Muñoz, disidentification represents the willing uptake of toxic elements to pose new figurations of identity and minoritarian-majoritarian politics.

Taking Muñoz's suggestions further, and taking toxicity's ontological shape-shifting from mercury to traumatic sociality seriously, I believe that we can, in a sense, claim toxicity as already "here," already a truth of nearly every body, and also as a biopolitically interested distribution (the deferral of toxic work to deprivileged or already "toxic subjects"). Such a distribution, in its failure to effectively segregate, leaks outside of its bounds to "return," and it might allow a queer theoretical move that readily embraces, rather than refuses in advance, heretofore unknown reflexes of raciality, gender, sexuality, (dis-)ability.[57] In assuming both individual and collective vulnerability, it suggests an ulterior ethical stance.[58] If we were to release toxicity from its own stalwart anti-ness, its ready definition as an unwelcome guest, it has the possibility to intervene into the binary between the segregated fields of "life" and "death," vitality and morbidity. Toxicity straddles boundaries of "life" and "nonlife," as well as the literal bounds of bodies (quite independently of toxicity's immunitary representation), in ways that introduce a certain complexity to the presumption of integrity of either lifely or deathly subjects.

Using the worldly ontologies described earlier, we might consider reframing the terms of intimacy itself, so that it might not be restricted to operating between only human or animate entities. *Intimacy* is, furthermore, temporalized, in the sense that it is cognate with *intimation*. Intimacy might be thought of as a temporalized notion insofar as it might provide a hint or prediction of the future. In these final paragraphs, I connect the "aberrant" socialities implicated within discourses of toxicity to those suggested in queer (political) futures. What futurity might such a present suggest, particularly if we read these futures back into politically sexualized and racialized maps of desirability and repulsion? Here I draw inspiration from the feminist disability theorist Alison Kafer, whose book theorizes a queer-crip approach to disability, one that, in its disentangling of the discourses of morbidity and sexual exile that contain and fix dis/abled bodies, refuses the "grim imagined futures" associated with them and moves toward a resolutely optimistic futurity.[59]

According to J. Jack Halberstam's *In a Queer Time and Place*, above and beyond the temporal closures and fissures wrought by (the U.S. advent of) AIDS, the queer life narrative necessarily has a trajectory very different from heterosexual, heteronormative, reproductive time.[60] Such a notion of queer time can be worked to emphasize its racial and gendered dimensions. On the "racial" dimension of time, or racialized temporality, David Eng has argued that it was Freud's attempt to negate the primitive that fundamentally motivated and underlaid his developmental narrative of sexuality, as well as his rendering of homosexuality.[61] The idea that ontogeny recapitulates phylogeny replicates itself teleologically in science and in public life alike, for instance, in the notion that child is to adult as primitive is to modern. Thus, the animalization of (queer) children cannot be divorced from the vote-bearing African American figure in the nineteenth-century *Harper's Weekly* cartoon considered in chapter 3. Interracial frameworks—whether human or animal or stone (which bears the mark of "nature")—are constantly haunted by the possibility of anachronism. Within global capitalism's racialized arrangements of labor, the racially marked body in the contemporary or modernist moment is a "freaky" subject of unacceptable temporal transit. It is not coincidental that in the United States the animality of childhood, in which a child represents an animalizable early evolutionary stage, is the only (marginally) acceptably queer one.

Thus, both queer and racial temporalities are a kind of shimmering presence. They are less easily bound to capital or to any other regimented time; or perhaps we could say that the time of capital is also no longer in the form it might have once been. And so queer and racially marked bodies are present (that is, in the present time) but *strangely* so, embracing anachronism and "touching the past" (to evoke the historian Carolyn Dinshaw).[62]

Heather Love suggests in her introduction to *Feeling Backward*, an exploration of literary texts that circle around queer suffering, that the contemporary juncture of affect studies and queer studies is attentive to the possibility that it is presently at a turning point, asking how to articulate or assume a queer political vision (within and beyond scholarship) that must do something with its history of shame, stigma, embarrassment, and pain. She describes this as "the emphasis on damage in queer studies."[63] Recent work has engaged a turn toward the embrace of acknowledgment of abjection as a site of work and healing in domains such as literature, the creative arts, and sexual practices, particularly in relation to queer of color proximities to racial abjection. Juana María Rodríguez theorizes the importance of politically incorrect desire, exercised in sexual fantasy, as one kind of utopic practice: she advises that "we must learn to read submission and service differently," even if—or as—we find ourselves occupying sexual positions written through with painful histories.[64] Indeed, the antipathy toward submission or service in and of itself does seem to collude too neatly with the autonomous urges of neoliberal culture, and would do well to think through the arguments for interdependence articulated within disability theory and activism.

Toxicity, at least in its mode of "intoxication," embraces the ambivalent, in Love's words, "abject/exalted" combination proper to queerness itself. (She even uses the words *damage* and *toxicity* to refer, as Muñoz and Sedgwick do, to the stigmatization of queerness and the painful affects associated with the recuperation of historical texts that represent "tear-soaked accounts of same-sex desire.")[65] Negativity and death, of course, also attach to disabled bodies with terrible regularity, and they appear in different valences. But affective nuances are informative. Ato Quayson's literary study *Aesthetic Nervousness: Disability and the Crisis of Representation* focuses on doubt: he traces a notion of "skeptical interlocution" through a number of literary works, suggesting that "there is always an anticipation of doubt within the perceptual and imagined horizon of the disabled character in literature, and that this doubt is incorporated into their representation."[66] Quayson's study suggests a complication of sociality by a negating affect.

In view of the attempts of these works to suggest a future politics, or the recommendations for politics that might be extracted from them, toxic affect is certainly not suggested as a panacea. It is a (re-)solution to the question of what to do with the ambivalence of queerness only to the extent that it does not represent a choice: it is *already here*, it is not a matter of queer political agency so much as a queered political state of the present. If toxicity is ambivalently constructed by a barely tenable political community, that fragility is not acknowledged. Nevertheless, an uptake, rather than a denial of, toxicity seems to have the power to turn a lens on the anxieties that produce it and allow for a queer knowledge production that gives some means for structural remedy while not abandoning a claim to being just a little bit "off." The growing acknowledgment of a shared condition of toxicity within the United States—not only in terms of citing numbers of toxins present in people's bodies, toxins whose hospitality toward the body is uncertain (or toward whom the body doesn't know whether it should be hospitable), but also in terms of the resigned acknowledgment that toxic assets were part of the fabric of U.S. capitalism—is not just evidence of a fall, or a radical shifting of political and economic fortunes. It is also evidence that the interstices of the otherwise suffocating cultures of neoliberalism may be engaged, productive, and immensely meaningful.

Thus, toxicity, as a queer thing or affect, both is and is more than horizon, which is unpredictable and, furthermore, synchronically traceable only to the extent that we not remain ontologically faithful. Toxicity fails over and again to privilege rationality's favorite partner, the *human* subject, rather defaulting to chairs, couches, and other sexual orientations, but we might be wrong to disavow its claim to rationality altogether. If we let affect fall to object life, or to the interanimation that surrounds us, one example of which toxicity illuminates very precisely, then perhaps there is a chance to take up (not revive, as it is far from "old and tired") *queer* as something both like itself and yet also entirely different.

The Spill and the Sea

On September 19, 2010, the oil well in the Macondo Prospect region of the Gulf of Mexico—which had ruptured five months earlier, on April 20, spilling an estimated two hundred million barrels of oil into the Gulf—was finally declared to be sealed. This closure led to a wave of relief that the threat had somehow been contained, and that further pollution of the Gulf would no longer occur (at least not at such an uncontrollable pace). The next day, the spill's National Incident Commander, Thad Allen, acknowledged in an interview that "we're actually negotiating how clean is clean," going on to explain that this phrase was "a euphemism we use at the end of an oil spill to say, is there anything else we can do? And, sometimes, there will still be oil there, but then the agreement is that there can be no more technical means applied to it, and we're all going to agree that this one is done as far as what we can do."[1]

Allen concluded the interview with a lively mixture of metaphors: both immediate "cleanup" and long-term "recovery" should be the goal; the residents of the coast have had "a lot of stuff laid at their door" and they "have a way of life that has been threatened down there." It was unclear whether "recovery" meant the health of the Gulf or the economic well-being of the human residents of the Gulf, but clearly some kind of affliction was implied. Of course, metaphors of health and treatment have a peculiar history in national economic discourses; consider the phrase *shock therapy* (commonly associated with the economist Jeffrey Sachs) used to describe a radical economic reform in the direction of free markets, deregulation, and public disinvestment.[2]

More often than not, articulations of the oil's danger, or the oil dispersant's toxicity (untested at such quantities), to sea creatures were made not for their sake but for the purpose of identifying a risk to an economic source of "livelihood" for the human professional residents of the U.S. Gulf shores, the fishermen and fisherwomen and the economy built around them. Many of the fishermen and -women (though it is unclear how many, and it is hard to disentangle such language from locally controlled BP media interests) were content to rely on their symbiotic relationship to their local environment, using cash payments and barter systems, and did not see fit to record and report income to the IRS tax system, habits of nonengagement which imperiled their future compensation by BP. In interviews with those workers, however, the distinction between "sources of revenue" and "living beings" was often blurred; their expressed pain did not appear to distinguish between the lost generations of shrimp and their own generativity of income.

The well was one of a newer generation of offshore deep-ocean wells, part of an adventurous effort by state governments and corporations to control heretofore inaccessible domestic resources by supporting deep-sea oil drilling offshore at ever-greater depths. When the well "blew," Allen acknowledged that containment efforts at such depths were "unprecedented," raising questions about what kinds of design principles and fail-safe procedures had been pursued in the case of the newer deep-well ventures. The politics of ownership of the well and its products and the responsibility for the spill's casualties are extremely complex, as with virtually any transnational projects involving property. While the Macondo well itself is owned by BP, the Exclusive Economic Zone where the Macondo Prospect was located is a geocapital entity that extends spatially into waters defined as "international" while retaining U.S. control over marine resources.[3] Additionally, BP was working with a leased drilling rig, the Deepwater Horizon, as well as subcontracting with Halliburton Energy Services, which was responsible for establishing the seal over the well. Under BP's directive, the seal process was hastened and security measures were reduced (some against Halliburton's recommendations). Due to an inappropriate seal, methane gas escaped and flew up the drill column, exploding upon its rapid expansion into the ship. A faulty blow-out preventer failed to cut off the gushing oil that ensued, at the level of an estimated tens of thousands of barrels a day.

Leading up to and following the sealing of the well on September 19, 2010, the news media stuck with extreme regularity to a number of phrases referring to the state of the well: "killed," "killed for good," "dead," "effectively dead," and even "permanently dead." Such deathly—and lifely—language was summoned to refer to a situation that was much more complicated and only raised further questions. To what degree was such language strategically used to motivate a wave of transformed affect of relief or newfound security across the United States and beyond, a wave of assurance that the monster had been vanquished?[4] How and in what sense was the well ever *alive*? Was the well conceivable, in strictly biological terms, as a single living unit? As the well is a general vessel for pools of oil, the burden of living proof then falls on the oil; hydrocarbons, oil's primary constituent, thus continue to comprise the matter of contemporary industrialized energy.

The well's excessive porosity, mainly in the form of a single leaching point, was used to deem its sudden *lifeliness*; indeed, the very fact that it was not generally containable rendered it alive, when common conceptions of the living body are that it is generally a contained unit. But if we accept this definition of "alive," then how "dead" was the well upon being sealed? In human cases, physicians declare death under certain precise neural conditions (generally the irreversible ceasing of all brain function), often while certain tissues and organs are still biologically valid. The preoccupation among media and among government and BP representatives with declaring the well "dead" is remarkable. Slippages occur, however, in the category of "dead": even though "effectively dead," the well had not yet been subjected to "plugging and abandonment," in the words of Allen, suggesting that irreversible containment needed to be complemented with a withdrawal of vital engagement.

Working with Allen's articulations of the closing process, we could say that the conceptions animated in the closure of this human-led natural disaster were, on the one hand, life and death and, on the other hand, dirtiness and cleanliness, where "dirtiness" was paired with "death" and "cleanliness" with "life." The pure animation of the oil—until some of it evaporated, and some of it settled, and some of it got consumed by the "naturally occurring" bacteria in the Gulf—

was dramatized and literalized by video coverage of the spewing drill pipe in the water. Its animacy, spectacular to the degree that it dramatized the uncontrollable shifting or transformation of matter at scales that dwarf and overwhelm human bodies, resembled other "natural disasters" like tornadoes, whose rapid shifting of matter occurs in the air rather than in the water, and even monster and horror movies such as *Godzilla* or *Twister*, whose horrific elements operate similarly as a threat of uncontrollable scale.

Visual and affective politics, and decisions thereof, surrounded the spill and its aftereffects at multiple levels. The people hired to clean up the surface oil included local fishermen in need of replacement income and so-called disaster migrants, largely made up of Latinos who relocate to work at changing disaster sites. We learned, in a few quietly released news stories, that initially the cleanup workers were not only not provided protective respirators but actively forbidden from wearing protective equipment, as reported in at least a few cases. While BP restricted news reporters from being anywhere in the area and should therefore theoretically have been safe from image-based indictment, it still desired any images of the cleanup to show humans free of apparent threat. (For reasons unknown, I was unsuccessful in obtaining permission from BP's Video Department for the publication of before and after—"alive" and "dead"—images of the Macondo well.) For BP, whatever threat existed seemed to be divided into two irreconcilable domains: any threat to the "environment" was to the aesthetic preservation of the shore, and any threat to "humans" was only economic (that is, the reproductive cycles of some Gulf seafood, the fishing that they depended on for income, might possibly be interrupted). The notion of toxicity, which would have connected these stories, was largely bypassed in favor of the cleavage of these narratives.

Still, clashing layers of disease discourse piled up on one another: the oil that "contaminated" the landscape had to be cleaned up by human workers, and a further contaminant was represented by the dispersants themselves. Human cleanup workers on the surface were being subjected to toxic exposures while "protecting" the contaminated environment. BP's attitude was that the mere viewing of safety equipment, presumably across the nation, could lead to mass "hysteria," an unacceptable gendering of a nation already on the (bio-) defense. It is no surprise, somehow, that "dead" and "killed" were recruited to perform a kind of cognitive blanket to augment BP's apparent power, control, and masculine righteousness over all forms of matter.

At bottom, the overbearing use of *dead* and *killed* functioned as an admission that a toxic spill was a *lifely* thing: lifely, perhaps, beyond its proper bounds. The well itself was alive, and not only because something had flowed out of it with such vivid animation. It was a threat *to* life in the Gulf, as well as to a *way* of life. This occlusion of life over marginal life speaks, as I see it, to the inadequacy of lifely notions as a framework for governance, medicine, and vernacular affect and makes room for a concept like animacy, which encodes forces without being beholden to the failing categories of life and nonlife. As I have argued in this book, animacy permits an even more thorough registration of the role of racial, geopolitical, affective, and sexualized politics therein.

This is one vision of a contemporary biopolitical "ending": the plugged Gulf well, good and dead, no longer a threat to a vulnerable sea. But I do not wish to end here, for the lessons of the Gulf spill feel disingenuous, particularly in a book that has been very much about places and sources of unexpected life. So let us also consider the inhabitants of Hayao Miyazaki's animated film *Ponyo*, released in 2008, which is, like the BP oil spill catastrophe, a land-water drama, though one revealingly designed as a dreamscape in which "the ocean is a living presence."[5] The titular character, Ponyo, is a little fish (ambiguously raced) who desires to become a human and has strong affective ties to a little boy, Setsuke. She is not alone: she has a father, a kind of magician of the ocean who tends to its health by summoning potions which move and transform ocean matter, living or dead; a mother-goddess who seems almost metaphysical in form, but who makes occasional human-size departures; and a whole lot of little sisters who resemble her fish form, but are smaller in size, literally her "little sisters" (figure 19). They are her comfort and support when she is in the ocean. And this sea, as Miyazaki comments, "is animated not as a backdrop to the story, but as one of its principal characters."[6] Animation here works in multiple ways: both conjuring animacy and referring to the illustrated style and fantastical figuration of the film itself.

In Miyazaki's visual narrative, however, the distinction between land and sea is blurred: indeed, it is hardly a hostile relationship or, as in the case of the BP spill, an economic one primarily. The border between land and sea simply shifts upward in the wake of a tsunami-

19. Ponyo's little sisters. *Ponyo* (dir. Hayao Miyazaki, 2008).

induced flood. Miraculously, despite the flood, death seems not what is at stake ("terror" and "contagion" is displaced by "magic," perhaps?), and the anxieties that exist are based on a disparate bunch of concerns, including electricity, protection for the elderly residents of the retirement home, and Setsuke's father being lost at sea. Ultimately, no one is killed; the big fish simply swim along what were formerly roads for automobiles; Setsuke's house remains above water; and the humans have simply remained buoyant, in boats, on the surface. Ponyo's little sisters are the ulterior oil plumes, animated little particles that have shared feelings. Collectively, they are affective matter.

I am reminded here of J. Jack Halberstam's work on animated movies featuring bees. Halberstam observes that animation films which center on bees display alternative political organizations despite not going so far as to observe, for instance, the matriarchal aspect of bee societies. That is, there are moments when more exact investigation of lived animal formations is generative. Halberstam nicely assumes this appropriability of reference not as a means of restoring final honesty to a signifier, but as a means toward political ends, suggesting that if mainstream animation filmmakers did study the lives of actual bees, bee fiction might do better than its currently middling job at representing a kind of feminist or otherwise progressive politics.[7] The case of Ponyo's little sisters presents an alternative political organization of a hybrid posthuman-goddess-fish family which, in Miyazaki's configuration, is matriarchally structured and, unlike what human procreation predicts, involves a set of hundreds and hundreds of siblings, siblings that are not necessarily the less-autonomous "little sister" deserving of protection.

Miyazaki's Studio Ghibli is known for being judicious about when it takes advantage of the convenience of computer-generated imagery (CGI) technologies, which Halberstam has observed is technology's latest imaginative feat in the representability of enormous collectivities ("hordes") and their accompanying political formations within animation. Ponyo's many little sisters, even if they were so numerous as to make up a "horde," were thus not multiply generated copies of a replicated single sister, launched at different points in her repeating dynamic smiling, speaking, and fluttering actions to induce the perception of difference and individuation. Rather, the supervising animator of the film, Katsuya Kondo, explained:

> It wasn't enough just to have a lot of sisters onscreen. Each sister needed to move as an individual character. The scene in which the sisters rescue the half-fish, half-human Ponyo was divided into three stages—beginning, middle, and end—and the assistant animators drew each sister carefully. We didn't use any copies or CG, of course, because everything was drawn by hand this time. While the work was painstaking, it was easier to create the movements of an ensemble by hand than by CG, and we took on this task because we wanted to render those movements to our hearts' content.[8]

The technicality of Kondo's focus on mobility did not mitigate its sweetness to me, for the sisters were "painstakingly" given life one by one to the animators' "hearts' content." The "animation" of Ponyo was enriched by the multiple factors of animacy: sentience, movement, faciality, speech, and action upon something else—as well as the many imaginative animations dreamed up by each creator for which the final embodiment of a single sister was the culmination. Animation is thus the end point of the setting-off of many different animacies; its careful consolidation of these animacies, particularly in the case of Ponyo, is what sets it apart.

In her attempt to transmogrify into a human, Ponyo enters intermediary stages where she sprouts chicken legs (figure 20). She experiences her greatest exhilaration and exuberance at that in-between juncture: that chickenlike embodied site of interstitial land-water and fish-human, rather than a site of confusing or distressing liminality,

20. Ponyo sprouts chicken legs. *Ponyo* (dir. Hayao Miyazaki, 2008).

yields an intensity easily read to viewers as pleasure. For Ponyo, the promise of humanness exists in spite of all that humans have done.

The fish/chicken/little girl is far from a binary logic; she is a blending that is partial and contingent and enacted across time, yet the blending is simultaneously robust and profound, effective and affective. Both air and seawater are the stuff of blends, the stuff of human, animal, and godly mattering. If lungs no longer critically matter for breathing, then the material difference between air and water also dissolves. The air-seawater is also the stuff of sex, of the sensuous, sensible exchange of breath, fluids, and parts; of meetings and interpenetrations which may be "actual" or "virtual," within which we need feel no particular responsibility to any exceptional organs; of reproduction, of penetration, of reception, of animacy itself.

Still, "the real world in which matter matters most" inevitably haunts even this promise of gratifying transmogrification. For all its fictive identity as the ostensible setting of an animation film, the "Japan" that quietly informs the villages, personalities, languages, and socialities of Ponyo, as I write in spring 2011, too easily comes up against the Japan that was devastated—in an overwhelming way in Fukushima, Miyagi, and Iwate prefectures, as well as economically and affectively in its national ensemble—by an earthquake-instigated tsunami ranging from eight to twenty meters high on March 11, 2011. The tsunami, engulfing smaller towns in the north of Japan that largely engaged in farming and fishing, disproportionately killed and displaced the elderly, putting into aching relief Miyazaki's rehabilitative image of elderly Japanese who have been submerged by a tsunami cavorting at the bottom of the ocean (to their surprise).

Yet to construe this contemporary and actual tsunami-radiation compound event exclusively in ready terms of failure, loss, and death risks a certain narrowing of imagination (surely justified for many closest to these events) that relies on the dubious construct of "natural disaster" and necessarily prioritizes economy, humans, locality, and national security. Once this kind of narrative is launched, it has only a narrow path that leads to blaming either "the Japanese," or the bad disaster preparation, or the nuclear industry, or energy dependence, or something else; perhaps there is even a quieter rejoicing at the apparent failure of Japanese industrialism's grasp on modernity, for all its recent decades of challenge to the United States's tale of economic dominance. In the opening song to Ponyo, "Umi no Okasan" (Mother sea), the lyrics sing of lost unity and beckon a return to the family of countless siblings:

The sea lilies sway
In a world of blue
To brothers and sisters uncountable
We spoke in the bubbly, watery language of the sea
Do you remember when
So very, very long ago
We dwelt there together
Deep in the blue, blue sea?
The jellyfish, the sea urchins, the fish and the crabs
Were our family.[9]

The ending scenes of the film execute this new possible kinship between land and sea with the long-desired transmogrification of Ponyo into a human (albeit one who has a memory of being a fish) and the compacting of this transition by an agreement between a human (Sosuke), who agrees to care for her, and Ponyo's mother who commands the sea and makes the transition so. The antinomic controlling magic of Ponyo's waterborne father Fujimoto (an "exhuman"), which allows him to transform and animate (and imprison) all kinds of matter, has been attenuated; in its place, we viewers have been transformed into such magicians of imaginary and imaginative possibility by our very witnessing of the transmogrifications that populate this animation film and the gratitude and affection that attends the new unities.

Memory here seems to be both the foundation of togetherness and the target of extinction: Fujimoto's "exhumanness" shifts from its substantive status as a toxic trace in his management of his world to a feckless trace barred from boundary-enforcing potency. At the same time, the memory that constitutes the longing opening song permeates the film: a longing for remembered togetherness can bring about that worldly interanimation which yields the possibility of new relations as well as beloved possibilities. Such contradictory tropes of time provide us with anachronisms not constrained by progressivist "healing," appropriative or recuperative phylogenetic racial longing, but rather by a queer "temporal drag," or the "pull of the past upon the present" (to use Elizabeth Freeman's words), that retains a critical ambivalence about where, what, and who we are.[10]

Following the ocean has its lessons, too, and does not necessitate a well-articulated cosmology like Miyazaki's. Nor is it necessary to simply *reverse* the affective response to either delight or numbness, only to attempt to keep labile the affective economies that necessarily subtend modern life, especially in late capitalism when one is considering something like a "natural disaster." "Following the ocean," beyond the histories that oceans keep and the transterritorial human epistemologies they provoke, helps us scramble and interrupt the animacies that are both known and felt at the linguistic level, akin but not limited to the paradigmatic plays of Derrida and the associative games of Gertrude Stein, moving beyond streams of consciousness to the affectively orthogonal disregard for the deeply vested intricacies of "standardness" characteristic of English as a second language.[11] And beyond language, it helps us consider the minor, subtle, boundary-leaping memory traces that intoxications leave with us.

Though I began with language in this book, nowhere did I depend upon a dry vision of resignification; rather, I remained attached to a feeling for affect that subtends, exceeds, richly accompanies such otherwise mechanistic understandings of words, animals, and metals. It was against my own expectation for this book that I went back to my roots in linguistics. My explicit return began when I became quite attached to thinking about mobility (for instance, asking to what degree cosmopolitanism played in the uptake of queer theory's transnational objects, or asking after mobility's connection to abled embodiment). I came to the understanding that different mobilities meant very different things, and that the differences often had something to do with the animacy of the mobile or immobile object. I realized that what might seem a stale debate about *queer*'s seemingly mobile meaning and effectivity could still be richly informed from the perspective of cognitive semantics. If any word's meaning could shift and flex according to its users, what was so special about the senses of *queer*?

While I could not, from this limited perspective, settle the debate of whether *queer* was finally and universally special, I did attempt to explain the reasons why it might be considered special by some. It came down to *queer*'s status as either matterlike (a noun) or something that affected, modified, the meaning, the very materiality, of other things (an adjective, verb, adverb). I began to realize that queerness had everything to do with animacy: it was an operator that shiftily navigated gradations of matter, including things, actions, and sensibilities. At the same moment, I took seriously the lessons of feminist, antiracist, and political-economic assertions that privilege had became solidified into a lexeme that otherwise got a lot of credit for being unfixable.

Privilege has ultimately played multiple roles in this book. For I attended, in some ways disproportionately, to the crafting of worldly matter by privileged beings. Animate hierarchies have settled into their current life as a palimpsest of a long journey through Aristotelian categorizations, Christian great chains of being, Linnaean typologies, biopolitical governances, capitalisms, and historical imperialisms; these are the traces and marks of privileged views upon the world. To the extent these hierarchies have been used to enact zones of deferral, they have produced extraordinary fungibilities of entities in the realms that lie below the white male at the top, the kinds of exchange of matter that allow humans to "be" animals to "be" inanimate objects, while that equally fungible zone of highest privilege has remained largely backgrounded. This is not to say, however, that only the privileged take up these perspectives on the matter around us. For their logics are written into the textures of this world, and our enmeshment within it bespeaks our vexed and often painful complicity. Those of us who can suitably duck them could be said perhaps to access the counterprivileges of biopolitical irrelevance.

Furthermore, my own location with regard to privilege is not lost on me. As much as I track the empire's traces, indelible marks, regurgitations, phobias, and abandonments—as much as I occupied a place of social toxicity by the genderings and transgenderings, dis- ablements, and racializations that have befallen and become me—I, too, write from the seat and time of empire. I have not forgotten Jacqui Alexander's prompt ever since I heard it: what can we do as intellectuals within and without academies from the seat of empire, particularly to encounter the problem of the "here and now" ver- sus the "then and there" that colonial and imperial time naturalize?[12] The concept of animacy has functioned for me in this book as one of many diverse and multimodal attempts to reach across this compacted condensation of time-space, always with the awareness that there is so much more to do and to imagine. With an eclectic traversal of ob- jects and affects, this book tracked both the paradoxical naturaliza- tions of animacy hierarchies (for instance, in the form of racialized animal anachronisms) and the rejoinders launched by contemporary animacies (unintended reimaginations of kinship and intense intima- cies), only some of which remain in a human domain of disidentifi- cation. Some animacies remained quite corrupt; others seemed par- ticularly enlivened by a capacity to romp through, under, and over such hierarchical knowledges. Finally, I claim the "eclectic," perhaps reflexively, while remaining keenly aware of its role as a disclaimer for exceedingly, rudely feral transdisciplinarity. My archive of apes, theo- ries, turtles, sensoria, cartoons, mercury particles, airborne skin, signi- fying lexemes, and racialized humans has seemed entirely logical that is, to *me*; yet the label of "eclecticism" rings true, in my view, from a perspective that is wedded to institutional typologies of intellectual reference and styles of thinking. At the same time, animate affinities *do* bring these bodies together, and that, whether delivered under the protective bandage of "eclectic," has ultimately been my point.

Animacy hierarchies slip and give, but they do not do so willy-nilly: I have suggested that they slip in particular privileged terms of sexu- ality, race, and ability, perhaps in part because these are the fragile grounds upon which they have been built in popular ontologies and political cultures in the United States: race because the formation of animal and animality has been enriched by colonial histories; sexuality because the discussions of kind, genre, production, and reproduction with regard to such an ontology inevitably call forth concerns of sexu- ality broadly conceived; ability because the human body and subject have resolutely been imagined as able-bodied, in a god's image. My conviction that hierarchies are contingent and mobile lies in my sense that their rigidity must be promulgated and not simply rest in truth. Not only, for instance, might stones be multivalent, as both building materials and divine representants in some aspects of Inkan or Japanese cultures,[13] but they are, despite their mainstream representation as dead and inanimate, dynamic and even moving, changing and shifting at a time scale that seems to outrun human life spans (if we ignore that human bodies themselves are capable of making calcium deposits that are, for all practical purposes, stones) and that lies beyond the narrower time cycles of capitalism. What might it be to take stones as "more than a thing to ignore"?[14]

I take inspiration here from the artist, disability rights activist, and animal rights advocate Sunaura Taylor, who writes: "In my life I have been compared to many animals. I have been told I walk like a monkey, eat like a dog, have hands like a lobster, and generally resemble a chicken or penguin. . . . The thing is, they were right. I do resemble a monkey when I walk—or rather I resemble an ape, specifically a chimpanzee. . . . This resemblance is simply true, as is the statement I eat 'like a dog' when I don't use my hands and utensils to eat. These comparisons have an element of truth that isn't negative—or, I should say that doesn't have to be negative."[15] Taylor uses the recognition of this likeness—we might say a being-like—as a basis for a revised ethics. Such radical thingness as stoneness, I insist, can be visited, can be felt, and can have been; if that still seems more plausible than humanness being visited and felt *by* stones (with thanks, say, to humans' being rendered so pervasively as commodity), I have at least attempted to plumb the boundaries and animate conditions of such orders of plausibility and suggested ways we might divest from such unthought conditions.

In her text "Animation, Apostrophe, and Abortion," Barbara Johnson writes of the peculiar "animation"—the strange personification—realized in the specific poetic apostrophe form in which the addressee "you" refers to an aborted fetus. She asks: "For if apostrophe is said to involve language's capacity to give life and human form to something dead or inanimate, what happens when those questions are literalized? What happens when the lyric speaker assumes responsibility for producing the death in the first place, but without being sure of the precise degree of human animation that existed in the entity killed? What is the debate over abortion about, indeed, if not the question of when, precisely, a being assumes a human form?"[16] I think this question is uncannily reproduced, albeit without a direct lyric addressee, in the animation of things unknown in their proximity to humanness, by their uneven agency, by their uncertain capacity to affect, by their unlikelihood of being "the effector of," by their uncertain possession of (human) life. For all its verbal coherence, with the exception of the interruption of a few pronouns, this book has also been a project of address, not so easily a diagnosable scene in which a living lyric speaker addresses a dead being whose animacy was uncertain, but a scene of engagement in which the "lives" on both sides are beholden to terms unknown. However you—my reader—have read this, I hope we have been engaged, you and I, in rediscovering existing forms of death, or deadness, as much as we have been engaged in the lifely absence of life and lively inanimation.

In deploying animacy and its forbidding hierarchies as a central figure in this book, I aimed to move beyond reifying its apparent hierarchal closures. I endeavored to show how animacy tends to hide its own contradictions, the transsubstantiations, the transmatterings that go on underneath, through, and across it: hence, my title *Animacies* is importantly plural. One could go so far as to argue that they are what keep it vital, they are that upon which it depends. However, that being said, I was interested in animacy in a very significant way *for* its assertion of hierarchical validity, an assertion that is found peppered across discourses of not only mainstream thinking but also science itself. The categorical humanism characteristic of such ontologies is one reason why the call for "new materialisms" has become so urgent. The new materialisms we can pursue are those that not only diagnose the "facts" by which humans are not animals are not things (or by which humans cannot be animals cannot be things), but simultaneously reveal such "facts" to be the real uncanny permeating the world we know. This is the beauty of *Ponyo*: it forgoes tensions borne of uncanniness, promising instead an airy *and* watery cosmology that animacy hierarchies only begrudgingly admit, one in which communing and transmogrification among unlikely kinds is not exceptional, but normal and unsurprising. Taking in animacy in this way also suggests an alternative means, outside of the strictly political or strictly emotional, to identify cross-affiliations—affinities—among groups as diverse as environmentalists, people with autism, social justice activists, feminists, religious believers in nature's stewardship, and antiracists, to mention just a few. It is also to refuse prescriptive closures around the possibility of metamorphosis, imaginative or otherwise. Not mimesis or partial-morphosis, but the stuff of transformative commitment. I take to heart the words of the political scientists Noenoe K. Silva and Jonathan Goldberg-Hiller when they say that the politics of indigenous sovereignty in Hawaii, given the critical relevance of competing ontologies including animals and landscape objects in which powerful spirits reside, comes down to questions of metamorphosis.[17]

These affinities, however, demand fierce sensitivity to their differences. In my own thinking I return often to Trinh T. Minh-ha's ethnographic ethics "not to speak about / Just speak nearby."[18] Well beyond rejecting either secularism or spirituality, I wish for an ethics of care and sensitivity that extends far from humans' (or the Human's) own borders. It is in queer of color and disability/crip circles, neither of which has enjoyed much immunity from the destructive consequences of contemporary biopolitics, that I have often found blossomings of this ethics of care and sensitivity, queerings of objects and affects accompanied by political revision, reworldings that challenge the order of things.

Thinking and feeling critically about animacy encourages opening to the senses of the world, receptivity, vulnerability. My care for a couch may well have stemmed from what some deem pathology, but that does not invalidate it as a peculiar kind of care that may at least truck with the more intensive valence that a couch acquires for one who cannot afford to replace it, and who cleans it; a dog who likes the taste of it and licks it; a relatively wealthy person who, due to some vague charting of proper liberal conduct, tries to give things away before sending them to the landfill; or a person of whatever neurological categorization who runs her finger along a slip of fabric ever so gently. Radical affection does not require intentional politics; and subjectivity itself, with its attendant danger zones of nationalism, individualism, whiteness, and rather anti-animate preference for typology and judgment, need not be core to this account. I seek not to end here with concluding words about animacy's ultimate failure or success, only that it is here and that it has its own regulatory forces which must be accounted for and met. If we must keep company with such ontological closure, it nevertheless remains eminently possible for us to seek out and affirm the wiliness within.

Notes

Introduction

1. Anatole Broyard describes his engagement with illness as an intoxication; in opposition to his "sobered" friends, he felt "vivid, multicolored, sharply drawn." Broyard, *Intoxicated by My Illness*, 6.

2. See, especially, Mbembe, "Necropolitics"; and Agamben, *Homo Sacer*.

3. I refer here to Ludwig Wittgenstein's notion of family resemblances, in which a group is defined not by a core criterion or essential meaning, but by multiple similarities.

4. Silverstein, "Hierarchy of Features and Ergativity."

5. Mak, Vonk, and Schriefers, "Animacy in Processing Relative Clauses."

6. Aristotle, *De Anima*.

7. Frede, "On Aristotle's Conception of the Soul," 94.

8. Dean, *A Culture of Stone*, 8.

9. Daston, *Things That Talk*.

10. Within the United States, material culture is examined both within the social sciences (that is, anthropology) and the humanities (that is, art history); for an overview, see Kingery, *Learning from Things*; and Lock and Farquhar, *Beyond the Body Proper*. Arjun Appadurai has also edited a book that considers commodification and culture from a global perspective; Appadurai, *The Social Life of Things*.

11. Coole and Frost, "Introducing the New Materialisms," 2. See also Colebrook, "On Not Becoming Man," for a reading of selected feminist approaches to matter.

12. Bennett, *Vibrant Matter*.

13. Haraway, *Simians, Cyborgs, and Women*; Latour, *We Have Never Been Modern*; Barad, *Meeting the Universe Halfway*; and Deleuze and Guattari, *A Thousand Plateaus*.

14. Shukin, *Animal Capital*, 11.

15. Puar, *Terrorist Assemblages*, 35.

16. Foucault, "The Birth of Biopolitics."

17. Yamamoto, *Animacy and Reference*, 1.

18. Ibid., 15.

19. "Animacy" conference, Radboud University, 2005.

20. Yamamoto, *Animacy and Reference*, 180. Emphasis mine.

21. See, for example, Checker, *Polluted Promises*.

22. Haraway's oeuvre is central here, as are critically important texts such as Franklin, *Dolly Mixtures*; Thompson, *Making Parents*; and Hayden, *When Nature Goes Public*.

23. Ngai, *Ugly Feelings*, 91.

24. Bennett, *Vibrant Matter*, vii.

25. Ahmed, "Affective Economies," 119.

26. Foucault, *The Order of Things*. The original French title was, perhaps more apt for this book, *Les mots et les choses* (words and things).

27. Cvetkovich, *An Archive of Feelings*; Love, *Feeling Backward*; Edelman, *No Future*; and Eng, *The Feeling of Kinship*.

28. See Moore, Kosek, and Pandian, *Race, Nature, and the Politics of Difference*.

29. Clare, *Exile and Pride*; McRuer, *Crip Theory*.

30. Ferguson, *Aberrations in Black*, 149.

31. Snyder and Mitchell, *Cultural Locations of Disability*, 195.

32. Gopinath, *Impossible Desires*, 6–10.

33. Santiago, "The Wily Homosexual."

34. See, for example, the feminist theorist and poet Susan Griffin's memoir *What Her Body Thought* and Audre Lorde's *The Cancer Journals*.

1. Language and Mattering Humans

1. Comrie, *Language Universals and Linguistic Typology*, 185.

2. Ibid.

3. Yamamoto, *Animacy and Reference*, 1.

4. Comrie, *Language Universals and Linguistic Typology*, 186.

5. Silverstein, "Hierarchy of Features and Ergativity."

6. Ibid., 168.

7. Ibid., 164.

8. Ibid., 211.

9. For a summary, see Yamamoto, *Animacy and Reference*, 24–35. Silverstein's animacy hierarchy depended on a number of contributing features, each of which could have a binary value, while Yamamoto's definition of animacy departs from this approach.

10. Cherry, *Animism in Thought and Language*.

11. Ibid., 314.

12. Comrie reports that in early Slavonic, the emergence of a new gram-

matical form "was used only for male, adult, freeborn, healthy humans, i.e. not for women, children, slaves, or cripples." Comrie, *Language Universals and Linguistic Typology*, 196.

13. Ibid., 62.

14. Yamamoto, *Animacy and Reference*, 1.

15. Ibid., 199.

16. Ibid., 43.

17. Cherry, *Animism in Thought and Language*, 217.

18. Langacker, *Concept, Image, and Symbol*, 248.

19. Yamamoto, *Animacy and Reference*, 9.

20. Approaches to some indigenous cosmologies are central to this critique. See, for instance, the exemplary article by Goldberg-Hiller and Silva titled "Sharks and Pigs."

21. Important debates about hate speech and state regulation have been vital to my own thinking on such topics. In particular, I am indebted to Brown, *States of Injury*; Butler, *Excitable Speech*; and Matsuda, *Words That Wound*.

22. WebbCampaign, "Allen's Listening Tour," YouTube, August 14, 2006. The video was recorded by S. R. Sidarth on August 11, 2006.

23. Brown, *States of Injury*.

24. Matsuda, "Public Response to Racist Speech," 2320–21.

25. Fanon, *Black Skin, White Masks*, 113.

26. Ibid., 111–13.

27. Rich, "2006: The Year of the 'Macaca.'"

28. Scherer, "Salon Person of the Year: S. R. Sidarth."

29. "Person of the Year: You"; and Grossman, "Citizens of the New Digital Democracy."

30. See Clifford, "The Humbling of Jimmy Lai."

31. The psychometric measure of intelligence dates back to 1917 and is attributed to the Englishman Sir Francis Galton, who believed in its heritability. Later, French theorist Alfred Binet's interest in the measurement of intelligence was less attached to interests in eugenics (he believed in the possible contribution of nurture to intelligence). However, the taking up of intelligence psychometrics in the United States revived an investment in eugenics in its application to the diagnosis of mental retardation in the Stanford-Binet test. Stephen Jay Gould popularized criticisms about IQ tests in his *The Mismeasure of Man*. For an excellent study of the history and contemporary institutional and philosophical treatment of intellectual disability, and the relationship to animality that it was perceived and theorized to have, see Carlson, *The Faces of Intellectual Disability*.

32. Fauconnier and Turner, *The Way We Think*.

33. Ibid., 46.

34. Riley, *Impersonal Passion*, 13.

35. Fauconnier and Turner, *The Way We Think*, 46.

36. Lacan, "The Agency of the Letter in the Unconscious or Reason since Freud," 152.

37. Haraway, *Modest_Witness@Second_Millennium.FemaleMan_Meets_Onco-Mouse*, 231.

38. Deleuze and Guattari, *A Thousand Plateaus*, 141, 135.

39. Tsing, *Friction*, 59, 76.

40. Kristeva, *Powers of Horror*, 5.

41. Bennett, *Vibrant Matter*, 39.

42. For more on the scientific and State discourses surrounding Schiavo, see Miller, "'Reading' the Body of Terri Schiavo."

43. Davis, "Life, Death and Biocultural Literacy" and "An End to It All."

44. Hayles, *How We Became Posthuman*, 279.

45. Currently there is some discussion of "inhumanization" in political theory, used to avoid the anthropocentrist idealization of the human in "dehumanization." See, for example, Feldman, "Mediating Inhumanization."

46. Kafer, "Accessible Futures."

47. Schweik, *The Ugly Laws*, 1.

48. Thompson, *Making Parents*, 265.

49. Marx, *Economic and Philosophical Manuscripts of 1844*, xxii.

50. Mulvey, "Visual Pleasure and Narrative Cinema."

51. Trinh, "II. The Language of Nativism: Anthropology as a Scientific Conversation of Man with Man," in *Woman, Native, Other*, 47–76.

52. See for instance Linda Williams's self-authored *Hard Core* and edited anthology *Porn Studies*.

53. Dworkin, *Pornography*.

54. Adams and Donovan, *Animals and Women*. For more positivist cultural-feminist and indigenous-feminist approaches that are less centered on critiques of negating objectifications, see Hogan, Metzger, and Peterson, *Intimate Nature*.

55. Adams, *The Sexual Politics of Meat*.

56. MacKinnon, *Only Words*, 22.

57. Rubin, "Misguided, Dangerous, and Wrong."

58. hooks, "The Oppositional Gaze."

59. See, for example, Clare, "Gawking, Gaping, Staring," in *The Marrow's Telling*, 81–90; and Thomson, *Staring*.

60. Wendell, *The Rejected Body*, 93.

61. Kafer, "Compulsory Bodies," 142.

62. Chinn, "Feeling Her Way," 184.

63. Nussbaum, "Objectification."

64. Ibid., 251.

65. See Memmi, *The Colonizer and the Colonized*. The history of what is called "colonialism" is still quite overwhelmingly European colonialism. For a look at a non-Western colonial discourse—the case of Japanese rule

in South Korea—see Choi, "The Discourse of Decolonization and Popular Memory."

66. Césaire, *Discourse on Colonialism*.

67. Fanon, *Wretched of the Earth*, 211.

68. See, for instance, Cheryl Harris, "Whiteness as Property"; and Stephen Best, *The Fugitive's Properties*.

69. For instance, the philosopher Donald Davidson's influential writings about mental capacity and speech, as in *Subjective, Intersubjective, Objective*.

70. Whorf, *Language, Thought, and Reality*.

71. Slobin, "From Thought and Language to Thinking for Speaking."

72. Taub and Galvan, "Patterns of Encoding in ASL Motion Descriptions."

73. See Langacker, *Concept, Image, and Symbol* and *Cognitive Grammar*; Fauconnier and Turner, *Mental Spaces*; Fauconnier, *Mappings in Thought and Language*.

74. For Butler, the body, if and where it matters, cannot simplistically precede the speech event. Butler, *Bodies That Matter*, 8.

2. Queer Animation

1. Freccero, "Queer Times," 491.

2. Butler, *Excitable Speech*.

3. Johnson, "'Quare' Studies, or (Almost) Everything I Learned about Queer I Learned from My Grandmother."

4. Munt, in her recent book on queer affect, *Queer Attachments*, advances connections between racialized religious Irish identity and queer sexuality in various cultural, temporal, and political locations and proposes that Irishness serves to falsify British whiteness via queer's meaning of "fake."

5. There exist many excurses of such wonderfully productive frictions among *queer*'s dictionary senses, particularly with regard to spoiled capital, strangeness, and oddity; I won't repeat them here.

6. Burrington, "The Public Square and Citizen Queer."

7. Before this sexually specific sense was added to the OED, queer scholars were artfully working around an even-more mystifying array of queer meanings defined therein than exist now, attempting to plumb an authoritative text that had in its turn only circumlocution to offer in both definition and documentation: for just two examples, see Cleto, "Introduction," 12–13; Umphrey, "The Trouble with Harry Thaw."

8. That the *Oxford English Dictionary* treats "transgenderism" as a "sexual lifestyle" rather than a gender identification drives home the importance of thinking majoritarian categories—even *queer*—through, and not over, subcultural lives.

9. Without addressing more recent meanings of homosexuality, Philip Durkin proposes that a word merger, a consolidation of "strange" and

"bad" senses to a singular meaning of "strange and bad," occurred. Durkin, *The Oxford Guide to Etymology*, 216–17.

10. Nikki Sullivan discusses this in *A Critical Introduction to Queer Theory*.

11. Chauncey, *Gay New York*, 15–16. For other histories, or notes on the historicity, of *queer*, see Zwicky, "Two Lavender Issues for Linguists"; and Butler, *Excitable Speech*.

12. Chauncey, *Gay New York*.

13. For an examination of the visual materials and slogans of ACT UP, see Crimp and Rolston, *AIDS Demo Graphics*.

14. See Berlant and Freeman, "Queer Nationality."

15. See Chasin, *Selling Out*.

16. Duggan, *The Twilight of Equality?*

17. For scholarship on mobile queer capital in the name of gay and lesbian tourism and its relationships to nationalism, race, and neoliberalism, see Puar, "A Transnational Feminist Critique of Queer Tourism"; Alexander, *Pedagogies of Crossing*, 21–90.

18. Anzaldúa, *Borderlands/La Frontera*. See also her "To(o) Queer the Writer," 208.

19. Anzaldúa, "La Prieta."

20. De Lauretis, "Queer Texts, Bad Habits, and the Issue of a Future."

21. Robert McRuer makes this point in *Crip Theory* as part of an extensive and careful derivation of his understanding of Anzaldúa's important place as a crip theorist: "Because the contributions of feminists of color are often far from central in the origin stories we construct for queer theory, Anzaldúa's 1981 assertion is an important and ongoing challenge to the field or movement" (37–38).

22. Butler, "Critically Queer."

23. Duggan, "Making It Perfectly Queer," 155.

24. Warner, "Introduction," xxvi.

25. Sedgwick, *Tendencies*, 9.

26. Cohen, "Gay and the Disappearing [+Female]," 22–24.

27. Smitherman, *Talkin and Testifyin*, 35, 41.

28. Hock, *Principles of Historical Linguistics*, 300.

29. Eng, *The Feeling of Kinship*, 25.

30. This was especially the case in the flurry of political activity surrounding the California Proposition 8 campaign of 2008.

31. For pointedly race-critical critiques of capital's consolidation to whiteness and its implications for queer politics, see Cohen, "Punks, Bulldaggers, and Welfare Queens."

32. For critiques and analysis, see, for example, Monroe, "Race, Religion, and Proposition 8," 3; Kim, "Marital Discord"; Cannick, "No-on-8's White Bias." For a similar argument made about Arizona's recent marriage contests, see Chávez, "Exploring the Defeat of Arizona's Marriage Amendment and the Specter of the Immigrant as Queer."

33. Zwicky, "Two Lavender Issues for Linguists," 22.

34. Brugman, *The Story of "Over."*

35. Sedgwick, *Tendencies*, 8.

36. Halperin, *Saint Foucault*, 62.

37. René Dirven and Marjolyn Verspoor define "concept" simply as "a person's idea of what something in the world is like"; categories are structured concepts that extend beyond individual entities (like proper name concepts) and thus "slice up reality into relevant units." *Cognitive Exploration of Language and Linguistics*, 13–14.

38. For one example, see Walters, *All the Rage*.

39. Goldberg, *Queering the Renaissance*, 13.

40. Gay, Lesbian, and Straight Education Network, *National School Climate Survey*.

41. Muñoz, *Disidentifications*.

42. Smitherman, *Word from the Mother*.

43. Baugh, "The Politicization of Changing Terms of Self-Reference among American Slave Descendants."

44. For more work on queer temporality, see Freccero, *Queer/Early/Modern*; Halberstam, *In a Queer Time and Place*; Elizabeth Freeman's edited special issue of *GLQ* titled *Queer Temporalities*; Freeman, *Time Binds*; Puar, *Terrorist Assemblages*, 204–22; and Dinshaw, *Getting Medieval*.

45. For more on category structure, see Lakoff, *Women, Fire and Dangerous Things*, 121.

46. "Graded centrality" in relation to prototype structure, with components of varying goodness-of-exemplar and degree-of-membership, is described in Croft and Cruse, *Cognitive Linguistics*, 77–106.

47. Butler, *Excitable Speech*.

48. Freud, "Remembering, Repeating, and Working-Through."

49. Butler, *Excitable Speech*, 100.

50. An excellent book considering many largely psychoanalytic approaches to loss is David L. Eng and David Kazanjian, *Loss*.

51. See, for example, work on trauma, activism, and affective politics in Ann Cvetkovich's *An Archive of Feelings*.

52. Sweetser, *From Etymology to Pragmatics*.

53. I am grateful to Eve Sweetser for providing me with this useful notion of prepackaging.

54. See Leap and Boellstorff, *Speaking in Queer Tongues*.

55. Duggan, *Twilight of Equality*; and Puar, *Terrorist Assemblages*.

56. In a book on language and sexuality, Mari Kleinfeld and Noni Warner do not mention the uptake of a sign or a finger spelling for *queer*: "Lexical Variation in the Deaf Community Relating to Gay, Lesbian, and Bisexual Signs." A YouTube demonstration by a young queer in the United States called Kaileno9 shows that, for some at least, *queer* has its own sign and is not just finger spelled: Kaileno9, "GLBT ASL Signs," July 27, 2009. How-

ever, the sign language interpreter Ric Owen notes that this sign does not circulate widely; it is still taken by some as deeply offensive (the signing in the YouTube video is hesitant enough to perhaps signify nonfluency in sign language). Owen also writes that both *queer* and *gay* continue to be finger spelled, and that region, community formation, and age have much to do with the preferences for which signs are used. Owen, e-mail communication.

57. Owen, e-mail communication.

58. Bacchetta, "Rescaling Transnational Queerdom," 949.

59. Chou, *Tongzhi*, 3.

60. Foucault, "Governmentality."

61. Benveniste, "Subjectivity in Language."

62. Fairclough, *Discourse and Social Change*.

63. Giffney and Hird, *Queering the Non/Human*, 4.

3. Queer Animality

1. See Nast, "Loving . . . Whatever: Alienation, Neoliberalism and Pet-Love in the Twenty-First Century," for a primarily political-economic mapping of such contradictions.

2. Derrida, "And Say the Animal Responded?"

3. Lippit, *Electric Animal*, 7.

4. Heidegger, "The Origin of the Work of Art," 73.

5. Agamben, *The Open*, 24.

6. Ibid., 26. Kelly Oliver points out that Agamben's evocations of the "slaughterhouse" and the "machine" of the anthropological machine oddly seem to leave unaddressed the positions of animals as well as of women. Oliver, *Animal Lessons*, 231.

7. Wolfe, "Introduction," xii.

8. Barrett, *Beyond the Brain*.

9. Sheets-Johnstone, *The Primacy of Movement*.

10. Austin, *How to Do Things with Words*.

11. Ibid., 14.

12. Ibid., 15.

13. Ibid., 24.

14. Sedgwick, "Queer Performativity."

15. For instance, as Greta Gaard writes in her carefully argued essay "Toward a Queer Ecofeminism," "the native feminized other of nature is not simply eroticized but also queered and animalized, in that any sexual behavior outside the rigid confines of compulsory heterosexuality becomes queer and subhuman" (30).

16. Felman, *The Scandal of the Speaking Body*, 85.

17. Weightman, *The Cat Sat on the Mat*.

18. Derrida, "Signature Event Context," 18.

19. This example can be compared to an HMO advertisement featuring a gorilla bride, which Haraway suggests is haunted by an animalized welfare queen image: Haraway, *Modest_Witness@Second_Millenium.FemaleMan_ Meets_OncoMouse*, 257–59.

20. Houlbrook, *Queer London*.

21. See, for instance, Spencer, *British Immigration Policy since 1939*; and Walvin, *Passage to Britain*.

22. Shukin, *Animal Capital*, 6.

23. Bhabha, *The Location of Culture*, 85.

24. Gates, *The Signifying Monkey*.

25. Heise, "From Extinction to Electronics."

26. See Thomson, *Freakery*, particularly the editor's introduction.

27. Aristotle, *The Politics of Aristotle*, xii.

28. Franklin, *Dolly Mixtures*.

29. Currently in the United States, domesticated pets are often excessively anthropomorphized or treated as accessories; see Serpell, "People in Disguise."

30. Lippit, *Electric Animal*, 1.

31. Schneider, *Donna Haraway*, 140.

32. Mbembe, *On the Postcolony*, 2. For more on a postcolonial take on animality, see Ahuja, "Postcolonial Critique in a Multispecies World."

33. See Foucault, *The History of Sexuality*; and Mortimer-Sandilands and Erickson, *Queer Ecologies*.

34. Haraway wrote of the dense collocations of race, nature, and women that came to bear in nineteenth- and twentieth-century primatology. See Haraway, *Primate Visions* and *Simians, Cyborgs, and Women*.

35. Terry, "Unnatural Acts in Nature," 152.

36. Thompson, *Good Science*.

37. Saenz de Rodriguez, Bongiovanni, and Conde de Borrego, "An Epidemic of Precocious Development in Puerto Rican Children."

38. Giffney and Hird, *Queering the Non/Human*. The exception is J. Jack Halberstam, "Animating Revolt/Revolting Animation."

39. Eng, *Racial Castration*; and Somerville, *Queering the Color Line*.

40. Marla Carlson attends to the variances that can exist among furries, as well as a contextualization of furry subcultures in relation to other contemporary phenomena that seem to depict the outlines of "humanness." Carlson, "Furry Cartography."

41. Deleuze and Guattari, *A Thousand Plateaus*, 233.

42. Kim, "The Racial Triangulation of Asian-Americans."

43. Roediger, *The Wages of Whiteness*.

44. Lowe, *Immigrant Acts*, 13.

45. Giles, *The Civilization of China*, 63.

46. Shah, *Contagious Divides*.

47. Many microcephalics, who were the subject of fascination in Euro-

pean and U.S. publics, were African American, even though they were often used to represent apes or exotic creatures from elsewhere. For example, William Henry Johnson (1842–1926), known as "Zip the Pinhead" of P. T. Barnum fame, was billed as a microcephalic, though his medical status remained uncertain. See Thomson, *Extraordinary Bodies*, for an excellent study of the historical figuration of disability within the United States, some of which was constructed within and through the figure of the "freak."

48. McClintock, *Imperial Leather*, 53.

49. Tchen, *New York before Chinatown*, 206.

50. Recent and distant multiracial dramas alike are shadowed by the logics of empire; for an insightful study of the interracial negotiations among Asian Americans, African Americans, and Chicana/os in literature, see Lee, *Urban Triage*.

51. Tchen elsewhere has argued that Nast's apelike Irish representations showed the clear influence of British animalizing representations of the Irish, particularly those in the English satirical journal *Punch*. Tchen, "Quimbo Appo's Fear of Fenians."

52. See, for instance, Chan, *Chinese American Masculinities*; and Kim, *Writing Manhood in Black and Yellow*.

53. Cartright, *Determinants of Animal Behavior*, 93.

54. De Kosnik, *Illegitimate Media*. The term *techno-orientalism* was popularized by David Morley and Kevin Robins, who used the term to refer primarily to the orientalism theoretically developed by Edward Said rather than East Asian orientalisms; Morley and Robins, *Spaces of Identity*.

55. Clegg, *Fu Manchu and the Yellow Peril*, 3.

56. These included: *The Yellow Claw* (1921), *The Mystery of Dr. Fu Manchu* (serial, 1923), *The Return of Dr. Fu Manchu* (1930), *The Drums of Fu Manchu* (1940), *The Face of Fu Manchu* (1965), *Vengeance of Fu Manchu* (1968), *The Castle of Fu Manchu* (1969), and *The Fiendish Plot of Dr. Fu Manchu* (1980).

57. See Chan, *Chinese American Masculinities*.

58. See Takaki, *Strangers from a Different Shore*.

59. Nayland Smith to Dr. Petrie. Rohmer, *The Insidious Dr. Fu Manchu*, 13.

60. Chen, "Dissecting the 'Devil Doctor,'" 232.

61. See Chin, "Confessions of a Chinatown Cowboy"; Kim, *Writing Manhood*; and Benshoff, *Monsters in the Closet*, 56–58. Elaine Kim has called Fu Manchu "asexual," in line with broader symbolic emasculations of Asian men. Kim, *Asian American Literature*, 8.

62. Baker, "Sloughing the Human."

63. Eng, *Racial Castration*.

64. Shimizu, *The Hypersexuality of Race*, 6.

65. For more on the spectacle of Asian trans bodies, see Chen, "Everywhere Archives."

66. Delonas, op-ed cartoon. For analysis of racialized images, including

this one in the wake of U.S. President Barack Obama's election, see Apel, "Just Joking?"

67. Tsao, Schweers, Moeller, and Freiwald, "Patches of Face-Selective Cortex in the Macaque Frontal Lobe."

68. "Chimp Victim Reveals Face on *Oprah*."

69. The activist group "Not Dead Yet" opposes euthanasia in large part because of its uncritical conflation of disability with lives less worth living.

70. Longmore, *Why I Burned My Book and Other Essays on Disability*, 149–214.

71. For two works on race in relation to Shelley's *Frankenstein*, see Malchow, *Gothic Images of Race in Nineteenth-Century Britain*; Young, *Black Frankenstein*.

4. Animals, Sex, Transsubstantiation

1. For two other studies on the intersection of transness and animals and animality, see Hansen, "Humans, Horses, and Hormones"; and Hayward, "Lessons from a Starfish."

2. Butler, *Bodies That Matter*.

3. In addition to Donna Haraway's corpus, some exemplary texts include Thompson, "When Elephants Stand In for Competing Philosophies of Nature"; Anderson, "The Beast Within"; Lutz and Collins, *Reading National Geographic*; and Shukin, *Animal Capital*.

4. Franklin, "The Cyborg Embryo."

5. Thompson, *Making Parents*.

6. Philo and Wilbert, "Introduction."

7. Hird, "Animal Transex."

8. See Zeng, "China Enters Dog-Eat-Dog Pet Industry."

9. Patton, "Stealth Bombers of Desire."

10. Wines, "Once Banned, Dogs Reflect China's Rise."

11. Ibid.

12. For a look at the gendered component of Chinese economics, see Chan, *Gender and Chinese Development*; Rofel, *Desiring China*.

13. Nast, "Critical Pet Studies?"

14. Nast, "Loving . . . Whatever," 306, 320.

15. Wines, "Once Banned, Dogs Reflect China's Rise."

16. From the website Love That Cat, www.lovethatcat.spayneuter.html.

17. Cohen, "Punks, Bulldaggers, and Welfare Queens."

18. Kluchin, *Fit to Be Tied*; Stubblefield, "Beyond the Pale."

19. For work that considers the queer-trans relationship, see Stryker, "Transgender Studies"; and Prosser, *Second Skins*.

20. Sullivan also discusses nonmainstream body modification such as tattooing, piercing, and cosmetic surgery; see Sullivan, "Transmogrification."

21. Hird, "Animal Transex," 35–50.

22. Ibid., 37.

23. Stryker, Currah, and Moore, "Introduction," 11.

24. Bersani, "Sexuality and Aesthetics."

25. Freud, "Fetishism," 154.

26. Williams, *Hard Core*, 34–57.

27. Ibid., 93–119.

28. Stevens, "Deadly Youth."

29. Turim, *The Films of Oshima Nagisa*, 210.

30. Bhabha, *The Location of Culture*, 123.

31. Creed, "A Darwinian Love Story."

32. Laqueur, *Making Sex*, 18. For studies of Victorian-era interests in non-human animals with significant treatment of visual representation, see the work of Harriet Ritvo, particularly *The Animal Estate* and *The Platypus and the Mermaid*.

33. Tropes of animality and primitivism in colonial spaces have been widely written about; for an overview of these tropes in visual cultures, see Shohat and Stam, *Unthinking Eurocentrism*.

34. Ian Condry describes tensions between Japanese self-identifications as monoracial and long-standing discrimination against Japanese of Korean heritage. Condry, "Yellow B-Boys, Black Culture, and Hip-Hop in Japan," 657–59. See also Steen, *Racial Geometries of the Black Atlantic, Asian Pacific and American Theatre*; and Raphael-Hernandez and Steen, *Afro Asian Encounters*.

35. For more on blackface in contemporary Japan, see Wood, "The Yellow Negro"; Cornyetz, "Fetishizing Blackness"; and Russell, "Consuming Passions."

36. Lippit, "The Films of Oshima Nagisa," 160.

37. However, Paul Coates sees Oshima's movies as resistant to any single lens of interpretation, preferring to discuss them as contradictory challenges to the viewer's sense of coherence; Coates, "Repetition and Contradiction in the Films of Oshima."

38. Xu Bing, personal conversation.

39. See Silbergeld and Ching, *Persistence-Transformation*.

40. Xu Bing, "A Case Study of Transference."

41. Lin, "Globalism or Nationalism?"

42. Quoted in Barboza, "Schooling the Artists' Republic of China."

43. Freccero, "Les chats de Derrida."

44. This is an iterativity whose central importance, particularly for heteronormativity, has been theorized by Butler. In the wake of Austin, Butler performs a Foucauldian reading on the entwined discursive lives of gender, sex, and the body, pointing to the iterativity that is necessary for the maintenance of a coherent normativity, and the likely fault lines that must be exposed. See Butler, *Gender Trouble*.

45. David Eng's *Racial Castration* offers a cogent psychoanalytic study of the vexed sexualization of the Asian American male. See also Richard

Fung's essay "Looking for My Penis," in which, against the popular gay and lesbian political motto "we are everywhere," he considers the relative paucity of Asians, and Asian sexuality in visual, particularly video, representation.

46. Fanon, *Black Skin, White Masks*.

47. Fuchs, "Michael Jackson's Penis," 17.

48. Jackson, interview.

49. Lauren Berlant comments on the panther in the video, suggesting that it represents Jackson's "amnesiac optimism or the absolute falseness of the utopian performative 'It don't matter if you're black or white.'" *The Queen of America Goes to Washington City*, 213.

50. Hartman, *Scenes of Subjection*.

51. Deleuze and Guattari, *Anti-Oedipus*, 9; *A Thousand Plateaus*.

52. The idea that each organ has a discrete function is contradicted by views that the systems of the body are in fact interdependent and in constant communicative flux. In neurobiology, the actual human body approaches the theoretical "body without organs" as it moves away from a regularized, systemic representation, both in the multifunctionality of a given organ and the increasing numbers of communicative relationships among "organs" that converge to produce behavioral or emotional appearances or effects (for example, neurophysiological constructs are understood to interact with bodily hormone systems in new ways that influence the measurable emotionality of a body).

53. Franklin, *Dolly Mixtures*.

54. Hayward, "More Lessons from a Starfish."

55. Ibid., 81.

56. McRuer, *Crip Theory*.

57. Basquin, "Range."

58. Basquin, "A Site for Queer Reproduction." See also Alfonso, "Nostalgia and Masculinities in Bill Basquin's Range."

59. See Basquin's website: http://www.billbasquin.com/catalog.o.html .o.html.

5. Lead's Racial Matters

1. I do not wish to fully privilege available medical evidence when I note that, to the degree that lead toxicity was medicalized, there were no known reports of poisoning from the specific toys recalled. It is the relationship between the high levels of panic and low levels of documented poisoning that points to a disproportionate response. I caution, however, that medically documented poisoning can often be an unreliable criterion, since documentation levels for testing may be calibrated to detect acute, rather than chronic, levels of poisoning.

2. See, for example, "Mattel Issues New Massive China Toy Recall."

3. Story, "Lead Paint Prompts Mattel to Recall 967,000 Toys."

4. Lipton and Barboza, "As More Toys Are Recalled, Trail Ends in China."

5. "New Worries over Lead."

6. See the essays in the excellent book edited by Evelyn Nakano Glenn, *Shades of Difference*, for a variety of approaches to the complex mappings between colorism and racism.

7. On April 29, 2011, the Illinois company RC2 was acquired by the Japanese toy-making corporation Tomy Company, Ltd.

8. Kang's essay focuses on the Asian female body's appropriation and decontextualized uptake for symbolic representation of transnational working bodies. Kang, "Si(gh)ting Asian/American Women as Transnational Labor."

9. See Jain, *Injury*, for a discussion of injury law and "American injury culture" from cultural anthropology and legal studies perspectives.

10. Lei, *Environmental Activism in China*; Tilt, *The Struggle for Sustainability in Rural China*.

11. Harvey, *A Brief History of Neoliberalism*, 108.

12. "WTO: China Overtakes U.S. in Exports; Asian Nation Set to Become the World's Biggest Exporter by 2008."

13. Lague, "China Output Not a Threat, Officials Say."

14. Lammers, "What to Do When Everything Is 'Made in China?'"

15. Such extravagant and rapid displacements in mainstream media do not, however, reflect the continued attention to this issue among environmental justice activists. Recently, the activist and artist Mel Chin has embarked on a campaign to raise awareness about lead levels in lower-income, historically black neighborhoods in post-Katrina New Orleans; for more on his "Operation Paydirt" project see Brookhardt, "Mel Chin's *Operation Paydirt* Aims to Get the Lead Out of New Orleans' Inner City Neighborhoods."

16. However, many scholars are taking more sensitive views to the permeability of national borders when it comes to industrial pollutants, including environmental studies such as Pulido, *Environmentalism and Economic Justice: Two Chicano Studies in the Southwest*.

17. Beck, *Risk Society*, 23.

18. For this phrasing I am indebted to Gabriele Schwab, who was responding to my talk at University of California, Irvine, on this topic on October 30, 2009.

19. Wald, *Contagious*. In the case of SARS, for instance, Gwen D'Arcangelis writes how microbial modes of transmission were explained by way of news media images and texts that placed people in proximity to nonhuman animals, linking these to U.S. imperialism in relation to China. See D'Arcangelis, "Chinese Chickens, Ducks, Pigs and Humans, and the Technoscientific Discourses of Global U.S. Empire."

20. Povinelli, *The Empire of Love*, 77.

21. Shah, *Contagious Divides*.

22. A phrase from Allen S. Williams, *The Demon of the Orient and His Satellite Fiends of the Joint: Our Opium Smokers as They Are in Tartar Hells and American Paradises* (1883), quoted in Shah, *Contagious Divides*, 54.

23. The Bioterrorism Act was enacted in 2002. According to Andrew Lakoff, concerns about bioterrorism merged with existing disease outbreaks in national security discourses in the late 1990s. Lakoff, "National Security and the Changing Object of Public Health."

24. A somewhat different argument is made by Marion Nestle, who writes about concerns over food safety and links them to rhetoric about bioterrorism; Nestle, *Safe Food*.

25. Austen, "Lead in Children's Toys Exceeds Limit, Magazine Says."

26. I am reminded here of Jake Kosek's articulation of another invisible threat, radiation near nuclear sites, and the fungibility it portends, precisely because it must be imagined: "Radiation is a strange beast. It is undetectable by our very senses. . . . Living next to a deeply secretive, historically deceptive nuclear research complex that produces a highly volatile, mobile, odorless, tasteless, invisible substance that is unimaginably enduring and deadly in its toxicity blurs the traditional boundaries between material and imaginary. The very essence of an object changes meanings: a dust cloud from the east, smoke from Los Alamos, firewood, drinking water, an elk steak, all become haunted by possibilities of what is not perceptively present but always a threat. What makes sense in a context where senses are useless?" Kosek, *Understories*, 258–59.

27. Adelaide Now Blog, "Why Is China Poisoning Our Babies?" This blog is by an Australian writer. Other ambiguous and not so ambiguous titles included the conservative website Americans Working Together, who posted an article called "Greed, China Poisoning Our Children with Lead."

28. Harris, "Heparin Contamination May Have Been Deliberate, F.D.A. Says."

29. Puar, *Terrorist Assemblages*.

30. For more accounts of the rhetorical strategies of environmental justice activism, see Sze, *Noxious New York*; Calpotura and Sen, "PUEBLO Fights Lead Poisoning." For general approaches to environmental justice, see Bullard, *The Quest for Environmental Justice*.

31. Wayne, "The Enemy at Home," 1. This was the print title; the online version is titled "Thousands of Homeowners Cite Drywall for Ills."

32. Chen, "Chinese Toy Terror." See also Cottle, "Toy Terror."

33. See, for example, Nash, "Fruits of Ill Health," and the film *Maquilopolis*, which refers to the poisoning of the environment in which maquiladoras are located as well as of the maquiladora workers' bodies themselves.

34. Pediatric mercury-laden vaccines serve as one example of such practices. The FDA and CDC bought up surpluses of thimerosal-preserved children's vaccines banned in the United States, then oversaw their exportation

to countries outside of the United States. On October 15, 2008, President Bush signed into law the Mercury Export Ban, which prohibits by 2013 the export of elemental mercury from the United States. The United States has been a top source of mercury distribution throughout the world, particularly by selling its stores of surplus mercury to industrializing countries. The ban does not however address the continuing export of electronic wastes (which contain lead, mercury, cadmium, and other toxic chemicals) to industrializing countries for resource mining, which results in highly toxic exposures.

35. Cheri Lucas Jennings and Bruce Jennings critique the shallow, still racist remedies inherent in "organic" and "sustainable" agricultural practice and policy developments. Jennings and Jennings, "Green Fields/Brown Skin," 180.

36. United States Consumer Product Safety Commission, Recall Release #08–247, April 10, 2008.

37. For more on the opposition between rural and metropolis and this divide's organizations based on class and sex, see Herring, *Another Country*.

38. Jennings, "Thomas the Tank Engine Toys Recalled Because of Lead Hazard."

39. David Eng discusses a photograph commemorating the construction of Western railroads that, through omission, performs the erasure of Chinese labor in the building of the railroads. He uses Walter Benjamin's considerations of history, temporality, and the photograph to perform a literary analysis of the rhetorical invisibilization of Asian American presence, building an argument about "racial melancholia" in the United States. Eng, *Racial Castration*.

40. There has been some popular attention to the conditions of Chinese labor, for example, Chang, *Factory Girls*, and the documentary directed by Micha Peled, *China Blue*, on the exploitive living and working conditions of young female Chinese workers who have come to the city to make blue jeans.

41. There are some exceptions. Among individual public responses to either professional journalism or blogged expressions of the toxicity of lead toys and the toxicity of Chinese products, one can find alerts to the more complex, sometimes imperial relationships between United States and transnational corporate interests, U.S. consumer interests, the Chinese government, and Chinese transnationalized labor. No mainstream publication to my knowledge, however, for all the complexity it might have included in its coverage, has not also symptomatically either assisted in retreating to occasional gestures of alarmism or conflations of biosecurity threats with the catch-all nomination of "China."

42. For a study of situations in which the employers of childcare are themselves people of color, see Qayum and Ray, "Traveling Cultures of Servitude."

43. Glenn, *Forced to Care*, 2. Glenn's book historicizes the long-standing racialization, gendering, and class structuring of all kinds of care work within the United States.

44. Briggs, "Foreign and Domestic."

45. Chang, *Disposable Domestics*.

46. Clough, *Autoaffection*.

47. See also Chun, *Control and Freedom*.

48. The first IQ measure in the United States was broadly and inaccurately adapted from the French Simon-Binet scale by H. H. Goddard. Goddard believed that intelligence was inborn and could not be altered environmentally; the IQ measure factored prominently in his and others' eugenicist efforts. Since then, several biases inherent in the test have been recognized, including the fact that IQ can dramatically change in relation to one's environment.

49. See Carter, *The Heart of Whiteness*. Carter discusses neurasthenia diagnoses of men and their associations with weakness and white vulnerability in general. Susan Schweik notes that neurasthenia was gendered as female and "turns out to be high-class mendicancy," illustrating to me the ease of alteration between one's vulnerability to disability and being disabled. Schweik, *The Ugly Laws*, 80.

50. Hartman, *Scenes of Subjection*, 206.

51. See Roig-Franzia, "Probe Opens on Study Tied to Johns Hopkins."

52. I heard this story when it aired in 2007 and immediately understood it as a symptom of willful forgetting in light of "Chinese lead." However, I am unable to find the exact citation since not all NPR programs are transcribed and archived.

53. "The Living Legacy of Lead."

54. Paul Gilroy implicitly arouses the specter of such a "savage" body when he critiques the naively rehabilitative reading of the contained and fluid image of the black athlete in Leni Riefenstahl's filming of Jesse Owens: "her superficially benign recognition of black excellence in physicality need not be any repudiation of raciological theory. In this world of overdetermined racial signs, an outstandingly good but temperamental natural athlete is exactly what we would expect a savage African to become." Gilroy, *Against Race*, 173.

55. Davis, "Masked Racism."

56. Lott, *Love and Theft*, 116.

57. In a chapter called "Animatedness," Sianne Ngai suggests the legacy of blackface minstrelsy haunts modern-day animation shows centering on black life, such as *The PJ's*; what Lott reads as Dickens's textual "jump-cuts" in describing minstrel dance might be found in the bodily displacements and exaggerations of the stop-motion sequencing of the *PJ's* characters. Ngai, *Ugly Feelings*, 89–125.

58. "A mind is a terrible thing to waste," reads The United Negro Col-

lege Fund's campaign to further blacks' access to education. Dan Quayle's perversion of this slogan, "What a terrible thing it is to lose one's mind," suggests what fantasies about blackness might underlie benevolent white liberal representations.

59. I thank Don Romesburg for first getting me to indulge in this sensory fantasy.

60. "Thomas the Tank Engine and Friends Recall."

61. See the Centers for Disease Control and Prevention's webpage on lead and toys, http://www.cdc.gov/nceh/lead/tips/toys.htm.

62. See Bruhm and Hurley, *Curiouser*; and Stockton, *The Queer Child*.

63. McRuer, *Crip Theory*, 88–89.

64. See, for instance, the website Lead in Mexican Candy, www.leadin mexicancandy.com.

6. Following Mercurial Affect

1. Buell, "Toxic Discourse," 645

2. For one such account and analysis, see Steingraber, *Living Downstream*.

3. Foucault, *The Order of Things*.

4. CNN Political Ticker, "Democratic Governor Candidate: Health Care Reform Could Be 'Toxic' in 2010."

5. Britney Spears's Grammy-winning hit song, "Toxic" (from the album *In the Zone*, 2003).

6. For a small sample of mass market books that use this metaphor (in categories from personal self-help to business), consider Brasher, *Toxic Relationships: How to Regain Lost Power in Your Relationship*; Glass, *Toxic People: 10 Ways of Dealing with People Who Make Your Life Miserable*; and Sue, *Toxic People: Decontaminate People at Work without Using Weapons*.

7. Kusy and Holloway, *Toxic Workplace! Managing Toxic Personalities and Their Systems of Power*, 3–4.

8. Wency Leung cites an interview with the author in an overview of the book. Leung, "How to Survive a Toxic Workplace."

9. Mitchell and Snyder, *Narrative Prosthesis*.

10. Davidson, "Universal Design."

11. Butler, *Bodies That Matter*.

12. Haraway, "Manifesto for Cyborgs."

13. Mbembe, "Necropolitics" and *On the Postcolony*.

14. Agamben, *Homo Sacer*.

15. Enstad, "Toxicity and the Consuming Subject," 57–58.

16. Donna Haraway has written of immune systems' constitution by biopolitical brokerages between "us" and "them." Haraway, "The Biopolitics of Postmodern Bodies" and "The Promises of Monsters."

17. Cohen, *A Body Worth Defending*.

18. Martin, *Flexible Bodies*, 38.

19. Esposito, *Bios*.

20. Edelman, *No Future*, 2.

21. Puar, *Terrorist Assemblages*.

22. Muñoz, *Cruising Utopia*.

23. Cvetkovich, *An Archive of Feelings*.

24. Berlant, "Intimacy: A Special Issue," 3.

25. Muñoz, *Cruising Utopia*, 185–89.

26. For complexities of passing and disclosure, see Samuels, "My Body, My Closet"; and Robert McRuer's chapter "Coming Out Crip" in *Crip Theory*, 33–76.

27. Siebers, *Disability Theory*, 101–8. On compulsory able-bodiedness in relation to queer-crip perspectives, see McRuer, *Crip Theory*; Kafer, "Compulsory Bodies"; Clare, *Exile and Pride*.

28. The sociologist Erving Goffman's *Stigma* considers visible disability, particularly disfigurement, as a kind of social stigma and the ways in which it is managed in conversation.

29. I am texturing an analysis of toxicity here to consider negatively racialized bodies as themselves "toxic bodies." See, for instance, the oft-cited scene from Fanon's *Black Skin, White Masks* in which the narrator considers his racialized objectification by a white child and by other whites.

30. Terry, "Objectum-Sexuality"; and Katayama, "Love in 2-D."

31. Thanks to Jennifer Terry for this suggestion.

32. Alaimo, *Bodily Natures*. This book rethinks agency through the materiality of bodies affected by environments. Alaimo considers Multiple Chemical Sensitivity as a phenomenon not easily captured by models of environmental justice and theorizes its relation to the body's resolutely inseparable material environment. Other ecofeminist perspectives include Gaard, *Ecofeminism*.

33. Rose, *The Politics of Life Itself*.

34. Clarkson, "Metal Toxicity in the Central Nervous System," 60.

35. Deleuze and Guattari, *A Thousand Plateaus*, 272–73.

36. Katherine Young, for instance, writes about the radical unconcern of Deleuze and Guattari for actual animals in their formulation of "becoming-animal." See her "Deleuze and Guattari: The Animal Question."

37. For an anthology theorizing violence in relation to a multiplicity of bodies (and landscapes), see Peluso and Watts, *Violent Environments*.

38. LaDuke, "Akwesasne: Mohawk Mother's Milk and PCBs."

39. Ahmed, *Queer Phenomenology*, 54.

40. Plotz, "Can the Sofa Speak? A Look at Thing Theory." The essay's titular citation of Gayatri Spivak's famous essay about human subalternity within the Indian context, "Can the Subaltern Speak?," is also never revisited.

41. Tuana, "Viscous Porosity," 199–200.

42. Three recent trade books include: Olmstead and Blaxill, *The Age of*

Autism: Mercury, Medicine and a Man-Made Epidemic; Kirby, *Evidence of Harm: Mercury in Vaccines and the Autism Epidemic: A Medical Controversy*; and Hightower, *Diagnosis Mercury: Money, Politics and Poison.*

43. Fleischman, "Language and Medicine."

44. Grandin, *Animals in Translation.*

45. Baggs, "In My Language."

46. See chapter 5, titled "The Face of the Beast," in Carlson, *The Faces of Intellectual Disability*, 131–61.

47. Cvetkovich, "Sexual Trauma/Queer Memory," 357.

48. McRuer and Wilkerson, "Introduction," 14.

49. If Baggs has been to any degree a controversial figure, the negative attention seems to be represented much more among non-disabled autism caregivers and nonautistic experts on autism (who say categorically, for instance, that she is so good with language that she can't possibly be autistic) than among autistics. Thanks to Eli Clare for discussing this with me.

50. In nominating this a crip-theoretical text, I am consciously calling up Robert McRuer's articulation of a crip theory that generates "ability trouble" without positivistic or purely identitarian completion. He looks for "crip actors who . . . will exacerbate, in more productive ways, the crisis of authority that currently besets heterosexual/able-bodied norms" (*Crip Theory*, 31).

51. Mukhopadhyay, *How Can I Talk If My Lips Don't Move?*, 27–28.

52. See the novel by Leslie Feinberg, *Stone Butch Blues*. For a reading of being stone in relation to trans identifications, see Halberstam, *Female Masculinity.*

53. Clare, "Stones in My Pocket, Stones in My Heart," *Exile and Pride*, 143–60. For more on what I read as the affects of gendered butchness in relation to illness, particularly cancer discourses, see Jain, "Cancer Butch."

54. Clare, *Exile and Pride*, 156.

55. Halberstam, *Female Masculinity*, 111–40.

56. Sedgwick, *Touching Feeling*; Muñoz, *Disidentifications.*

57. Christine Bacareza Balance, for instance, juxtaposes public health's indictment of queer Filipino bodies with disproportionately high HIV rates as "toxic subjects" with the possibility of shared queer Filipino American drug trips as pleasurable and intimate counterpublics. Balance, "On Drugs."

58. Thinking more specifically about the ethical and affective politics of geopolitical strife, in particular those of war, Judith Butler writes of vulnerability as a given condition, a condition that might inform a radically changed ethics were it to be acknowledged. See, for example, *Precarious Life.*

59. Kafer, "Accessible Futures."

60. Halberstam, *In a Queer Time and Place.*

61. Eng, *Racial Castration*, 4–13.

62. Freeman, *Time Binds*; Dinshaw, *Getting Medieval*, 1–54.

63. Love, *Feeling Backward*, 3.

64. Rodríguez is drawing here on work by Nguyen Tan Hoang that articulates a critical possibility in racialized bottoming. See Rodríguez, "Queer Sociality and Sexual Fantasies," 338. See also Scott, *Extravagant Abjection*.

65. Love, *Feeling Backward*, 3.

66. Quayson, *Aesthetic Nervousness*.

Afterword

1. Allen, interview with Jeffrey Brown.

2. For more on the idea of "shock therapy" in contemporary capitalist formations, see Klein, *The Shock Doctrine*.

3. Exclusive economic "sea zones" are defined under the United Nations Convention on the Law of the Sea (UNCLOS), developed over several decades of the twentieth century. UNCLOS took effect in 1994 and has legal force for the approximately 160 signees.

4. Such a state-facilitated affect of new security would be in close company with the affective economy of fear about which Sara Ahmed writes in "Affective Economies."

5. Miyazaki, *The Art of Ponyo*, 11.

6. Ibid.

7. Halberstam, *The Queer Art of Failure*.

8. Miyazaki, *The Art of Ponyo*, 116.

9. Lyrics: Wakako Kaku and Hayao Miyazaki; music composition and arrangement: Joe Hisaishi; performance: Masako Hayashi; translation: Rieko Izutsu-Vajirasarn. Reported in Miyazaki, *The Art of Ponyo*, 268.

10. Freeman, *Time Binds*.

11. I am thinking here of Paul Gilroy's *The Black Atlantic* and of newer work that departs from or reworks his fundamental insight about the generativity of the Middle Passage. For recent queer-theory work, see Alexander, *Pedagogies of Crossing*; and Tinsley, "Black Atlantic, Queer Atlantic."

12. Alexander, "Race, Gender, and Sexuality."

13. See, for example, Dean, *A Culture of Stone*; Parkes, "The Awareness of Rock."

14. Savarese, "More Than a Thing to Ignore." In a discussion of learning her tribe's language, Potowatomi, and its revelation of Anishinaabe (a First Nations tribal grouping) cosmology, the botanist Robin Wall Kimmerer uses stones, deemed animate in Potawatomi, to contrast with inanimate, generally human-made objects. "Of an inanimate being like a table we say, 'What is it?' And we answer *Dopwen yewe*. Table it is. But of apple, we must say 'Who is it?' And reply *Mshimin yawe*. Apple he is." Kimmerer, "Learning the Grammar of Animacy," 174.

15. Taylor, "Beasts of Burden," 191–92.

16. Johnson, "Apostrophe, Animation, and Abortion," 32.

17. Silva and Goldberg-Hiller, "Taking Indigenous Cosmologies Seriously."

18. *Reassemblage*; Trinh and Chen, "Speaking Nearby."

Bibliography

Adams, Carol J. *The Sexual Politics of Meat: A Feminist-Vegetarian Critical Theory*. New York: Continuum, 1990.

Adams, Carol J., and Josephine Donovan, eds. *Animals and Women: Feminist Theoretical Explorations*. Durham: Duke University Press, 1995.

The Adelaide Now Blog. "Why Is China Poisoning Our Babies?" Blog entry by Samela Harris, November 9, 2007.

Agamben, Giorgio. *Homo Sacer: Sovereign Power and Bare Life*. Translated by Daniel Heller-Roazan. Stanford: Stanford University Press, 1998.

———. *The Open: Man and Animal*. Translated by Kevin Attell. Stanford: Stanford University Press, 2004.

Ahmed, Sara. "Affective Economies." *Social Text* 22, no. 2 (2004): 117–39.

———. *The Cultural Politics of Emotion*. New York: Routledge, 2004.

———. *Queer Phenomenology: Orientations, Objects, Others*. Durham: Duke University Press, 2006.

Ahuja, Neel. "Postcolonial Critique in a Multispecies World." PMLA 124, no. 2 (March 2009): 556–63.

Alaimo, Stacy. *Bodily Natures Science, Environment, and the Material Self*. Bloomington: Indiana University Press, 2010.

Alaimo, Stacy, and Susan Hekman, eds. *Material Feminisms*. Bloomington: Indiana University Press, 2008.

Alexander, Jacqui. *Pedagogies of Crossing: Meditations on Feminism, Sexual Politics, Memory and the Sacred*. Durham: Duke University Press, 2005.

———. "Race, Gender, and Sexuality: Transnational Feminism as Radical Praxis." Center for Race and Gender Distinguished Lecture, Berkeley, California, November 7, 2006.

Alfonso, Rita. "Nostalgia and Masculinities in Bill Basquin's Range." Paper delivered at "Transomatechnics" conference, Simon Fraser University, Vancouver, 2008.

Allen, Thad. Interview with Jeffrey Brown, PBS Newshour, PBS, September 20, 2010.

American Heritage Dictionary of the English Language. 4th ed. New York: Houghton Mifflin, 2010.

Americans Working Together. "Greed, China Poisoning Our Children with Lead." www.americans-working-together.com, 2008.

Anderson, Kay. "'The Beast Within': Race, Humanity, and Animality." Environment and Planning D: Society and Space 18, no. 3 (2000): 301–20.

Anzaldúa, Gloria. Borderlands/La Frontera: The New Mestiza. San Francisco: Aunt Lute Books, 1987.

———. "La Prieta." In This Bridge Called My Back: Writings by Radical Women of Color, edited by Cherríe Moraga and Gloria Anzaldúa, 198–209. New York: Kitchen Table Press, 1983.

———. "To(o) Queer the Writer—Loca, escritora y chicana." In Inversions: Writing by Dykes, Queers, and Lesbians, edited by Betsy Warland, 249–64. Vancouver: Press Gang, 1991.

Apel, Dora. "Just Joking? Chimps, Obama and Racial Stereotype." Journal of Visual Culture 8, no. 2 (2009): 134–42.

Appadurai, Arjun, ed. The Social Life of Things: Commodities in Cultural Perspective. Cambridge: Cambridge University Press, 1998.

Aristotle. De Anima. Translated by J. A. Smith. In The Basic Works of Aristotle, edited by Richard McKeon, 534–603. New York: Modern Library, 2001.

———. The Politics of Aristotle. Translated with an introduction by J. E. C. Welldon. London: Macmillan, 1883.

Austen, Ian. "Lead in Children's Toys Exceeds Limit, Magazine Says." New York Times, October 19, 2007.

Austin, J. L. How to Do Things with Words: The William James Lectures Delivered in Harvard University in 1955. Oxford: Clarendon Press, 1962.

Bacchetta, Paola. "Rescaling Transnational 'Queerdom': Lesbian and 'Lesbian' Identitary-Positionalities in Delhi in the 1980s." Antipode 34, no. 5 (2002): 947–73.

Baggs, Amanda. "In My Language." YouTube, January 14, 2007.

Baker, Steve. "Sloughing the Human." In Zoontologies, edited by Cary Wolfe, 147–64. Minneapolis: University of Minnesota Press, 2003.

Balance, Christine Bacareza. "On Drugs: The Production of Queer Filipino America through Intimate Acts of Belonging." Women and Performance: A Journal of Feminist Theory 16, no. 2 (July 2006): 269–82.

Barad, Karen. Meeting the Universe Halfway: Quantum Physics and the Entanglement of Matter and Meaning. Durham: Duke University Press, 2007.

Barboza, David. "Schooling the Artists' Republic of China." New York Times, March 30, 2008.

Barrett, Louise. Beyond the Brain: How Body and Environment Shape Animal and Human Minds. Princeton: Princeton University Press, 2011.

Basquin, Bill. "A Site for Queer Reproduction." GLQ: A Journal of Lesbian and Gay Studies 14, no. 1 (2008): 122–24.

Baugh, John. "The Politicization of Changing Terms of Self-Reference among American Slave Descendants." *American Speech* 66, no. 2 (1991): 133–46.

Beck, Ulrich. *Risk Society: Towards a New Modernity*. Translated by Mark Ritter. London: Sage, 1992.

———. *World at Risk*. English ed. Cambridge: Polity, 2009.

Bennett, Jane, ed. *In the Nature of Things: Language, Politics, and the Environment*. Minneapolis: University of Minnesota Press, 1993.

———. *Vibrant Matter: A Political Ecology of Things*. Durham: Duke University Press, 2010.

Benshoff, Harry M. *Monsters in the Closet: Homosexuality and the Horror Film*. Manchester: Manchester University Press.

Benveniste, Emile. "Subjectivity in Language." In *Problems in General Linguistics*, translated by Mary Elizabeth Meek, 223–30. Miami: University of Miami Press, 1971.

Berlant, Lauren. "Intimacy: A Special Issue." *Critical Inquiry* 24, no. 2 (Winter 1998): 281–88.

———. *The Queen of America Goes to Washington City: Essays on Sex and Citizenship*. Durham: Duke University Press, 1997.

———. "Queer Nationality." *boundary 2* 19, no. 1 (Spring 1992): 149–80.

Bersani, Leo. "Is the Rectum a Grave?" *October* 43 (Winter 1987): 197–222.

———. "Sexuality and Aesthetics." *October* 28 (Spring 1984): 27–42.

Best, Stephen. *The Fugitive's Properties: Law and the Poetics of Possession*. Chicago: University of Chicago Press, 2004.

Bhabha, Homi. *The Location of Culture*. London: Routledge, 1994.

Brasher, Kimberly. *Toxic Relationships: How to Regain Lost Power in Your Relationship*. Charleston, WV: Better Life Publishing Company, 2003.

Briggs, Laura. "Foreign and Domestic: Adoption, Immigration, and Privatization." In *Intimate Labors*, edited by Eileen Boris and Rhacel Parreñas, 49–62. Stanford: Stanford University Press, 2010.

Brookhardt, D. Eric. "Mel Chin's *Operation Paydirt* Aims to Get the Lead Out of New Orleans' Inner City Neighborhoods." *Art Papers*, January/February 2009.

Brown, Wendy. *States of Injury: Power and Freedom in Late Modernity*. Princeton: Princeton University Press, 1995.

Broyard, Anatole. *Intoxicated by My Illness, and Other Writings on Life and Death*. New York: C. Potter, 1992.

Brugman, Claudia. *The Story of "Over": Polysemy, Semantics and the Structure of the Lexicon*. New York: Garland, 1988.

Bruhm, Steven, and Natasha Hurley, eds. *Curiouser: On the Queerness of Children*. Minneapolis: University of Minnesota Press, 2004.

Buell, Lawrence. "Toxic Discourse." *Critical Inquiry* 24, no. 3 (1998): 639–65.

Bullard, Robert, ed. *The Quest for Environmental Justice: Human Rights and the Politics of Pollution*. San Francisco: Sierra Club Books, 2005.

Burrington, Debra. "The Public Square and Citizen Queer: Toward a New Political Geography." *Polity* 31, no. 1 (Autumn 1998): 107–31.

Butler, Judith. *Bodies That Matter: On the Discursive Limits of Sex*. London: Routledge, 1993.

———."Critically Queer." GLQ: *A Journal of Lesbian and Gay Studies* 1, no. 1 (1993): 17–31.

———. *Excitable Speech*: *A Politics of the Performative*. New York: Routledge, 1997.

———. *Gender Trouble: Feminism and the Subversion of Identity*. New York: Routledge, 1990.

———. *Precarious Life: The Power of Mourning and Violence*. London: Verso, 2004.

Calpotura, Francis, and Rinku Sen. "PUEBLO Fights Lead Poisoning." In *Unequal Protection: Environmental Justice and Communities of Color*, edited by Robert Bullard, 234–55. San Francisco: Sierra Club Books, 1994.

Campbell, Fiona. *Contours of Ableism: The Production of Disability and Abledness*. New York: Palgrave Macmillan, 2009.

Cannick, Jasmyne A. "No-on-8's White Bias." *Los Angeles Times*, November 8, 2008.

Carlson, Licia. *The Faces of Intellectual Disability*. Bloomington: Indiana University Press, 2010.

Carlson, Marla. "Furry Cartography: Performing Species." *Theatre Journal* 63, no. 2 (May 2011): 191–208.

Carter, Julian B. *The Heart of Whiteness: Normal Sexuality and Race in America, 1800-1940*. Durham: Duke University Press, 2007.

Cartright, Jo-Anne. *Determinants of Animal Behavior*. New York: Routledge, 2002.

Césaire, Aimé. *Discourse on Colonialism*. Translated by Joan Pinkham. New York: Monthly Review Press, 1972.

Chan, Jachinson. *Chinese American Masculinities: From Fu Manchu to Bruce Lee*. New York: Routledge, 2001.

Chan, Lanyan. *Gender and Chinese Development: Towards an Equitable Society*. London: Routledge, 2008.

Chang, Grace. *Disposable Domestics: Women Workers in the Global Economy*. Cambridge: South End, 1999.

Chang, Leslie. *Factory Girls: From Village to City in a Changing China*. New York: Spiegel and Grau, 2008.

Chasin, Alexandra. *Selling Out: The Gay and Lesbian Movement Goes to Market*. New York: Palgrave, 2000.

Chauncey, George. *Gay New York: Gender, Urban Culture, and the Making of the Gay Male World, 1890-1940*. New York: Basic, 1994.

Chávez, Karma R. "Exploring the Defeat of Arizona's Marriage Amendment and the Specter of the Immigrant as Queer." *Southern Communication Journal* 74, no. 3 (July 2009): 314–24.

Checker, Melissa. *Polluted Promises: Environmental Racism and the Search for Justice in a Southern Town*. New York: New York University Press, 2005.

Chen, Mel Y. "Everywhere Archives: Transgendering, Trans Asians, and the Internet." *Australian Feminist Studies* 25, no. 64 (June 2010): 199–208.

Chen, Shu-Ching Jean. "Chinese Toy Terror." *Forbes*, August 2, 2007.

Chen, Tina. "Dissecting the 'Devil Doctor': Stereotype and Sensationalism in Sax Rohmer's *Fu Manchu*." In *Re-Collecting Early Asian America*, edited by Josephine Lee, Imogene Lim, and Yuko Matsukawa, 218–37. Philadelphia: Temple University Press, 2002.

Cheng, Anne. *The Melancholy of Race*. New York: Oxford University Press, 2000.

Cherry, John. "Animism in Thought and Language." Ph.D. diss., Department of Linguistics, University of California, Berkeley, 2002.

"Chimp Victim Reveals Face on *Oprah*." *New Haven Register*, November 12, 2009.

Chin, Frank. "Confessions of a Chinatown Cowboy." In *Bulletproof Buddhists, and Other Essays*, 63–110. Honolulu: University of Hawaii Press, 1998.

China Blue. Directed by Micha Peled. San Francisco: Teddy Bear Films and Independent Television Service, 2005.

Chinn, Sarah. "Feeling Her Way: Audre Lorde and the Power of Touch." GLQ: *A Journal of Lesbian and Gay Studies* 9, no. 1–2 (2003): 181–204.

Choi, Chungmoo. "The Discourse of Decolonization and Popular Memory: South Korea." In *The Politics of Culture in the Shadow of Capital*, edited by Lisa Lowe and David Lloyd, 461–84. Durham: Duke University Press, 1997.

Chun, Wendy Hui Kyong. *Control and Freedom: Power and Paranoia in the Age of Fiber Optics*. Cambridge: MIT Press, 2006.

Clare, Eli. *Exile and Pride: Disability, Queerness and Liberation*. Cambridge, MA: South End, 1999.

———. *The Marrow's Telling: Words in Motion*. Ypsilanti, MI: Homofactus, 2007.

Clarkson, Thomas W. "Metal Toxicity in the Central Nervous System." *Environmental Health Perspectives* 75 (1987): 59–64.

Clegg, Jenny. *Fu Manchu and the Yellow Peril: The Making of a Racist Myth*. Stoke-on-Trent, UK: Trentham, 1994.

Cleto, Fabio. "Introduction: Queering the Camp." In *Camp: Queer Aesthetics and the Performing Subject: A Reader*, edited by Fabio Cleto, 1–42. Ann Arbor: University of Michigan Press, 1999.

Clifford, Mark. "The Humbling of Jimmy Lai." *Business Week*, October, 23, 2000.

Clough, Patricia Ticineto. *Autoaffection: Unconscious Thought in the Age of Teletechnology*. Minneapolis: University of Minnesota Press, 2000.

CNN Political Ticker Blog. "Democratic Governor Candidate: Health Care

Reform Could Be 'Toxic' in 2010." Blog entry by Peter Hamby, October 12, 2010.

Coates, Paul. "Repetition and Contradiction in the Films of Oshima." *Quarterly Review of Film and Video* 11, no. 4 (1990): 65–71.

Cohen, Cathy. "Punks, Bulldaggers, and Welfare Queens: The Radical Potential of Queer Politics?" *GLQ: A Journal of Lesbian and Gay Studies* 3, no. 4 (1997): 437–66.

Cohen, Ed. *A Body Worth Defending: Immunity, Biopolitics, and the Apothesosis of the Modern Body*. Durham: Duke University Press, 2009.

Cohen, T. "Gay and the Disappearing [+Female]: Using the Word to Include Lesbians Strains Linguistic Credibility." *Gay and Lesbian Review* 9, no. 6 (2002): 22–24.

Colebrook, Claire. "On Not Becoming Man: The Materialist Politics of Unactualized Potential." In *Material Feminisms*, edited by Stacy Alaimo and Susan Hekman, 52–84. Bloomington: Indiana University Press, 2008.

Comrie, Bernard. *Language Universals and Linguistic Typology*. Chicago: University of Chicago Press, 1981.

Condry, Ian. "Yellow B-Boys, Black Culture, and Hip-Hop in Japan: Toward a Transnational Cultural Politics of Race." *positions: East Asia Cultures Critique* 15, no. 3 (Winter 2007): 657–59.

Coole, Diana, and Samantha Frost. "Introducing the New Materialisms." In *New Materialisms: Ontology, Agency, and Politics*, edited by Diana Coole and Samantha Frost, 1–46. Durham: Duke University Press, 2010.

Cornyetz, Nina. "Fetishizing Blackness: Hip Hop and Racial Desire in Contemporary Japan." *Social Text* 41 (Winter 1994): 113–39.

Cottle, Michelle. "Toy Terror." *New Republic*, August 13, 2007.

Creed, Barbara. "A Darwinian Love Story: *Max mon amour* and the Zoo-centric Perspective in Film." *Continuum: Journal of Media and Cultural Studies* 20, no. 1 (March 2006): 45–60.

Crimp, Douglas, and Adam Rolston. *AIDS Demo Graphics*. Seattle: Bay, 1991.

Croft, William. "Modern Syntactic Typology." In *Approaches to Language Typology*, edited by Masayushi Shibatani and Theodora Bynon, 85–144. New York: Oxford University Press, 1995.

Croft, William, and D. Alan Cruse. *Cognitive Linguistics*. Cambridge: Cambridge University Press, 2004.

Cvetkovich, Ann. *An Archive of Feelings: Trauma, Sexuality, and Lesbian Public Cultures*. Durham: Duke University Press, 2003.

———. "Sexual Trauma/Queer Memory: Incest, Lesbianism, and Therapeutic Culture." *GLQ: A Journal of Lesbian and Gay Studies* 2, no. 4 (1995): 351–77.

Dahl, Osten, and Kari Fraurud. "Animacy in Grammar and Discourse." In *Reference and Referent Accessibility*, edited by Thorstein Freitheim and Jeannette Gundel, 47–64. Philadelphia: John Benjamins, 1996.

D'Arcangelis, Gwen. "Chinese Chickens, Ducks, Pigs and Humans, and the Technoscientific Discourses of Global U.S. Empire." In *Tactical Biopoli-*

tics: Art, Activism, and Technoscience, edited by Beatriz da Costa and Kavita Philip. Cambridge: MIT Press, 2008.

Daston, Lorraine, ed. *Things That Talk: Object Lessons from Art and Science.* New York: Zone, 2004.

Davidson, Donald. *Subjective, Intersubjective, Objective.* Oxford: Clarendon Press, 2001.

Davidson, Michael. "Universal Design: The Work of Disability in an Age of Globalization." In *Disability Studies Reader,* edited by Lennard Davis, 117–28. New York: Routledge, 1996.

Davis, Angela. "Masked Racism: Reflections on the Prison Industrial Complex." *Color Lines,* September 10, 1998, 12–17.

Davis, Lennard. "An End to It All." *Chicago Tribune,* March 27, 2005.

———. "Life, Death, and Biocultural Literacy." *Chronicle Review,* January 6, 2006.

Dean, Carolyn. *A Culture of Stone: Inka Perspectives on Rock.* Durham: Duke University Press, 2010.

De Kosnik, Abigail. *Illegitimate Media: Minority Discourse and the Censorship of Digital Remix Culture.* Athens: University of Georgia Press, forthcoming.

de Lauretis, Teresa. "Queer Texts, Bad Habits, and the Issue of a Future." *GLQ: A Journal of Lesbian and Gay Studies* 17, no. 2–3 (2011): 243–63.

———. "Queer Theory: Lesbian and Gay Sexualities." *differences: A Journal of Feminist Cultural Studies* 3 (1991): iii–xviii.

Deleuze, Gilles, and Félix Guattari. *Anti-Oedipus: Capitalism and Schizophrenia.* New York: Penguin Classics, 1977.

———. *A Thousand Plateaus: Capitalism and Schizophrenia.* Translated by Brian Massumi. Minneapolis: University of Minnesota Press, 1987.

Delonas, Sean. Op-ed cartoon. *New York Post,* February 18, 2009.

Derrida, Jacques. "And Say the Animal Responded?" In *The Animal That Therefore I Am,* edited by Marie-Louis Mallet, translated by David Wills, 119–40. New York: Fordham University Press, 2008.

———. "Signature Event Context." Translated by Samuel Weber and Jeffrey Mehlman. *Glyph* 1 (1977): 172–97.

Di Chiro, Giovanna. "Polluted Politics? Confronting Toxic Discourse, Sex Panic, and Eco-Normativity." In *Queer Ecologies: Sex, Nature, Politics, Desire,* edited by Catriona Mortimer-Sandilands and Bruce Erickson, 199–230. Bloomington: Indiana University Press, 2010.

Dinshaw, Carolyn. *Getting Medieval: Sexualities and Communities, Pre- and Postmodern.* Durham: Duke University Press, 1999.

Dirven, René, and Marjolyn Verspoor. *Cognitive Exploration of Language and Linguistics.* Amsterdam: John Benjamins, 2004.

Dixon, Robert M. W. *Ergativity.* Cambridge: Cambridge University Press, 1994.

Duggan, Lisa. "Making It Perfectly Queer." In *Sex Wars: Sexual Dissent and Political Culture,* edited by Lisa Duggan and Nan Hunter, 155–72. New York: Routledge, 1995.

———— *The Twilight of Equality? Neoliberalism, Cultural Politics, and the Attack on Democracy*. Boston: Beacon, 2003.

Durkin, Philip. *The Oxford Guide to Etymology*. Oxford: Oxford University Press, 2009.

Dworkin, Andrea. *Pornography: Men Possessing Women*. New York: Dutton, 1981.

Edelman, Lee. *No Future: Queer Theory and the Death Drive*. Durham: Duke University Press, 2004.

Eng, David. *The Feeling of Kinship: Queer Liberalism and the Racialization of Intimacy*. Durham: Duke University Press, 2010.

————. *Racial Castration: Managing Masculinity in Asian America*. Durham: Duke University, 2001.

Eng, David L., and David Kazanjian, eds. *Loss: The Politics of Mourning*. Berkeley: University of California Press, 2003.

Enstad, Nan. "Toxicity and the Consuming Subject." In *States of Emergency: The Object of American Studies*, edited by Russ Castronovo and Susan Gillman, 55–68. Chapel Hill: University of North Carolina Press, 2009.

Esposito, Roberto. *Bios: Biopolitics and Philosophy*. Minneapolis: University of Minnesota Press, 2008.

Fairclough, Norman. *Discourse and Social Change*. Cambridge: Polity, 1992.

Fanon, Frantz. *Black Skin, White Masks*. Translated by Charles Lan Markmann. New York: Grove, 1967. First French edition published in 1952 by Editions du Seuil.

————. *Wretched of the Earth*. Translated by Richard Philcox. New York: Grove, 2005. First published 1963.

Fauconnier, Gilles. *Mappings in Thought and Language*. Cambridge: Cambridge University Press, 1997.

Fauconnier, Gilles, and Mark Turner. *Mental Spaces: Aspects of Meaning Construction in Natural Language*. Cambridge: Cambridge University Press, 1994.

————. *The Way We Think: Conceptual Blending and the Mind's Hidden Complexities*. New York: Basic, 2002.

Feinberg, Leslie. *Stone Butch Blues*. Ithaca: Firebrand, 1993.

Feldman, Alan. "Mediating Inhumanization: The Emblem and the Animorph." *Television and New Media* 10, no. 1 (January 2009): 52–54.

Felman, Shoshana. *The Scandal of the Speaking Body: Don Juan with J. L. Austin, or Seduction in Two Languages*. Stanford: Stanford University Press, 1993.

Ferguson, Roderick. *Aberrations in Black: Toward a Queer of Color Critique*. Minneapolis: University of Minnesota Press, 2004.

Fleischman, Suzanne. "Language and Medicine." In *Handbook of Discourse Analysis*, edited by Deborah Schiffrin, Deborah Tannen, and Heidi E. Hamilton, 470–502. Malden, MA: Blackwell, 2001.

Foucault, Michel. "The Birth of Biopolitics." In *Michel Foucault, Ethics: Subjectivity and Truth*, edited by Paul Rabinow, 73–79. New York: New Press, 1997.

————. "Governmentality." Translated by Rosi Braidotti. Revised by

Colin Gordon. In *The Foucault Effect: Studies in Governmentality*, edited by Graham Burchell, Colin Gordon, and Peter Miller, 87–104. Chicago: University of Chicago Press, 1991.

———. *The History of Sexuality*. Vol. 1, *An Introduction*. New York: Pantheon, 1978.

———. *The Order of Things: An Archaeology of the Human Sciences*. New York: Pantheon, 1971.

Franklin, Sarah. "The Cyborg Embryo: Our Path to Transbiology." *Theory, Culture and Society* 23, no. 7–8 (2006): 167–87.

———. *Dolly Mixtures: The Remaking of Genealogy*. Durham: Duke University Press, 2007.

Freccero, Carla. "Les chats de Derrida." In *Derrida and Queer Theory*, edited by Michael O'Rourke. Basingstoke, UK: Palgrave, 2012.

———. *Queer/Early/Modern*. Durham: Duke University Press, 2005.

———. "Queer Times." *South Atlantic Quarterly* 106, no. 3 (Summer 2007): 485–93.

Frede, Michael. "On Aristotle's Conception of the Soul." In *Essays on Aristotle's De Anima*, edited by Martha Nussbaum and Amélie Oksenberg Rorty, 93–108. Oxford: Oxford University Press, 2003.

Freeman, Elizabeth, ed. "Queer Temporalities." Special issue, GLQ: *A Journal of Lesbian and Gay Studies* 13, no. 2–3 (2007).

———. *Time Binds: Queer Temporalities, Queer Histories*. Durham: Duke University Press, 2010.

Freud, Sigmund. "Fetishism" In *Standard Edition of the Complete Psychological Works of Sigmund Freud*, vol. 2, translated by Joan Riviere, edited by James Strachey, 147–57. New York: W. W. Norton, 1976. First published 1927.

———. "Remembering, Repeating, and Working-Through: Further Recommendations on the Technique of Psychoanalysis II." In *Standard Edition of the Complete Psychological Works of Sigmund Freud*, vol. 2, translated by Joan Riviere, edited by James Strachey, 145–56. New York: W. W. Norton, 1976. First published 1914.

Fuchs, Cynthia. "Michael Jackson's Penis." In *Cruising the Performative*, edited by Sue-Ellen Case, Philip Brett, and Susan Leigh Foster, 13–33. Bloomington: Indiana University Press, 1995.

Fung, Richard. "Looking for My Penis: The Eroticized Asian in Gay Video Porn." In *Asian American Sexualities: Dimensions of the Gay and Lesbian Experience*, edited by Russell Leung, 181–98. New York: Routledge, 1996.

Gaard, Greta Claire. *Ecofeminism: Women, Animals, Nature*. Philadelphia: Temple University Press, 1993.

———. "Toward a Queer Ecofeminism." *Hypatia* 12, no. 1 (Winter 1997): 114–37.

Gates, Henry Louis, Jr., *The Signifying Monkey: A Theory of African-American Literary Criticism*. New York: Oxford University Press, 1988.

Gay, Lesbian, and Straight Education Network. *National School Climate Survey*. New York: GLSEN, 2009.

Giffney, Noreen, and Myra Hird, eds. *Queering the Non/Human*. Burlington, VT: Ashgate, 2008.

Giles, Herbert. *The Civilization of China*. Los Angeles: Indo-European Publishing, 2010. First published 1921.

Gilroy, Paul. *Against Race: Imagining Political Culture Beyond the Color Line*. Cambridge: Harvard University Press, 2002.

———. *The Black Atlantic*. Cambridge: Harvard University Press, 1993.

Glass, Lillian. *Toxic People: 10 Ways of Dealing with People Who Make Your Life Miserable*. New York: St. Martin's Griffin, 1997.

Glenn, Evelyn Nakano. *Forced to Care: Coercion and Caregiving in America*. Cambridge: Harvard University Press, 2010.

———, ed. *Shades of Difference: Why Skin Color Matters*. Stanford: Stanford University Press, 2009.

Goffman, Erving. *Stigma: Notes on the Management of Spoiled Identity*. Upper Saddle River, NJ: Prentice Hall, 1963.

Goldberg, Jonathan. *Queering the Renaissance*. Durham: Duke University Press, 1995.

Goldberg-Hiller, Jonathan, and Noenoe K. Silva. "Sharks and Pigs: Animating Hawaiian Sovereignty against the Anthropological Machine." *South Atlantic Quarterly* 110, no. 2 (Spring 2011): 429–46.

Gopinath, Gayatri. *Impossible Desires: Queer Diasporas and South Asian Public Cultures*. Durham: Duke University Press, 2005.

Gould, Stephen Jay. *The Mismeasure of Man*. New York: W. W. Norton, 1981.

Grandin, Temple. *Animals in Translation: Using the Mysteries of Autism to Decode Animal Behavior*. New York: Simon and Schuster, 2005.

Griffin, Susan. *What Her Body Thought: A Journey into the Shadows*. New York: Harper Collins, 1999.

Grossman, Lev. "Citizens of the New Digital Democracy." *Time*, December 25, 2006.

Grosz, Elizabeth. *Volatile Bodies: Toward a Corporeal Feminism*. Bloomington: Indiana University Press, 1994.

Halberstam, Judith. "Animating Revolt/Revolting Animation: Penguin Love, Doll Sex, and the Spectacle of the Queer Nonhuman." In *Queering the Non/Human*, edited by Noreen Giffney and Myra Hird, 265–81. Burlington, VT: Ashgate, 2008.

———. *Female Masculinity*. Durham: Duke University Press, 1998.

———. *In a Queer Time and Place: Transgender Bodies, Subcultural Lives*. New York: New York University Press, 2005.

———. *The Queer Art of Failure*. Durham: Duke University Press, 2011.

Halperin, David M. *Saint Foucault: Towards a Gay Hagiography*. New York: Oxford University Press, 1994.

Hansen, Natalie Corinne. "Humans, Horses, and Hormones: (Trans) Gendering Cross-Species Relationships." *WSQ: Women's Studies Quarterly* 36, no. 3–4 (2008): 87–105.

Haraway, Donna. "The Biopolitics of Postmodern Bodies: Determinations of Self in Immune System Discourse." *differences: A Journal of Feminist Cultural Studies* 1, no. 1 (1989): 3–43.

———. "Manifesto for Cyborgs: Science, Technology, and Socialist Feminism in the 1980s." *Socialist Review* 15, no. 80 (1985): 65–108.

———. *Modest_Witness@Second_Millenium.FemaleMan_Meets_OncoMouse: Feminism and Technoscience*. London: Routledge, 1997.

———. *Primate Visions: Gender, Race, and Nature in a World of Modern Science*. New York: Routledge, 1989.

———. "The Promises of Monsters: A Regenerative Politics for Inappropriate(d) Others." In *Cultural Studies*, edited by Lawrence Grossberg, Cary Nelson, and Paula A. Treichler, 295–337. New York; Routledge, 1992.

———. *Simians, Cyborgs, and Women: The Reinvention of Nature*. London: Routledge, 1990.

Harris, Cheryl L. "Whiteness as Property." *Harvard Law Review* 106, no. 8 (June 1993): 1701–91.

Harris, Gardiner. "Heparin Contamination May Have Been Deliberate, F.D.A. Says." *New York Times*, April 30, 2008.

Hartman, Saidiya. *Scenes of Subjection: Terror, Slavery, and Self-Making in Nineteenth-Century America*. Oxford: Oxford University Press, 1997.

Harvey, David. *A Brief History of Neoliberalism*. Oxford: Oxford University Press, 2007.

Hayden, Cori. *When Nature Goes Public: The Making and Unmaking of Bioprospecting in Mexico*. Princeton: Princeton University Press, 2003.

Hayles, N. Katherine. *How We Became Posthuman: Virtual Bodies in Cybernetics, Literature, and Informatics*. Chicago: University of Chicago Press, 1999.

Hayward, Eva. "Lessons from a Starfish." In *Queering the Non/Human*, edited by Noreen Giffney and Myra Hird, 249–63. Burlington, VT: Ashgate, 2008.

———. "More Lessons from a Starfish: Prefixial Flesh and Transspeciated Selves." *Women's Studies Quarterly* 36, no. 3–4 (Fall/Winter 2008): 64–85.

Heidegger, Martin. "The Origin of the Work of Art." In *Poetry, Language, Thought*, translated by Albert Hofstadter. New York: Harper and Row, 1971.

Heise, Ursula. "From Extinction to Electronics: Dead Frogs, Live Dinosaurs, and Electric Sheep." *Zoontologies: The Question of the Animal*, edited by Cary Wolfe, 59–81. Minneapolis: University of Minnesota Press, 2003.

Herring, Scott. *Another Country: Queer Anti-Urbanism*. New York: New York University Press, 2010.

Hightower, Jane M. *Diagnosis Mercury: Money, Politics and Poison*. Washington, DC: Island Press/Shearwater Books, 2009.

Hird, Myra. "Animal Transex." *Australian Feminist Studies* 21, no. 49 (March 2006): 35–50.

Hock, Hans. *Principles of Historical Linguistics*. 2nd ed. Berlin: Mouton de Gruyter, 1986.

Hogan, Linda, Deena Metzger, and Brenda Peterson, eds. *Intimate Nature: The Bond between Women and Animals.* New York: Fawcett Columbine, 1998.

hooks, bell. *Black Looks: Race and Representation.* London: Turnaround, 1992.

———. "The Oppositional Gaze: Black Female Spectators." In *Black Looks: Race and Representation*, 115–31 Boston: South End, 1992.

Houlbrook, Matt. *Queer London: Perils and Pleasures in the Sexual Metropolis, 1918-1957.* Chicago: University of Chicago Press, 2005.

Jackson, Michael. Interview with interviewer unknown. *100 Greatest Videos*, MTV, 1999.

Jain, S. Lochlann. "Cancer Butch." *Cultural Anthropology* 22, no. 4 (2007): 501–38.

———. *Injury: The Politics of Product Design and Safety Law in the United States.* Princeton: Princeton University Press, 2006.

Jennings, Angel. "Thomas the Tank Engine Toys Recalled Because of Lead Hazard." *New York Times*, June 15, 2007.

Jennings, Cheri Lucas, and Bruce H. Jennings. "Green Fields/Brown Skin: Posting as a Sign of Recognition." In *The Nature of Things: Language, Politics, and the Environment*, edited by Jane Bennett and William Chaloupka, 173–94. Minneapolis: University of Minnesota Press, 1993.

Johnson, Barbara. "Apostrophe, Animation, and Abortion." *Diacritics* 16, no. 1 (Spring 1986): 28–47.

Johnson, E. Patrick. "'Quare' Studies, or (Almost) Everything I Learned about Queer I Learned from My Grandmother." In *Black Queer Studies: A Critical Anthology*, edited by E. Patrick Johnson and Mae G. Henderson, 124–57. Durham: Duke University Press, 2005.

Kafer, Alison. "Accessible Futures: Feminist, Queer, Crip." Unpublished book manuscript, Southwestern University.

———. Compulsory Bodies: Reflections on Heterosexuality and Able-Bodiedness." *Journal of Women's History* 15, no. 3 (2003): 77–89.

———. "Inseparable: Gender and Disability in the Amputee-Devotee Community." In *Gendering Disability*, edited by Bonnie G. Smith and Beth Hutchison, 107–18. New Brunswick, NJ: Rutgers University Press, 2004.

Kang, Laura Hyun Yi. "Si(gh)ting Asian/American Women as Transnational Labor." *positions: East Asia Cultures Critique* 5, no. 2 (1997): 403–37.

Katayama, Lisa. "Love in 2-D." *New York Times*, July 26, 2009.

Kim, Claire Jean. "The Racial Triangulation of Asian-Americans." *Politics and Society* 27, no. 1 (March 1999): 105–38.

Kim, Daniel Y. *Writing Manhood in Black and Yellow.* Stanford: Stanford University Press, 2005.

Kim, Elaine. *Asian American Literature: An Introduction to the Writings and Their Social Context.* Philadelphia: Temple University Press, 1982.

Kim, Richard. "Marital Discord: Why Prop 8 Won." *The Nation*, November 5, 2008.

Kimmerer, Robin Wall. "Learning the Grammar of Animacy." In *Colors of*

Nature: Culture, Identity, and the Natural World, edited by Alison H. Deming and Lauret E. Savoy, 167–77. Minneapolis: Milkweed Editions, 2002.

Kingery, W. David. *Learning from Things: Method and Theory of Material Culture Studies*. Washington, DC: Smithsonian Institute, 1998.

Kirby, David. *Evidence of Harm: Mercury in Vaccines and the Autism Epidemic: A Medical Controversy*. New York: St. Martin's Press, 2006.

Kittay, Eva. *Love's Labor Essays on Women, Equality and Dependency*. London: Routledge, 1999.

Klein, Naomi. *The Shock Doctrine: The Rise of Disaster Capitalism*. New York: Henry Holt, 2007.

Kleinfeld, Mari, and Noni Warner. "Lexical Variation in the Deaf Community Relating to Gay, Lesbian, and Bisexual Signs." In *Queerly Phrased: Language, Gender, and Sexuality*, edited by Anna Livia and Kira Hall, 58–84. Oxford: Oxford University Press, 1997.

Kluchin, Rebecca M. *Fit to Be Tied: Sterilization and Reproductive Rights in America, 1950-1980*. New Brunswick, NJ: Rutgers University Press, 2009.

Kosek, Jake. *Understories: The Political Life of Forests in Northern New Mexico*. Durham: Duke University Press, 2006.

Kristeva, Julia. *Powers of Horror: An Essay on Abjection*. Translated by Leon S. Roudiez. New York: Columbia University Press, 1982.

Kusy, Mitchell, and Elizabeth Holloway. *Toxic Workplace! Managing Toxic Personalities and Their Systems of Power*. San Francisco: John Wiley and Sons, 2009.

Lacan, Jacques. "The Agency of the Letter in the Unconscious or Reason since Freud." In *Écrits: A Selection*, translated by Alan Sheridan, 146–78. New York: W. W. Norton, 1977.

LaDuke, Winona. "Akwesasne: Mohawk Mother's Milk and PCBs." In *Sing, Whisper, Shout, Pray! Feminist Visions for a Just World*, edited by M. Jacqui Alexander, Lisa Albrecht, Sharon Day, and Mab Segrest, 158–71. Fort Bragg, CA: EdgeWork, 2003.

Lague, David. "China Output Not a Threat, Officials Say." *New York Times*, April 1, 2006.

Lakoff, Andrew. *Biosecurity Interventions: Global Health and Security in Question*. New York: Columbia University Press, 2008.

———. "National Security and the Changing Object of Public Health." In *Biosecurity Interventions: Global Health and Security in Question*, edited by Andrew Lakoff and Stephen J. Coller, 33–60. New York: Columbia University Press, 2008.

Lakoff, George. *Women, Fire, and Dangerous Things*. Chicago: University of Chicago Press, 1987.

Lammers, Dirk. "What to Do When Everything Is 'Made in China?'" MSNBC.com, June 29, 2007.

Langacker, Ronald. *Cognitive Grammar: A Basic Introduction*. New York: Oxford University Press, 2008.

—. *Concept, Image, and Symbol: The Cognitive Basis of Grammar.* Berlin: Mouton de Gruyter, 1990.

Laqueur, Thomas. *Making Sex: Body and Gender from the Greeks to Freud.* Cambridge: Harvard University Press, 1990.

Latour, Bruno. *We Have Never Been Modern.* Translated by Catherine Porter. Cambridge: Harvard University Press, 1993. First French edition published 1991 as *Nous n'avons jamais ete modernes: Essais d'anthropologie symmétrique.*

Leap, William, and Tom Boellstorff, eds. *Speaking in Queer Tongues: Globalization and Gay Language.* Urbana: University of Illinois Press, 2004.

Lee, James Kyung-jin. *Urban Triage: Race and the Fictions of Multiculturalism.* Minneapolis: University of Minnesota Press, 2004.

Lei, Xie. *Environmental Activism in China.* London: Routledge, 2009.

Leung, Wency. "How to Survive a Toxic Workplace." *Globe and Mail,* March 22, 2010.

Lin, Xiaoping. "Globalism or Nationalism?" *Third Text* 18 (2004): 4279–95.

Lippit, Akira Mizuta, *Electric Animal: Toward a Rhetoric of Wildlife.* Minneapolis: University of Minnesota Press, 2000.

—. "The Films of Oshima Nagisa: Images of a Japanese Iconoclast." *Monumenta Nipponica* 54, no. 1 (Spring 1999).

Lipton, Eric S., and David Barboza. "As More Toys Are Recalled, Trail Ends in China." *New York Times,* June 19, 2007.

"The Living Legacy of Lead." *Living on Earth,* National Public Radio, November 2, 2007.

Lock, Margaret, and Judith Farquhar, eds. *Beyond the Body Proper: Reading the Anthropology of Material Life.* Durham: Duke University Press, 2007.

Longmore, Paul. *Why I Burned My Book, and Other Essays on Disability.* Philadelphia: Temple University Press, 2003.

Lorde, Audre. *The Cancer Journals.* Argyle, NY: Spinsters Ink, 1980.

Lott, Eric. *Love and Theft: Blackface Minstrelsy and the American Working Class.* New York: Oxford University Press, 1993.

Love, Heather. *Feeling Backward: Loss and the Politics of Queer History.* Cambridge: Harvard University Press, 2007.

Lowe, Lisa. *Immigrant Acts: On Asian American Cultural Politics.* Durham: Duke University Press, 1996.

Lutz, Catherine A., and Jane L. Collins. *Reading National Geographic.* Chicago: University of Chicago Press, 1993.

MacKinnon, Catherine. *Only Words.* Cambridge: Harvard University Press, 1994.

Mak, W. M., W. Vonk, and H. Schriefers. "Animacy in Processing Relative Clauses: The Hikers That Rocks Crush." *Journal of Memory and Language* 54, no. 4 (2006): 466–90.

Malchow, Howard L. *Gothic Images of Race in Nineteenth-Century Britain.* Stanford: Stanford University Press, 1996.

Maquilopolis: City of Factories. Produced by Vicky Funari and Sergio de la Torrc, 2006. Distributed by California Newsreel.

Martin, Emily. *Flexible Bodies: Tracking Immunity in American Culture from the Days of Polio to the Age of AIDS*. Boston: Beacon Press, 1994.

Marx, Karl. *Economic and Philosophical Manuscripts of 1844*. Translated by Martin Mulligan. Moscow: Progress Publishers, 1959.

Matsuda, Mari. "Public Response to Racist Speech: Considering the Victim's Story." *Michigan Law Review* 87, no. 8 (August 1989): 2320–21.

———. *Words That Wound: Critical Race Theory, Assaultive Speech, and the First Amendment*. Boulder, CO: Westview, 1993.

"Mattel Issues New Massive China Toy Recall." MSNBC.com, August 14, 2007.

Mbembe, Achille. "Necropolitics." Translated by Libby Meintjes. *Public Culture* 15, no. 1 (2003): 11–40.

———. *On the Postcolony*. Berkeley: University of California Press, 2001.

McClintock, Anne. *Imperial Leather: Race, Gender and Sexuality in the Colonial Conquest*. New York: Routledge, 1995.

McRuer, Robert. *Crip Theory: Cultural Signs of Queerness and Disability*. New York: New York University Press, 2006.

McRuer, Robert, and Abby Wilkerson. "Introduction." GLQ: *A Journal of Lesbian and Gay Studies* 9, no. 1–2 (2003): 1–23.

Memmi, Albert. *The Colonizer and the Colonized*. New York: Beacon, 1965. First published 1957.

Miller, Terri Beth. "'Reading' the Body of Terri Schiavo: Inscriptions of Power in Medical and Legal Discourse." *Literature and Medicine* 28, no. 1 (Spring 2009): 33–54.

Mitchell, David T., and Sharon L. Snyder. *Narrative Prosthesis: Disability and the Dependencies of Discourse*. Ann Arbor: University of Michigan Press, 2001.

Miyazaki, Hayao. *The Art of Ponyo: Ponyo on the Cliff by the Sea*. San Francisco: Viz Media, 2009.

Mollow, Anna. "No Safe Place." WSQ: *Women's Studies Quarterly* 39, no. 1–2 (Spring/Summer 2011): 188–99.

Monroe, Irene. "Race, Religion, and Proposition 8." *The Advocate*, November 12, 2008.

Moore, Donald, Jake Kosek, and Anand Pandian, eds. *Race, Nature, and the Politics of Difference*. Durham: Duke University Press, 2003.

Morley, David, and Kevin Robins. *Spaces of Identity: Global Media, Electronic Landscapes and Cultural Boundaries*. London: Routledge, 1995.

Mortimer-Sandilands, Catriona, and Bruce Erickson, eds. *Queer Ecologies: Sex, Nature, Politics, Desire*. Bloomington: Indiana University Press, 2010.

Mukhopadhyay, Tito Rajarshi. *How Can I Talk If My Lips Don't Move? Inside My Autistic Mind*. New York: Arcade, 2008.

Mulvey, Laura. "Visual Pleasure and Narrative Cinema." *Screen* 16, no. 3 (Autumn 1975): 6–18.

Muñoz, José Esteban. *Cruising Utopia: The Then and There of Queer Futurity.* New York: New York University Press, 2009.

―――. *Disidentifications: Queers of Color and the Performance of Politics.* Minneapolis: University of Minnesota Press, 1999.

Munt, Sally. *Queer Attachments: The Cultural Politics of Shame.* Burlington, VT: Ashgate, 2007.

Nash, Linda. "Fruits of Ill-Health: Pesticides and Workers' Bodies in Post–World War II California." In *Landscapes of Exposure: Knowledge and Illness in Modern Environments,* edited by Greg Mitman, Michelle Murphy, and Christopher Sellers, 203–19. Chicago: University of Chicago Press, 2004.

Nast, Heidi J. "Critical Pet Studies?" *Antipode* 38, no. 5 (November 2006): 894–906.

―――. "Loving . . . Whatever: Alienation, Neoliberalism and Pet-Love in the Twenty-First Century." *ACME: An International E-Journal for Critical Geographies* 5, no. 2 (2006): 300–27.

Nestle, Marion. *Safe Food: Bacteria, Biotechnology, and Bioterrorism.* Berkeley: University of California Press, 2003

"New Worries over Lead." *Consumer Reports,* December 2007.

Ngai, Sianne. *Ugly Feelings.* Cambridge: Harvard University Press, 2005.

Nussbaum, Martha. "Objectification." *Philosophy and Public Affairs* 24, no. 4 (October 1995): 249–83.

Oliver, Kelly. *Animal Lessons: How They Teach Us to Be Human.* New York: Columbia University Press, 2009.

Olmstead, Dan, and Mark Blaxill. *The Age of Autism: Mercury, Medicine and a Man-Made Epidemic.* New York: Thomas Dunne Books/St. Martin's Press, 2010.

Osteen, Mark, ed. *Autism and Representation.* New York: Routledge, 2007.

Parkes, Graham. "The Awareness of Rock: East Asian Understandings and Implications." In *Mind That Abides: Panpsychism in the New Millennium,* edited by David Skirbina, 325–40. Amsterdam: John Benjamins, 2009.

Patton, Cindy. "Stealth Bombers of Desire: The Globalization of 'Alterity' in Emerging Democracies." In *Queer Globalizations: Citizenship and the Afterlife of Colonialism,* edited by Arnaldo Cruz-Malavé and Martin F. Manalansan, 195–218. New York: New York University Press, 2002.

Peluso, Nancy Lee, and Michael Watts, eds. *Violent Environments.* Ithaca: Cornell University Press, 2001.

"Person of the Year: You." *Time,* December 25, 2006.

Philo, Chris, and Chris Wilbert. "Introduction." In *Animal Spaces, Beastly Places,* edited by Chris Philo and Chris Wilbert. London: Routledge, 2000.

Plotz, John. "Can the Sofa Speak? A Look at Thing Theory." *Criticism* 47, no. 1 (2006): 109–18.

Povinelli, Elizabeth. *The Empire of Love: Toward a Theory of Intimacy, Genealogy, and Carnality.* Durham: Duke University Press, 2006.

Prosser, Jay. *Second Skins: The Body Narratives of Transsexuality*. New York: Columbia University Press, 1998.

Puar, Jasbir K. *Terrorist Assemblages: Homonationalism in Queer Times*. Durham: Duke University Press, 2007.

———. "A Transnational Feminist Critique of Queer Tourism." *Antipode* 34, no. 5 (2002): 935–46.

Pulido, Laura. *Environmentalism and Economic Justice: Two Chicano Studies in the Southwest*. Tuscon: University of Arizona Press, 1996.

Qayum, Seemin, and Raka Ray. "Traveling Cultures of Servitude." In *Intimate Labors: Cultures, Technologies, and the Politics of Care*, edited by Eileen Boris and Rhacel Parreñas, 101–16. Stanford: Stanford University Press, 2010.

Quayson, Ato. *Aesthetic Nervousness: Disability and the Crisis of Representation*. New York: Columbia University Press, 2007.

"Range." Directed by Bill Basquin, 8 minutes, 16 mm. 2005.

Raphael-Hernandez, Heike, and Shannon Steen, eds. *Afro Asian Encounters. Culture, History, Politics*. New York: New York University Press, 2006.

Reassemblage. Directed by Trinh T. Minh-ha. Wychoff, NJ: Women Make Movies, 1982.

Rich, Frank. "2006: The Year of the 'Macaca.'" *New York Times*, November 12, 2006.

Riley, Denise. *Impersonal Passion: Language as Affect*. Durham: Duke University Press, 2005.

Ritvo, Harriet. *The Animal Estate: The English and Other Creatures in the Victorian Age*. Cambridge: Harvard University Press, 1987.

———. *The Platypus and the Mermaid, and Other Figments of the Classifying Imagination*. Cambridge: Harvard University Press, 1997.

Rodríguez, Juana María. "Queer Sociality and Sexual Fantasies." Lecture at Center for Study of Sexual Cultures, University of California, Berkeley, February 8, 2010.

Roediger, David. *The Wages of Whiteness: Race and the Making of the American Working Class*. London: Verso, 1991.

Rofel, Lisa. *Desiring China: Experiments in Neoliberalism, Sexuality, and Public Culture*. Durham: Duke University Press, 2007.

Rohmer, Sax. *The Insidious Dr. Fu Manchu*. New York: Kensington, 1985. First published 1913.

Roig-Franzia, Manuel. "Probe Opens on Study Tied to Johns Hopkins." *Washington Post*, August 23, 2001.

Rose, Nikolas. *The Politics of Life Itself: Biomedicine, Power, and Subjectivity in the Twenty-First Century*. Princeton: Princeton University Press, 2007.

Rubin, Gayle. "Misguided, Dangerous, and Wrong: An Analysis of Anti-Pornography Politics." In *Bad Girls and Dirty Pictures: The Challenge to Reclaim Feminism*, edited by Allison Assiter and Avedon Carol, 18–40. Boulder, CO: Pluto, 1993.

Russell, John G. "Consuming Passions: Spectacle, Self-Transformation, and the Commodification of Blackness in Japan." *positions: East Asia Cultures Critique* 6, no. 1 (1998): 113–77.

Saenz de Rodriguez, Carmen, Alfred Bongiovanni, and Lillian Conde de Borrego. "An Epidemic of Precocious Development in Puerto Rican Children." *Journal of Pediatrics* 107, no. 3 (September 1985): 393–96.

Samuels, Ellen. "My Body, My Closet: Invisible Disability and the Limits of Coming-Out Discourse." GLQ: *A Journal of Lesbian and Gay Studies* 9, no. 1–2 (Spring 2003): 233–55.

Santiago, Silviano. "The Wily Homosexual." In *Queer Globalizations: Citizenship and the Afterlife of Colonialism*, edited by Arnaldo Cruz-Malavé and Martin Manalansan, 13–19. New York: New York University Press, 2002.

Savarese, Ralph James. "More Than a Thing to Ignore: An Interview with Tito Rajarshi Mukhopadhyay." *Disability Studies Quarterly* 30, no. 1 (2010), http://dsq-sds.org/.

Scherer, Michael. "Salon Person of the Year: S. R. Sidarth," *Salon*, December 16, 2006,

Schneider, Joseph. *Donna Haraway: Live Theory*. London: Continuum, 2005.

Schweik, Susan M. *The Ugly Laws: Disability in Public*. New York: New York University Press, 2009.

Scott, Darieck. *Extravagant Abjection: Blackness, Power, and Sexuality in the African American Literary Imagination*. New York: New York University Press, 2010.

Sedgwick, Eve Kosofsky. "Queer Performativity: Henry James' *The Art of the Novel*." GLQ: *A Journal of Lesbian and Gay Studies* 1, no. 1 (1993): 1–32.

———. *Tendencies*. Durham: Duke University Press, 1993.

———. *Touching Feeling: Affect, Pedagogy, Performativity*. Durham; Duke University Press, 2000.

Serpell, James A. "People in Disguise: Anthropomorphism and the Human-Pet Relationship." In *Thinking through Animals: New Perspectives on Anthropomorphism*, edited by Lorraine Daston and Gregg Mitman, 121–36. New York: Columbia University Press, 2005.

Shah, Nayan. *Contagious Divides: Epidemics and Race in San Francisco's Chinatown*. Berkeley: University of California Press, 2001.

Sheets-Johnstone, Maxine. *The Primacy of Movement*. Amsterdam: John Benjamins, 1999.

Shibatani, Masayoshi, and Theodora Bynon, eds. *Approaches to Language Typology*. New York: Oxford University Press, 1995.

Shimizu, Celine Parreñas. *The Hypersexuality of Race: Performing Asian/American Women on Screen and Scene*. Durham: Duke University Press, 2007.

Shohat, Ella, and Robert Stam, *Unthinking Eurocentrism: Multiculturalism and the Media*. New York: Routledge, 1994.

Shukin, Nicole. *Animal Capital: Rendering Life in Biopolitical Times*. Minneapolis: University of Minnesota Press, 2009.

Siebers, Tobin. *Disability Theory*. Ann Arbor: University of Michigan, 2008.

Silbergeld, Jerome, and Dora C. Y. Ching, eds. *Persistence-Transformation: Text as Image in the Art of Xu Bing*. Princeton: Princeton University Press, 2006.

Silva, Noenoe, and Jon Goldberg-Hiller. "Taking Indigenous Cosmologies Seriously." Paper delivered at "Why the Animal?" symposium, University of California, Berkeley, Science, Technology, and Society Center, April 12, 2011.

Silverstein, Michael. "Hierarchy of Features and Ergativity." In *Grammatical Categories in Australian Languages*, edited by R. M. W. Dixon, 112–71. Canberra: Australian Institute of Aboriginal Studies, 1976.

Slobin, Dan. "From Thought and Language to Thinking for Speaking." In *Rethinking Linguistic Relativity*, edited by J. J. Gumperz and S. C. Levinson, 70–96. Cambridge: Cambridge University Press, 1996.

Smith, Bonnie. *Gendering Disability*. New Brunswick, NJ: Rutgers University Press, 2004.

———, ed. *Haunted by Empire: Geographies of Intimacy in North American History*. Durham: Duke University Press, 2006.

Smitherman, Geneva. *Talkin and Testifyin: The Language of Black America*. Boston: Houghton Mifflin, 1977.

———. *Word from the Mother: Language and African Americans*. New York Routledge, 1996.

Snyder, Sharon L., and David T. Mitchell. *Cultural Locations of Disability*. Chicago: University of Chicago Press, 2006.

Somerville, Siobhan. *Queering the Color Line: Race and the Invention of Homosexuality in America*. Durham: Duke University Press, 2000.

Spencer, Ian R. G. *British Immigration Policy since 1939: The Making of Multi-Racial Britain*. London: Routledge, 1997.

Spivak, Gayatri. "Can the Subaltern Speak?" In *Marxism and the Interpretation of Culture*, edited by Cary Nelson and Lawrence Grossberg. London: Macmillan, 1988.

Steen, Shannon. *Racial Geometries of the Black Atlantic, Asian Pacific and American Theatre*. Basingstoke, UK: Palgrave Macmillan, 2010.

Steingraber, Sandra. *Living Downstream: An Ecologist Looks at Cancer and the Environment*. Reading: Addison-Wesley, 1997.

Stevens, Chuck. "Deadly Youth: Nagisa Oshima's *Gohatto*." *Film Comment* 36, no. 6 (November/December 2000): 22–26.

Stockton, Kathryn Bond. *The Queer Child: Or Growing Sideways in the Twentieth Century*. Durham: Duke University Press, 2009.

Stoler, Ann. *Carnal Knowledge and Imperial Power: Race and the Intimate in Colonial Rule*. Berkeley: University of California Press, 2002.

Story, Louise. "Lead Paint Prompts Mattel to Recall 967,000 Toys." *New York Times*, August 2, 2007.

Stryker, Susan. "Transgender Studies: Queer Theory's Evil Twin." GLQ: *A Journal of Lesbian and Gay Studies* 10, no. 2 (2004): 212–15.

Stryker, Susan, Paisley Currah, and Lisa Jean Moore. "Introduction: Trans-,

Trans, or Transgender?" *Women's Studies Quarterly* 36, no. 3–4 (Fall/Winter 2008): 11–22.

Stubblefield, Anna. "'Beyond the Pale': Tainted Whiteness, Cognitive Disability, and Eugenic Sterilization." *Hypatia* 22, no. 2 (Spring 2007): 162–81.

Sue, Marsha Petrie. *Toxic People: Decontaminate People at Work without Using Weapons.* Hoboken, NJ: John Wiley and Sons, 2007.

Sullivan, Nikki. *A Critical Introduction to Queer Theory.* New York: New York University Press, 2004.

———. "Transmogrification: (Un)Becoming Other(s)." In *The Transgender Studies Reader*, edited by Susan Stryker and Stephen Whittle, 552–65. New York: Routledge, 2006.

Sweetser, Eve. *From Etymology to Pragmatics: Metaphorical and Cultural Aspects of Semantic Structure.* Cambridge: Cambridge University Press, 1990.

Sze, Julie. *Noxious New York: The Racial Politics of Urban Health and Environmental Justice.* Cambridge: MIT Press, 2007.

Takaki, Ronald. *Strangers from a Different Shore: A History of Asian Americans.* Boston: Little, Brown, 1989.

Taub, Sarah, and Dennis Galvan. "Patterns of Encoding in ASL Motion Descriptions." *Sign Language Studies* 1, no. 2 (2001): 175–200.

Taylor, Sunaura. "Beasts of Burden: Disability Studies and Animal Rights." *Qui Parle* 19, no. 2 (2011): 191–222.

Tchen, John Kuo Wei. *New York before Chinatown: Orientalism and the Shaping of American Culture.* Baltimore: Johns Hopkins University Press, 1999.

———. "Quimbo Appo's Fear of Fenians: Chinese-Irish-Anglo Relations in New York City." In *The New York Irish*, edited by Ronald Bayor and Timothy Meagher, 125–52. Baltimore: Johns Hopkins University Press, 1996.

Terry, Jennifer. "Objectum-Sexuality." Paper presented at "Rethinking Sex: A State of the Field Conference in Gender and Sexuality Studies," University of Pennsylvania, March 4–6, 2009.

———. "Unnatural Acts in Nature: The Scientific Fascination with Queer Animals." *GLQ: A Journal of Lesbian and Gay Studies* 6, no. 2 (2000): 151–93.

Thompson, Charis. *Good Science.* Cambridge: MIT Press, 2012.

———. *Making Parents: The Ontological Choreography of Reproductive Technologies.* Cambridge: MIT Press, 2007.

———. "When Elephants Stand In for Competing Philosophies of Nature." In *Complexities: Social Studies of Knowledge Practices*, edited John Law and Annamarie Mol, 166–90. Durham: Duke University Press, 2002.

Thomson, Rosemarie Garland. *Extraordinary Bodies: Figuring Physical Disability in American Culture and Literature.* New York: Columbia University Press, 1997.

———. *Freakery: Cultural Spectacles of the Extraordinary Body.* New York: New York University Press, 1996.

———. *Staring: How We Look*. Oxford: Oxford University Press, 2009.

Tilt, Bryan. *The Struggle for Sustainability in Rural China: Environmental Values and Civil Society*. New York: Columbia University Press, 2010.

Tinsley, Omise'eke Natasha. "Black Atlantic, Queer Atlantic: Queer Imaginings of the Middle Passage." GLQ: *A Journal of Lesbian and Gay Studies* 14, no. 2–3 (2008): 191–216.

Trinh T. Minh-ha. *Woman, Native, Other: Writing Postcoloniality and Feminism*. Bloomington: Indiana University Press, 1989.

Trinh T. Minh-ha and Nancy N. Chen. "Speaking Nearby." In *Feminism and Film*, edited by E. Ann Kaplan, 317–35. Oxford: Oxford University Press, 2000.

Tsao, Doris, Nicole Schweers, Sebastian Moeller, and Winrich A. Freiwald. "Patches of Face-Selective Cortex in the Macaque Frontal Lobe." *Nature Neuroscience* 11 (2008): 877–79.

Tsing, Anna Lowenhaupt. *Friction: An Ethnography of Global Connection*. Princeton: Princeton University Press, 2005.

Tuana, Nancy. "Viscous Porosity: Witnessing Katrina." In *Material Feminisms*, edited by Stacy Alaimo and Susan Hekman, 188–213. Bloomington: Indiana University Press, 2008.

Turim, Maureen Cheryn. *The Films of Oshima Nagisa: Images of a Modern Japanese Iconoclast*. Berkeley: University of California Press, 1990.

Umphrey, Martha M. "The Trouble with Harry Thaw." In *Queer Studies: An Interdisciplinary Reader*, edited by Robert Corber and Stephen Valocchi, 21–30. Malden, MA: Blackwell, 2003.

Wald, Priscilla. *Contagious: Cultures, Carriers, and the Outbreak Narrative*. Durham: Duke University Press, 2007.

Walters, Suzanna Danuta. *All the Rage: The Story of Gay Visibility in America*. Chicago: University of Chicago Press, 2001.

Walvin, James. *Passage to Britain: Immigration in British History and Politics*. London: Penguin, 1984.

Warner, Michael. "Introduction." In *Fear of a Queer Planet: Queer Politics and Social Theory*, edited by Michael Warner, vi–xxxi. Minneapolis: University of Minnesota Press, 1993.

Wayne, Leslie. "The Enemy at Home." *New York Times*, October 8, 2009. The online version is titled "Thousands of Homeowners Cite Drywall for Ills."

Weightman, John. *The Cat Sat on the Mat: Language and the Absurd*. London: Weech, 2002.

Wendell, Susan. *The Rejected Body: Feminist Philosophical Reflections on Disability*. New York: Routledge, 1996.

Whorf, Benjamin Lee. *Language, Thought, and Reality: Selected Writings of Benjamin Lee Whorf*, edited by John B. Carroll. Cambridge: MIT Press, 1956.

Williams, Allen S. *The Demon of the Orient and His Satellite Fiends of the Joint:*

Our Opium Smokers as They Are in Tartar Hells and American Paradises. New York: Allen S. Williams, 1883.

Williams, Linda. *Hard Core: Power, Pleasure, and the Frenzy of the Visible.* Berkeley: University of California Press, 1989.

———, ed. *Porn Studies.* Durham: Duke University Press, 2004.

Wines, Michael. "Once Banned, Dogs Reflect China's Rise." *New York Times*, October 25, 2010.

Wolfe, Cary. "Introduction." In *Zoontologies: The Question of the Animal*, edited by Cary Wolfe, ix–xxiii. Minneapolis: University of Minnesota Press, 2003.

Wood, Joe. "The Yellow Negro." *Transition* 73 (1997): 40–66.

"WTO: China Overtakes U.S. in Exports; Asian Nation Set to Become the World's Biggest Exporter by 2008." MSNBC.com, April 12, 2007.

Xu Bing. "A Case Study of Transference." Video documentation. Directed and edited by Ma Yingli and Ai Weiwei. Translated by Kris Torgeson. New York, July 1994.

———, Personal conversation with author. Translation by Tonglin Lu. Held by Species Spectacles Residential Research Group, University of California Humanities Research Institute, Irvine, CA, December 2009.

Yamamoto, Mutsumi. *Animacy and Reference: A Cognitive Approach to Corpus Linguistics.* Amsterdam: John Benjamins, 1999.

Young, Elizabeth. *Black Frankenstein: The Making of an American Metaphor.* New York: New York University Press, 2008.

Young, Katherine. "Deleuze and Guattari: The Animal Question." In *An (Un)likely Alliance: Thinking Environment(s) with Deleuze/Guattari*, edited by Bernd Herzogenrath, 245–65. Newcastle upon Tyne, UK: Cambridge Scholars Publishing, 2008.

Zeng, Candy. "China Enters Dog Eat-Dog Pet Industry." *Asia Times*, July 19, 2006.

Zhou, Huashan. *Tongzhi: Politics of Same-Sex Eroticism in Chinese Societies.* Binghamton: Haworth Press, 2000.

Zwicky, Arnold. "Two Lavender Issues for Linguists." In *Queerly Phrased: Language, Gender, and Sexuality*, edited by Kira Hall and Anna Livia, 21–34. New York: Oxford University Press, 1997.

Index

Mel Y. Chen is assistant professor
of gender and women's studies at
the University of California,
Berkeley.

Library of Congress Cataloging-in-Publication Data
Chen, Mel Y., 1969–
Animacies : biopolitics, racial mattering, and queer affect /
Mel Y. Chen.
p. cm. — (Perverse modernities)
Includes bibliographical references and index.
ISBN 978-0-8223-5254-9 (cloth : alk. paper)
ISBN 978-0-8223-5272-3 (pbk. : alk. paper)
1. Grammar, Comparative and general — Animacy.
2. Ontology. 3. Perception. 4. Biopolitics. 5. Sex role.
I. Title. II. Series: Perverse modernities.
P240.65.C44 2012
302'.1 — dc23
2012011589